SHAKESPEARE AND JUNGIAN TYPOLOGY

SHAKESPEARE AND JUNGIAN TYPOLOGY

A Reading of the Plays

Kenneth Tucker

McFarland & Company, Inc., Publishers
Jefferson, North Carolina, and London

Library of Congress Cataloguing-in-Publication Data

Tucker, Kenneth, 1940–
    Shakespeare and Jungian typology : a reading of the plays /
Kenneth Tucker.
      p.   cm.
    Includes bibliographical references and index.

    ISBN 0-7864-1647-5 (softcover : 50# alkaline paper)

    1. Shakespeare, William, 1564–1616 — Knowledge —
Psychology.   2. Shakespeare, William, 1564–1616 — Characters.
3. Jung, C. G. (Carl Gustav), 1875–1961.   4. Typology
(Psychology) in literature.   5. Drama — Psychological aspects.
6. Psycyhology in literature.   7. Typology (Psychology).
PR3065.T83   2003
822.3'3 — dc21   2003013296

British Library cataloguing data are available

Cover images ©1996 Eclecticollections Publishing Ltd. and
©2003 Clipart.com

Manufactured in the United States of America

McFarland & Company, Inc., Publishers
 Box 611, Jefferson, North Carolina 28640
  www.mcfarlandpub.com

Contents

Roughly three hundred years ago, Western civilization emerged into what is frequently called the Age of Reason. As far as I know, we are still in it.

— M. Scott Peck, *In Search of Stones*, 1995, 3

A massive intellectual revolution is taking place that is perhaps as great as that which marked off the modern world from the Middle Ages. The foundations of the modern world are collapsing, and we are entering a postmodern world. The principles forged during the Enlightenment (c. 1600–1780), which formed the foundations of the modern mentality, are crumbling.

— Diogenes Allen, *Christian Belief in a Postmodern World*, 1989, 2

...for there is nothing either good or bad but thinking makes it so.

— *Hamlet,* II. ii. 250.

Preface

Phenomenal. That exuberant and overused adjective may be the just word to describe Carl Jung's influence on literary criticism of the twentieth century. For decades critics have used Jungian theories of psychology to interpret imaginative works from *The Odyssey* to *Star Wars*, but these approaches have focused almost exclusively on Jung's theory of archetypes. In following the celebrated Swiss psychoanalyst, literary scholars, however, have given scant attention to Jung's theory of the four functions, i.e., personality types—feeling, thinking, sensation, and intuition—first outlined in his ground-breaking study *Psychological Types* (1921). Jung himself placed as much significance on his theory of psychological types as he did on archetypes, and believed that understanding one's own psychetype was vital to each person's individuation or self-realization. Yet literary scholars, ranging from the so-called New Critics of the forties and fifties to the more recent deconstructionists, feminists, and new historicists, have avoided Jungian typology.

Over twenty years ago Michael Malone, in his seminal work *Psychetypes: A New Way of Exploring Personality*, attempted to link Jungian typology with literary interpretation. Admittedly, Malone's central purpose was to explain Jung's theories to the educated public, but to do so, he drew heavily on authors and literary characters as well as historical figures in his efforts to explain these fundamental personality traits. He did offer provocative insights into both fictional and historical personages, but his study produced few ripples in the literary world.

What, then, may account for this neglect? One reason is that the very notion of typing individuals arouses distrust and even hostility in some persons. In discussing psychetypology with colleagues and other interested individuals, I have at times encountered spirited resistance. Some persons fear that any system of classifying personalities will lead to psychological pigeonholes and to stereotypes. These opponents suspect that psychetypology will sanction unyielding and hidebound modes of personality classification such as the Medieval and Renaissance system of the four humors. Of course, any system that attempts to understand the human personality may be abused, but psychetypology, used cautiously, should help our understanding of ourselves and works of literature, not constrict or thwart these efforts. Jung himself never envisioned his study of psychetypes would lead to a close-minded system which would ignore human complexity and unpredictability by reducing persons to their lowest possible psychological common denominators. Rather, he saw typology as a tool to be used along with many others to improve humankind's understanding of itself.

A second reason for the neglect of psychetypology by literary scholars is the very climate of criticism for the past twenty years or so. Feminism, race and gender studies, and New Historicism, while providing useful insights, have tended to concentrate on humanity in its social roles rather than delving into the depths of psychology.

The neglect of Jung's typological theories in literary studies is unfortunate because just as they can help explain the personalities of living persons, they also can also illuminate those of fictional characters and even of authors themselves. Here we encounter what at times may be a third objection to psychetypology as a literary tool: the question of the validity of exploring the psychetypes of such characters as Othello and Hamlet and their creator, Shakespeare. This current study, of course, is predicated upon the belief that psychetypological theory offers valid judgments. I will briefly touch upon this complex issue here (a detailed consideration appears in the appropriate place in the text). Also at this point, it behooves me to approach the tricky and indeed troubling question of what "literary knowledge" is.

Quite clearly, within the last few decades and with the advent of deconstruction, new historicism, and postmodernism, literary scholars and critics—and indeed the intellectual community as a whole—have found themselves vexed with the question of what knowledge in general is and the question of if, in fact, knowledge exists. We approach turbulent and baffling waters, but for the sake of clarity I would like to "chart" three major currents or understandings as to what knowledge is: *one*, the modern view; *two*, the postmodern view; and *three*, critical realism.

One. The modern view. Actually the scientific view which, once germinated in western culture, steadily developed from the seventeenth century to flower in the first half of the twentieth. Central to this view is the belief that the world's phenomena can be broken down into component parts, analyzed and comprehended. A rainbow can be looked at objectively and understood not as a bridge to the gods but as an atmospheric and optical phenomenon. Sociological phenomena may also be studied in the same way. The sociologist, by interviewing divorced persons, can determine why the number of divorces has skyrocketed in the twentieth century and can, therefore, rank the causes of divorces in order of their relative importance. Likewise, the literary critic can come up with certain understandings of literature and authors. For instance, the psychoanalytically-minded critics, by detailed study of *Hamlet's* text, can "prove" that the melancholy prince and his creator both suffer from Oedipus complexes.

Two. The postmodern view. This approach to understanding knowledge spread rapidly during the latter half of the twentieth century from intellectual circles via the more esoteric media to mass circulation magazines and daily newspaper columns. Yet it in itself is not entirely new. The ancient Hermetic philosophers, as well as Shakespeare's contemporary Montaigne, would have readily understood its theoretical basis. In essence, this view holds that there is no objective knowledge, since what we call knowledge is filtered through the subjective minds of observers—that is, fallible, confused, biased, and emotional human beings. Even scientific knowledge, according to some theoreticians, is not objective. But for simplicity's sake, let us return to our example drawn from sociology. Suppose a team of sociologists, after many time-consuming interviews, has come up with a list of the causes of divorce, such as alcoholism, problems with in-laws, and conflicts over religious differences. The postmodern critic would object that such a study is at base valueless because the data have been forced into arbitrary patterns having little accord with reality. For instance, the critic might object that the researchers' definition of divorce might be faulty. Can a couple whose marriage has been legally ended but who are still much attracted to each other and seeking a reconciliation be in fact "divorced"? And what about gradated causes of divorce? Suppose the study concluded that alcoholism was the number one cause of divorce while conflicts with in-laws and religious differences were numbers two and three? How can we determine that alcoholism was the major cause in a divorce case in which all three factors, and perhaps others, were present? How are we to judge a broken marriage in which one former partner declares that the interference of in-laws was a factor and the other minimizes or even denies the unfortunate influence of relatives? In other words, any number of possible errors in definition or faulty sampling or conscious or unconscious bias might be marshaled to attack the validity of the study. To some such skeptics the obvious conclusion is that no analysis of the causes of divorce can be correct. If I wish to believe alcoholism is the number one cause of divorce and you believe it should be ranked number four, let us both believe as we wish. Neither of us can prove the other's view invalid. This stance has its literary counterpart and may be couched in the following example. If my Hamlet suffers from an Oedipus complex, fine. If yours doesn't, that's also fine. I have my view; you have yours. Nobody can decide which is correct. Although in some instances such intellectual relativity may be irrefutable, few of us would wish to adopt such pyrrhonism as a credo concerning all possible knowledge. (Indeed, if we could not agree in some measure about the nature of physics, history, and moral values, our civilization would be disastrously more chaotic than it is!) Few literary critics would welcome every literary interpretation as valid, especially when cockeyed ones abound. For instance, a case could be made (and as far as I know it never has been) that Shakespeare admired Iago's ruthlessness and ingenuity to such an extent that he actually applauds the ancient's machinations and wishes for us to honor him. In other words, Iago is the hero of *Othello*.

Three. Critical realism. This approach draws on the best of both intellectual stances and strives, in some measure, to bring them into harmony. It admits that in a very important sense all knowledge is subjective, yet argues that, to a reliable extent, external phenomena can be understood. We may not be able to prove that alcoholism is the number one cause of divorce, but we can agree that it is an important factor in a number of divorces. Likewise, we may not be able to agree upon the applicability of Freud's concept of the Oedipus complex to Hamlet, yet we can agree that Hamlet is disturbed, suffers mood swings and depression, and experiences suicidal impulses and surges of violent behavior even though we may not be able to prove that he is manic depressive, borderline, or schizophrenic. Similarly, we can agree that while Shakespeare may secretly admire Iago's intellectual ingenuity and daring resourcefulness, the poet does not consider his character's villainy admirable and wish us to imitate it.

"In sum, 'critical realism' believes there is something to be known, and that our perceptions do have something to do with a reality external to ourselves. Therefore…critical realism expects and demands that we test such knowledge by every means at our disposal, including empirical verification/falsification in areas where that is appropriate and possible" (*The New Testament* 61).[1]

In essence, critical realism is the bedrock of the current study. The use of psychetypes, like other tools of literary criticism, can deliver not scientifically verifiable data but provocative theoretical insights or "pseudo-statements"—to use I. A. Richard's useful term (329–30)—about literary characters. It can illuminate important psychological currents in characters and provide new perspectives on their conflicts. Of course, some relativity appears regarding potential characters for study. Some are more amenable to psychetypological analysis than others. Important psychological currents in authors may also be illuminated, although here the results may be more provisional in the sense that they may or may not be relatable to biographical data. For instance, this study argues that Shakespeare's personality reveals a recurrent conflict between thinking and feeling modes of interpreting reality. We can say that the opposition of thinking and feeling modes shows itself recurrently in the plays and presumably in Shakespeare's psyche without our being able to say what particular family conflicts, financial problems, or personal demons might have caused this pattern to emerge in a particular play in a specific manifestation.

This study is also predicated upon the belief that advances in the sciences, sociology, psychology, and other disciplines can immeasurably aid literary interpretation by providing new labels for old, recurrent phenomena of the human race — labels that are not idle nor pretentious, but provocative and stimulating. In essence, they make critical discussion more immediate, more relevant to the present, indeed to the ever-changing zeitgeist itself. Jungian psychetypology is long overdue in gaining recognition as such a tool for literary analysis. This study seeks in part to remedy the situation in the hope that readers may find it worthwhile to apply their own psychetypological observations to Shakespeare and other writers.

I wish to thank Dr. Paul Neumarkt, editor of *The Journal of Evolutionary Psychology*, for allowing me to make use of two articles published in that journal in which I originally offered some of the ideas presented here in my discussions of *Antony and Cleopatra* and *Troilus and Cressida*. I would also like to thank my colleague Dr. Thayle Anderson of Murray State University for helping me clarify some of my ideas about Conrad. Thanks goes also to a second colleague, Mrs. Helen Roulston, who as usual employed her considerable skills in getting the proofs read for the press.

Introduction

Shakespeare was a Roman Catholic.

Shakespeare was gay.

Shakespeare was an arrant skirt-chaser.

The young man celebrated in the sonnets was the Earl of Southampton.

The young man celebrated in the sonnets was the Earl of Pembroke.

The Dark Lady of the sonnets was Emilia Lanier.

Shakespeare had no religion whatsoever.

Shakespeare was a covert Roman Catholic.

These are all propositions about Shakespeare which have been advanced — often vehemently by their adherents— since 1990. None of them is in fact new, and all are contestable. Their supporters have not been able to amass enough data to refute counterclaims and to make their opponents shamefacedly retire from the scholarly fields of battle. Unfortunately (or perhaps fortunately) not enough primary data has come to light concerning Shakespeare's life to settle these intellectual skirmishes, and barring the discovery of a major biographical tool — for instance, the personal diary of William Shakespeare — students and scholars will have to remain content with their surmises, congratulating themselves that they are absolutely right while enduring the repeated unsettling invasions of their private intellectual kingdoms by the unsettling forces of skepticism, whispering that they may well be wrong.

Still it is impossible to refrain from delving into Shakespeare's life, hoping by conjecture to hit upon some happy truth. Stephen Greenblatt wrote that his book *Shakespearean Negotiations* was born of the desire to speak with the dead (1). We would also like to converse with the dead, Shakespeare in particular. We would like to ask him why Hamlet delays in killing the king, whether Henry V is in fact his ideal ruler, whether he himself fell in love with his character Rosalind. We would like to know whether his marriage to Anne Hathaway was in fact happy, whether he

6

fully approved of his daughter Susanna's husband Dr. John Hall, what his reaction was to the accusation that Susanna had misbehaved with Rafe Smith. By forming such a desired, but impossible acquaintance with the poet, we hope on some level that we would then achieve a greater, more thorough, and indeed more meaningful understanding of his achievements. Theoretically, then, all questions would be asked, and all answers would be given. A pipe dream, obviously, but one we like to pursue.

Our hopes, of course, are inevitably disappointed, for strictly biographical attempts to understand Shakespeare inevitably founder if they are to be understood as excavations of the hidden truth about the Bard and his views. A case in point is that of Ted Hughes' recent study *Shakespeare and the Goddess of Complete Being*. Basing his study on the supposition that Shakespeare was in fact bisexual, Hughes sees *Venus and Adonis* as a paradigm of Shakespeare's concerns, with Shakespeare himself experiencing the love for his own Adonis, the Earl of Southampton, which he ascribes to Venus. Moreover, Hughes sees the Venus and Adonis relationship obliquely mirroring that of the poet and the Dark Lady. The Dark Lady turns into Venus, and Venus into the boar which strikes down Adonis. Thus a recurrent pattern is formulated, resulting from Shakespeare's own entangled sex life, a pattern repeated throughout his works as the poet in varying ways compulsively retells the story of Venus and Adonis (64-67). Since no one can prove that Shakespeare was bisexual or that the young man of the sonnets was indeed Southampton, Hughes's thesis must remain at best conjecture. The result is a complex book showcasing Hughes' erudition — which is considerable — and providing intriguing insights, but it simply cannot take us to the heart of the essential Shakespeare.

A similar well-intended excursion into Shakespeare's life which founders in a biographical wilderness is Ian Wilson's *Shakespeare: The Evidence*. A formidable and wide-ranging scholar, Wilson has written provocative volumes on the Shroud of Turin, possible pre-Columbian European discoverers of America, after-death experiences, and the life of Christ. In turning his attention to Shakespeare, Wilson follows the route of Father Peter Milward and others who have argued that Shakespeare and his family were in fact closet Roman Catholics. To support his view, Wilson marshals such often-presented quasi-evidence as "the will" of the poet's father John Shakespeare and Susanna Shakespeare's apparent recusancy. He also provides some thoughtful possibilities of his own, such as Shakespeare's having bought Blackfriar's Gatehouse in London to provide a haven for on-the-run priests. Wilson's central thesis leads him to far more detailed biographical assumptions, such as suggesting that Shakespeare, having become a member of Lord Strange's men, enjoyed a par-

ticularly vital relationship with the company's patron, Ferdinando Stanley, because of their shared Catholicism. Wilson then uses his thesis of
Shakespeare's supposed adherence to Rome to comment upon and interpret the plays; for instance, he argues that the murder of the elder Hamlet is a veiled commentary upon the poisoning of Ferdinando Stanley and
that Portia's often-anthologized speech on mercy refers to the execution
of the Jesuit Robert Southwell. Wilson also views Richard II's harsh treatment of John of Gaunt as a reflection of Henry VIII and Elizabeth's suppression of old Catholic England (201). Moreover, Wilson views Shakespeare's
alleged Catholicism as playing a vital behind-the-scenes role in the dramatist's collaboration with John Fletcher in the writing of *Henry VIII;* staunch
in his Catholicism, Shakespeare assigned the most protestant segment of
the play, Act five, with the famous encomium of Queen Elizabeth, to
Fletcher.

Again the argument rests upon an unstable foundation of conjectures. That the Blackfriar's Gatehouse was earlier used as a hiding place
for priests does not prove that Shakespeare bought it for that purpose.[1]
That Ferdinando Stanley was very likely poisoned does not prove his death
served as the springboard for *Hamlet.* To be fair to Wilson, one needs to
observe that he often calls his "discoveries" possibilities. For instance,
when discussing Fletcher and *Henry VIII,* Wilson writes, "So could it be
that Shakespeare's true *valete* not only to *Henry VIII* but to his whole career
as a dramatist was with Queen Katherine's deathbed scene? And that — in
whatever circumstances — it was to Fletcher that he passed the task of giving the play its final Protestant twist...?" (370). To be sure, Wilson does
not arrogantly assert half-truths or present utterly senseless fabrications.
Such frequent caveats, however, disclose that Wilson himself realizes the
tenuousness of many of his suppositions.[2]

Of course, one must also grant that Wilson *could be* correct in endors-
ing Shakespeare's supposed Catholicism. Wilson might have made true
suppositions and valid deductions, but unless indisputable evidence comes
to light, Wilson's theories can be only theories and cannot by any means
be claimed as a can opener that has removed the lid to Shakespeare's hidden life. Wilson's Shakespeare must remain a fictional construct, whose
relevance to the historical Shakespeare is uncertain.

Even biographers without such overriding agendas may often pro-
vide us with conjectures in the place of certainties. For instance, Gary
O'Connor, in his intriguing, fetchingly-written *William Shakespeare: A
Popular Life,* argues that Berowne's dispraise of learning in *Love's Labour's
Lost* equates with Shakespeare's own distrust of formal education (actu-
ated in part at least because he was not a university man) (102). Elsewhere

O'Connor asserts that Shakespeare's relationship with his father was strained: "William loved his father, but John Shakespeare pushed that love away from him, mistaking it for an emotional demand he could not satisfy" (26). Likewise, in *Ungentle Shakespeare: Scenes from his Life*, the often conscientious Katherine Duncan-Jones succumbs at times to the temptation to allow possibility to replace fact. For instance, she had earlier sailed against the wind of prevailing critical opinion by asserting that Shakespeare secretly worked with Thomas Thorpe to publish the apparently unauthorized first edition of the sonnets (Introduction *Sonnets*). The biography theory silently undergoes transformation into certainty (214-17).

Of course, one may be too critical of such biographers. After all they often rely upon educated guesses, and the critic might well recollect that without such authorial leaps of faith, biographies as a rule would be as dry as bales of straw. Still, one writer's educated guess might well be another writer's wild surmise. Thus the student of Shakespeare's life would do well to recall S. Schoenbaum's wise cautionary skepticism. In general his attitude toward such vexing questions as the identity of the Dark Lady and the nature of Shakespeare's religion was, in essence, "Theory X is indeed interesting. Certainly there are likelihoods, some connections, but show the proof!"

The case would be different, we may believe, for an author whose life is well-documented. Numerous letters written by F. Scott Fitzgerald have come down to us as well as letters written to him. Recollections of him by friends and associates have been recorded, and biographies of him have been written by his contemporaries. Hence, we are better able to discern Fitzgerald's opinions on various matters than we can Shakespeare's. For instance, by flipping open a biography of Fitzgerald, we can learn the novelist's opinions on his Roman Catholic background, on Princeton, on the excesses of the Jazz Age, and on the psychiatric care given to his wife Zelda. Likewise, on a more philosophical level, we can learn about Fitzgerald's views on organized religion, the rich who attracted him, and his thirst for literary fame that long troubled him. Yet even here we experience some level of difficulty in attempting to understand "the essential Fitzgerald" and its relationship to his writings, for Fitzgerald could be ambiguous and inconsistent in his attitudes and stances. It is well known that he both glamorized and condemned the rich, often at the same time or within the same story as in "The Diamond as Big as the Ritz" or "The Last of the Belles." Known as a religious skeptic by his contemporaries, even by his friends as a mocker of Christianity in his letters, Fitzgerald upon occasion could display an otherwise closeted religiosity. Joan Allen, a biographer who has deeply mined his Irish Catholic background, recounts an unexpected happening. Once Fitzgerald persuaded Charles Warren, a young writer, to be baptized and even took part in the service — a bizarre episode held in the wee hours with an Episcopal priest. Even though he was intoxicated, Fitzgerald read the appropriate responses (123). Hence, to conclude that Fitzgerald consistently mocked Christianity or that whatever need he had initially possessed to believe in Christianity had been eradicated would be inaccurate.

As Shakespeare's perceptive contemporary Montaigne stressed, we are all basically tumultuously inconsistent. In observing himself, the French sage wrote the following:

> Every sort of contradiction can be found in me, depending upon
> some twist or attribute: timid, insolent; ... chaste, lecherous; ...
> talkative, taciturn; tough, sickly; clever, dull; brooding, affable,
> lying, truthful; ... learned, ignorant; generous, miserly and then
> prodigal... I can see something of all that in myself, depending
> on how I gyrate; and anyone who studies himself attentively
> finds in himself and in his very judgment this whirring about
> and this discordancy [377].

Not only are we unable to capture the essential author while pursuing our quarry through his/her daily Protean shifts of perceptions, moods and attitudes, but also, in a sense, we cannot ever know precisely how our subject felt on a particular day at a particular time about a particular subject when a particular line was written. In other words, we cannot learn the pitch of a past emotion nor the color of a past mood.

Thus, even if we have "pinned down" an author's religious affiliation or political membership, can we say for certain how the given beliefs are manifested in a drama or poem? Let us suppose that Wilson's ideas about Shakespeare's Catholicism were proved. What then would this knowledge allow us to say about King Richard's treatment of John of Gaunt? Is Richard allegorically both Henry VIII and Elizabeth? Or one or the other? Does John of Gaunt stand for a particular Catholic nobleman, Catholics *en masse*, or Roman Catholicism? These possible distinctions may seem to be quibbles, yet they demonstrate the difficulty of pinpointing exact interpretations. And, of course, we must be aware of another possibility: That our Catholic Shakespeare made no conscious identification whatsoever of these characters as ardent Catholics or Catholic bashers. He could simply have been writing a play in which happenstance parallels to sixteenth century religious conflicts and to many other political confrontations emerge.

Of course, in some literary areas that might have led to contested interpretations, authors have left signposts to point the way, but still problems abound in attempting to come up with unassailable readings. The problem of attempting to comprehend the essential author is simply one aspect of the postmodern enigma of attempting to understand the past. After surveying many postmodern views of history, Linda Hutcheon succinctly and ably couched the overriding problem: "There is not so much 'a loss of belief in a significant external reality ... as there is a loss of faith in our ability to (unproblematically) *know* that reality, and therefore to be able to represent it in language" (139).

In a sense, then, the Protean psyche of an author, on one level, eludes our attempt to capture it, and our attempts to understand an author fully are doomed to frustration. We continue, however, to pursue our goal because we are convinced of its importance. Like Fitzgerald's Nick Carraway in *The Great Gatsby*, we long for achievement of our quest and secretly sympathize with Carraway's deluding optimism that one day his generation will gain its "green light"—the symbol of success—"that year by year recedes before us. It eluded us then, but that's no matter — tomorrow we will run faster, stretch out our arms farther.... So we beat on , boats against the current..." (168).

However, the hopes of our biographical quests need not be wholly frustrated. Although we may be unable to understand the essential author, we can understand *aspects* of the author. Hence, few of us would be willing to consign our literary biographies to the bonfire. Even though we are well aware of these studies' limitations, we recognize that every attempt to unfold a writer's personality helps us toward our impossible goal.

Surprisingly enough, in endeavoring to understand the essential author, scholarship has made little use of Jung's typological theories, which concern the four basic personality types based upon thinking, feeling, sensation, and intuition. Literary analysts have made far more use of Jungian archetypes—the shadow, the anima, the animus, and persona, among others—in attempts to define authors' essences and clarify their works. Jung's typology is as central to his psychological theories as is his concern with archetypes. The process of individuation — or becoming oneself— depends on recognizing one's psychological type as well as undergoing archetypal struggles.

Jung's theories of typology hold that the personality of each of us is based primarily upon two of the four functions or orientations listed above. Our primary and secondary functions determine how we perceive and relate to the world (of course, no one lacks any of the functions in his or her make up). Moreover, our dominant functions wall us within ourselves, cutting us off from the understanding and comprehension of others whose psychetypes differ from ours. For instance, a predominantly thinking person may not understand a sensation type's impulsive decision to buy a television set marked on sale. A feeling-oriented person may not understand a thinking colleague's relative indifference to St. Valentine's Day. In essence, our psychetypologies, to an extent many of us do not wish to recognize, predetermine how we react to the world.

Writers at times are able to endow their characters with imaginary but understandable psychetypes. These psychetypes can be understood as projections of psychological currents within the personalities of the authors themselves. The arch-romantic Gatsby can be viewed as an embodiment of Fitzgerald's capacity to feel. Likewise, Iago can be viewed as a projection of Shakespeare's rational function, whereas Othello embodies the expression of the dramatist's capacity to experience emotion. Thus Jungian typology initiates a quasi-biographical approach to understanding writers and their works. Instead of directing attention toward an author's alcoholism, education, class prejudices, or whatever, it routes our interest toward important emotional currents within the writings, which in turn express similar currents within the author's psyches. While not allowing us to totally comprehend "the essential author," it allows us to gain a deeper understanding of a writer's significant inner conflicts, modes of adapting to the world, and methods of determining reality. It helps us further along the path to realizing our impossible goal.

This study is predicated on the assumption that a number of important conflicts, such as those involving the need to validate love, to avoid political upheavals, to return to an Edenic state within nature, recur throughout Shakespeare's plays. One of the most frequently recurring conflicts involves the necessity of reacting to chaos, chaos within the realm, within human relationships, and within the human psyche — or, if you will, within the soul itself. In other words, chaos in the outer worlds of the plays calls forth chaos in the inner worlds of the psyches of Shakespeare's characters.

Of course, that events in the outer world influence our inner worlds may seem a truism hardly worth recalling, but its very obviousness may well cause it to recede from our awareness. For instance, the report on the six o'clock news of the discovery of contaminated canned meat on supermarket shelves may darken a person's mood for the evening without that person's being fully aware of the cause of the lingering doldrums. Often moderns tend to minimize the connection between outer events and their inner moods or forget the disturbing interrelationship as when one says, "I'll tough it out on my own!" Such a strategy recalls the attitude of the classical stoics that, in an important sense, one's mind and the outer world are fundamentally distinct, that one can make oneself emotionally impervious to life's misfortunes.[3]

Of course, stoicism was one of the favorite classical philosophies res- urrected by the Renaissance. Caught in the throes of their era's upheavals in cosmology, religion, politics and war, many Renaissance intellectuals found stoicism a desirable mental armor to don in defense against life's painful vicissitudes. Nowadays few thinking persons, of course, would deny that "the stiff upper lip" approach to life's mishaps has its rewards. But we may well wonder about the feasibility of practicing stoicism in its ideal form. After all, to become completely unresponsive to pleasure and impervious to sorrow and pain would be to make oneself into a kind of living stone. We would be dehumanized. To most persons, complete mas- tery of one's inner self seems an impossible aim. Even Epictetus, that staunch classical exponent of stoicism, complained that few truly stoic persons existed.

Although they valued the stoic's presumed control of turbulent emo- tions, thinkers throughout the ages were well aware that such control could never be complete.[4] In fact, throughout the Renaissance the belief that outer events ineluctably influenced those within persisted in opposition to Stoicism. On the grandest level, this concept appeared in the belief that disturbances in the cosmos were connected with and thus presaged those on earth. Meteor showers, storms, earthquakes foretold disasters in the realm, in politics, in personal lives of monarchs. As Shakespeare's dream- unnerved Calpurnia admonishes Julius Caesar, "When beggars die there are no comets seen; / The heavens themselves blaze forth the death of princes" (II. ii 30-31). This pattern of similitude also expressed itself in the repeated microcosm-macrocosm analogies of Renaissance thought and writing which E. M. W. Tillyard long ago emphasized (*Elizabethan World Picture*, 82-92). According to this belief, the individual human being was a miniature world or microcosm similar to the great world outside or macrocosm. Renaissance authors repeatedly drew parallels between trou- bles in the cosmos, politics, and the individual psyche. Such a mental habit permeated early modern culture and gave an especial dimension to the conflict of inner and outer that modern readers of Renaissance literature might miss. The belief that these were inextricably bound together cre- ated a stronger sense of threat of outside chaos than we ordinarily expe- rience today.

Of course, with the exception of those who believe in astrology, few moderns would assert that mystical forces from beyond influence our lives. For us, however, the Renaissance microcosm-macrocosm analogy still maintains its value as a powerful metaphor of the disturbing intercon- nection of outer and inner events. We can still respond emotionally and intellectually to its profound symbolic meaning.

Taking as its point of departure the pervasive sense of the micro-cosm-macrocosm interconnection in Shakespeare's work, this study high-lights certain plays in which the chaos calls forth complex, deeply-rooted reactions from the feeling function in Shakespeare's psyche. These reac-tions also call forth corollary actions and counteractions from the play-wright's thinking function. In essence, the plays show a struggle to use the thinking-feeling internal nexus to understand, if not, in fact, to control, chaos. By focusing attention on what I shall call "kernel" plays—ones in which problems in the interaction of thinking and feeling functions result in emphatic and illustrative portrayals—my study will trace and clarify this unending conflict during Shakespeare's career. Chapter Three will dis-cuss in detail Jungian theories of typology and illustrate their usefulness for literary studies. Chapter Four will examine the relatively stable fusion of thinking and feeling functions in the comedies. Subsequent chapters will examine plays such as *Troilus and Cressida, Hamlet, Othello, Antony and Cleopatra* and *Timon of Athens*. The concluding chapter will examine the final romances in which unity of thinking and feeling are again sought and will comment upon the usefulness of the psychetypological approach for Shakespearean studies. But first we shall look at one of Shakespeare's most emphatic portrayals of chaos in *King John*.

ONE

"Cry, havoc!" *King John* and the Darkling Plain

Among Shakespeare's history plays *King John* has seldom received accolades. Early in the twentieth century, E. K Chambers, in his *Shakespeare: A Survey*, dubbed it an "incoherent patchwork" (102). E. M. W. Tillyard in his classic, if controversial, *Shakespeare's History Plays*, though finding the drama "full of promise and new life," laments that "as a whole it is uncertain of itself" (266). More recently Russell Fraser has aligned himself with its detractors, marshaling a battalion of judgments against it. Fraser finds the play "all carapace, and you look in vain for interior logic" (154). Maurice Charney remarks upon "the shapelessness of the play" (151). Deeming it an early work, Ian Wilson judges "the play as a whole [lacks] the quality" of the plays Shakespeare was scripting in the mid-nineties (209). More recently still, Park Honan judges that "King John's overall form is poorer than in its best scenes, and the play is not a strong one" (195).

Some reasons for the general reader's neglect are not hard to come by. For one, the play stands by itself. Not part of either Shakespearean historical tetralogy, it does not beckon readers to follow the fortunes of its characters in continuing plays. Although King John abounds with villains, none of them fascinates us like Richard III. Nor does its dramatis personae boast a rogue as beguiling as Sir John Falstaff. To be sure, whether we place it among the earliest plays or give it a somewhat later date, it does contain dramaturgic immaturity. Constance's prolonged lamentations verge upon the wearisome. Arthur's sufferings, though moving, seem protracted in order to mist our eyes. Concluding events are so huddled together that we may well wonder whether the most attentive Elizabethan left the theater without furrowed brows.

Despite these blemishes, the play has peculiar power. The Time-Life

15

BBC version, featuring Leonard Rossiter in the title role, bears witness to the play's often overlooked force. Similarly, the Royal Shakespeare Company's recent production, with Guy Henry as the treacherous monarch, succeeded in bringing this undeservedly musty old play to throbbing life. Although some of King John's blank verse might have been composed by a fledgling playwright, the drama is not the work of a jejune dramatist unacquainted with "this world's false subtleties" (138 l. 4). Nor, as we shall see, is the play utterly without form. King John takes a sharp-sighted view of the gap between expressed political ideals and Machiavellian realities. It speculates on human helplessness before dominating powers which might be called fate, chance, and, in some instances, providence. Perhaps, most centrally, it speculates upon the frightening role of the unexpected in human affairs and raises one of Shakespeare's recurring themes—the question of the reality of values, be they practical or transcendent. It is, in essence, about the intrusion of chaos into crucial events and the subversion of order politically, socially, and personally.

The opening scenes of the play introduce us to a thematic baseline of confusion and perplexity. These episodes concern the validity of claims. The first, involving Chatillon, the French ambassador, raises the very question of John's right to occupy the throne in place of his nephew, Arthur. The second, although less important politically, receives more attention. The younger son of Lady Faulconbridge argues that his elder brother is the illegitimate offspring of Richard the Lion-Hearted, and therefore, is ineligible to inherit the family's fortune. This scene invites us to switch our attentions back to the previous episode and the question of the contested throne of England, a central dramatic motif. Who is indeed the rightful ruler? Is it John, or Arthur?

Although willing to defend his claim as Sir Robert's elder son, the Bastard, nevertheless, relinquishes his birthright upon John's invitation for him to embrace a new identity as the illegitimate son of Richard Coeur de Lion. The Bastard, rebellious, exuberant, willing to follow a shadowed path to presumed fortunes, readily accedes to the course of uncertain adventures.

Once King John, his mother, and the others have left the room, the question of the Bastard's legitimacy is resolved. His mother arrives, eager to stop the dispute between her sons before her reputation can be tarnished. After telling her his decision, the Bastard prevails upon her to admit the truth, that he is Richard's son.

At this point the play may seem to be suggesting a simplistic attitude toward discerning the truth of claims. For we also have Eleanor's admission that John's title depends upon "Your strong possession much more than your right" (I. i. 40).[5] The easy solution to the problem of the Bastard's birthright may suggest that the question of John's claim also has a simple resolution.

But the complex world of *King John* offers no such palliating assurances. It is a world of constant flux, of frightening, destructive change, of black turning to white and then to black again. The questions of right and legitimacy are asked more than once. As the play moves forward, answers become less and less certain.

The world of *King John* is one of arrant Machiavellianism and power plays. Despite Arthur's clearer title, John clings tenaciously to his throne, and Constance, Arthur's mother, cleaves with equal tenacity to her son's claim. Philip, the French king, also supports Arthur. But both monarchs reveal their willingness to depart from moral paths when doing so benefits them. As the Bastard cynically notes, John is willing to depart with a portion of his kingdom so that he might retain the bulk of it. Likewise, Philip sets aside Arthur's claim so that he may aggrandize himself by marrying his son Lewis to John's niece Blanche. Perhaps the most ruthless expression of Machiavellianism occurs when Pandulph, the papal legate, eggs Lewis into invading England so that John, out of desperation, will order young Arthur's death, thereby clearing the way for Lewis's claim. Even in our own brutal time, the conniving of a high-ranking churchman in a child's murder is shocking.

As the Bastard cynically analyzes the situation, commodity makes the world spin:

> Mad world, mad kings, mad composition!
> John, to stop Arthur's title in the whole,
> Hath willingly departed with a part;
> And France, whose armor conscience buckled on,
> Whom zeal and charity brought to the field
> As God's own soldier, rounded in the ear
> With that same purpose-changer, that sly devil,
> That broker that still breaks the pate of faith,
> That daily break-vow, he that wins of all,
> Of kings, of beggars, old men, young men, maids—
> Who, having no external thing to lose
> But the word "maid," cheats the poor maid of that —
> That smooth-faced gentleman, tickling Commodity,
> Commodity, the bias of the world —
> The world, who of itself is peisèd well,
> Made to run even upon even ground,
> Till this advantage, this vile-drawing bias,
> This sway of motion, this Commodity,

Makes it take head from all indifferency,
From all direction, purpose, course, intent.
And this same bias, this Commodity,
This bawd, this broker, this all-changing word,
Clapped on the outward eye of fickle France,
Hath drawn him from his own determined aid,
From a resolved and honorable war,
To a most base and vile-concluded peace.
And why rail I on this Commodity?
But for because he had not wooed me yet.
Not that I have the power to clutch my hand
When his fair angels would salute my palm,
But for my hand, as unattempted yet,
Like a poor beggar, raileth on the rich.
Well, whiles I am a beggar, I will rail
And say there is no sin but to be rich;
And being rich, my virtue then shall be
To say there is no vice but beggary.
Since kings break faith upon Commodity.
Gain, be my lord, for I will worship thee [II. ii. 562-599].

In a world so dominated by power plays, scheming, and ruthlessness, little political, moral, or social stability remains. All events, all positions of power, all tactics are subject to reversal and painfully so. The theme of unexpected reversals is introduced early in the play with the Bastard's abrupt decision to drop his claim to the Faulconbridge birthright, and the siege of Angiers makes this dominating theme disturbingly apparent. The French forces approach the city, demanding entry and claiming victory. Almost immediately the English, under John, likewise claim victory and demand entrance into the city. These counterclaims lead to another reversal. Since Angiers will admit neither force, both armies decide to join and attack Angiers. Just when the dual-pronged onslaught is to commence, the people of Angiers instigate another turnabout by suggesting that Lewis, Philip's son, marry Blanche, John's niece. Suddenly John and Philip become friends, allies; Constance, Philip's suppliant, then becomes his victim. The marriage is performed, but the relentless reversals are far from ending.

Pandulph, the legate from Rome, arrives, and, scornful of John's unwillingness to submit himself to papal rule, excommunicates him and forbids the compact of the two monarchs, provoking Philip into resuming hostilities toward John.

John's fortunes decline, but only momentarily. In the ensuing conflict, his forces capture Arthur and spirit the lad to England, where John plans his murder. Then we have another shift. The scepter of victory slips from

John's grasp as Pandulph stirs the coals of war into a blaze by rousing Lewis, Philip's son, to claim the throne through Blanche's right. The downward spiral of John's fortunes continues as he plans Arthur's murder, which he believes will ensure his claim. Hubert, the chosen executioner, overcome by his love for the boy and by Arthur's pleading, refuses to murder the lad and lets John believe the atrocity has been committed. Salisbury and other nobles, fearing that Arthur is dead, plan to revolt against their king. John, fearing mass desertions, wishes that Arthur had not been slain, whereupon Hubert declares that Arthur lives. John feels himself reprieved, but before Hubert can return to the boy, Arthur dies in an attempt to escape by leaping from the castle. In a twist of fortune suggestive of such darker novels as Thomas Hardy's *The Return of the Native* and *Two on a Tower*, Salisbury and other nobles, believe Arthur has been murdered. John, though innocent, is judged guilty of the murder he had authorized. The nobles then desert to the French.

The string of reversals not only claims John but victimizes the Machiavellian Pandulph as well. John, fearing the invading French, the desertion of his nobles, and the splintering of his realm, makes obeisance to the Pope. Pandulph glibly promises to curtail Lewis' invasion, but the fiery young Frenchman will not retrench. Having begun the foray, he will not withdraw, despite Pandulph's entreaties and commands. Only another reversal — one perhaps supernatural, the unexpected flood — halts the French advance, coercing Lewis to seek peace. Perhaps I have belabored the plot, but I have run this risk to underscore that the play is far from formless. The motifs of Machiavellianism and reversals of fortune give the drama shape and depth.

The reversals I have outlined are but some of many shifts that make the world of King John unsure, unsteady, and indeed, painful. Particularly poignant are the fortunes of the innocent, those individuals not guilty of Machiavellianism who find themselves psychologically torn asunder by machinations they cannot avoid or combat. Especially unfortunate is Blanche. Recently married to Lewis to cement the jerrybuilt alliance between England and France, she finds herself pulled between her uncle and her new husband:

> Which is the side that I must go withal?
> I am with both: each army hath a hand,
> And in their rage, I having hold of both,
> They whirl asunder and dismember me.
> Husband, I cannot pray that thou mayst win;
> Uncle, I needs must pray that thou mayst lose;
> Father, I may not wish the fortune thine;

> Grandam, I will not wish thy wishes thrive:
> Whoever wins, on that side I shall lose;
> Assurèd loss before the match be played [III. i. 327-336].

Likewise, Constance feels herself torn asunder. First, she is laid low by Philip's betrayal which threatens Arthur's claim. Then, when, because of Pandulph, the war between England and France indeed breaks out, Arthur is captured. Constance is lacerated by the pain of separation from her son and by the probability of his death:

> I am not mad. This hair I tear is mine;
> My name is Constance; I was Geoffrey's wife;
> Young Arthur is my son; and he is lost;
> I am not mad; I would to heaven I were... [III. iv. 45-48].

Despite her assertions, Constance borders on madness; she is never reunited with Arthur and dies. Without question Arthur joins the ranks of unfortunate innocents.

But in the violent world of *King John* not only the innocent but the ruthless suffer. The Machiavellian Eleanor dies in France, never reunited with her son, John. Pandulph endures the humiliation of not being able to curb Lewis's rampages. John himself must surrender his crown to the Pope and meets his death, poisoned by a treacherous monk. The would-be monarch of England, Lewis, sees his forces scattered by a flood.

Not all reversals in the play are disastrous. Curiously, as the drama moves toward its close, we encounter one of the most intriguing alterations, that of the Bastard from cynical opportunist to champion of British patriotism. As John's fortunes slide irreversibly downward, the Bastard's rise. As John loses more and more control over pell-mell events, the Bastard becomes more and more England's moral and political shepherd. It is he who rebukes the nobles because of their desertion of John; he who castigates Hubert when he believes the latter has murdered Arthur; he who seeks to preserve the boy's life; he who allows John's son, Prince Henry, to assume the throne upon the monarch's death. It is he, the Bastard, who speaks the well-known, triumphant lines: "This England never did, nor never shall, / Lie at the proud foot of a conqueror, / But when it first did help to wound itself" (V. vii. 112-114). In a final stroke of irony, the Bastard, the seemingly irredeemable scalawag, becomes the savior of Britain.

Madness, confusion, chaos— these are the elements of the world of King John. But the world of the play is not godless. Hints of providential concern form the backdrop. Imperiled by the invading French, the Bastard observes that "heaven itself doth frown upon the land" (IV. iii. 159).

Lewis's needed supplies "Are cast away and sunk on Goodwin sands" (V. v. 13)—possibly within the context of the play a providential intervention. The supernatural apparition of five moons appears in the sky, one moon whirling about the stationary other four. Peter of Pomfret's prophecy that John will hand over his crown before Ascension Day also suggests divine manipulations. But can clear patterns of divine approval or disapproval be drawn from these events? Perhaps we can conclude that heavenly powers cause John's humiliation. But do they also decree his death? Very likely they work the defeat of Lewis. Why do they not also supernaturally punish other Machiavellians such as Philip and Pandulph? Why do they not intervene to save the defenseless such as Constance or the innocent such as Arthur? One could, of course, continue asking questions about the fortunes of the play's many characters, but doing so would be pointless.

Little evidence of divine intervention emerges from the intertwining events of King John. There are some miraculous occurrences which are clearly preternatural, e. g., the apparition of the moons; other apparently preternatural occurrences, such as the discovery of Arthur's body, could simply result from happenstance. The overtly supernatural occurrences— the apparition and the fulfilled prophecy—imbue the action with an ambiance of superstition and folklore rather than illustrate unambiguous theological patterns. At best, what one can say of the play's theological perspective is that it exists. As stated before, the world of the play is not godless, but the extent of the theological manipulations is murky. On one hand the world of *King John* offers hope, with the other it places a counterbalancing weight. The play leaves readers with uneasy, partial comfort.

Distinctions whirl into darkness. Right and wrong change places. What Terry Eagleton said of *Macbeth* may well be applied to King John: "meaning falters and slides ... firm definitions are dissolved and binary oppositions eroded: fair is foul and foul is fair, nothing is but what is not" (2). Even the question of legitimacy ultimately becomes blurred, as Lewis, claiming through Blanche the right left her by Arthur's death, declares himself England's monarch, a claim, however legal it may be, is not acceptable to the play's English, to the Bastard, and, if we take into account the Bastard's often quoted patriotic lines, not even to Shakespeare himself.

Perhaps Salisbury best encapsulates the play's obsession with confusion:

> But such is the infection of the time
> That, for the health and physic of our right,
> We cannot deal but with the very hand

Of stern injustice and confused wrong.
And is't not pity, O my grieved friends
That we, the sons and children of this isle,
Were born to see so sad an hour as this,
Wherein we step after a stranger, march
Upon her gentle bosom and fill up
Her enemies' ranks—[V. ii. 20-29].

The achievement of *King John* can perhaps best be illustrated by stressing that the play first of all presents not a realistic portrayal of humanity and historical conflicts but a territory in Shakespeare's mind, an imaginary world in which Shakespeare juggles discrete historical events to provide a sense of complex interaction. For instance, Lewis's marriage to Blanche had nothing to do with the siege of Angiers, and his invasion of England took place years after Arthur's death.[6] However much of Shakespeare's play may frustrate the historian, *King John* offers us a meaningful interpretation of experience. This point might be made better by drawing upon J. R. R. Tolkien's concept of the artist as "sub-creator," as one who establishes in a literary work a "Secondary World which your mind can enter," that is, an imagined realm with its own principles of pseudo-reality. Tolkien continues, "Inside it, what he [the artist] relates is 'true': it accords with the laws of that world" (60). Of course, Tolkien is referring to works of fantasy, or, as he calls them, "fairy stories." But the basic terminology may be applied to the fantastic world of *King John*, a world not of elves, trolls, ents, hobbits, and ring-wraiths but a world of bizarre reversals, rampant treachery, and murky supernaturalism. The nightmarish vision of King John presents us something like a surrealistic interpretation of what the Elizabethan world could become, a world spinning without order.

For, along with political and psychological chaos, the world of King John offers a region that defies logical patterns of analysis and predictability. In a territory where patriots become traitors because of their patriotism, where the identity of England's rightful heir is obscured, where the snickering Machiavel can become the nation's savior, the result is a poignant air of indecipherability of truth, the unreliability of proposed action — in effect, chaos.

Indeed the world of *King John* lends itself to interpretation in accord with contemporary chaos theory. Known to the general public through Michael Crichton's novels *Jurassic Park* and *The Lost World* and their movie incarnations, chaos theory suggests an innate unpredictability of such phenomena as thunderstorms, tornadoes, the stock market, genetic selection, and the outbreaks of wars. This unpredictability results from unforeseen influences. Former physicist and now Anglican priest John

Polkinghorne thus delineates the predicament as he explains meteorologist Edward Lorenz's celebrated "butterfly effect."

> ...one of the earliest examples of this [chaotic] behaviour
> came to light during attempts to understand the
> Earth's weather systems. They are so sensitive
> that a butterfly stirring the air with its wings
> in the African jungle today will have consequences
> for the storms over London in three or four weeks'
> time. Because we can't know about all these
> African butterflies, I can say with confidence
> that detailed long-term weather forecasting
> is never going to work [57].

This factor of unpredictability, the stunning consequences of the interrelatedness of apparently discrete phenomena, severely limits and at times obviates humankind's ability to cope with life. In the novel version of *Jurassic Park* Crichton offers a grim application of chaos theory not only to the hope of creating a scientific Utopia but to the hope of human progress as well. As the mathematician Ian Malcolm speculates,

> And, like the medieval system before it, science is starting not to
> fit the world any more.... Ever since Newton and Descartes, sci-
> ence has explicitly offered us the vision of total control. Science
> has claimed the power to eventually control everything, through
> its understanding of natural laws. But in the twentieth century
> that claim has been shattered beyond repair.... And now, chaos
> theory proves that unpredictability is built into our daily lives.
> It is as mundane as the rainstorm we cannot predict [312].

Dwelling on the "end of the scientific era," Malcolm judges the hope of understanding and controlling much of the phenomena of existence as "an idle boast. As foolish and as misguided as the child who jumps off a building because he believes he can fly"(312).

Of course, chaos theory does not mean utter turmoil. Mathematical investigations reveal that amid whirls of chaos, patterns of order may be born when the chaotic phenomena begin to coalesce or fall into a design about some hitherto unforeseen and unpredictable factor or "strange attractor," to use the technical term. In other words, the rampages of chaos are not unending, leading to ever more dissolution and disorder. For instance, stock markets rebound, slumps in business can be followed by periods of growth, and civilizations fall and rise. Some scientists, in fact, nowadays prefer the term "complexity theory " to "chaos theory" to designate the phenomena under consideration. Yet whatever underlying principles of order mathematical inquiry may uncover, the dark implications of chaos theory are not abrogated. In the words of mathematician John Casty,

> It may well be the case that after the smoke and fire clear away, science will render the verdict that certain phenomena, like long-range weather patterns, that have resisted prediction for ages really are governed by chaotic laws of motion. This conclusion, suitably buttressed by convincing theoretical and empirical evidence, would certainly merit high marks for explanation. But the scientific laws of explanation would then be basically useless for any sort of prediction [76].

In other words, the emergent patterns of order are themselves unpredictable and, therefore, cannot be regulated or controlled. Or as Polkinghorne explains the hub of the impasse, "These systems are unpredictable in behaviour because they can never be insulated from the smallest nudges given them by their environment" (66).[7]

The Elizabethan fear of chaos, documented and explained by E. M. W. Tillyard and Theodore Spencer in the 1940s, receives new focus and emphasis from contemporary science. Although *King John* ends with a quasi-obligatory promise of hope with the dawning reign of King Henry III, only a careless reader would rejoice. The play ends not with a firm platform of social regeneration, but a somber conviction that whatever humankind may do, its endeavors are in the end mocked by chaos.

Although the fear of chaos runs deep through the works of Shakespeare — especially in the history plays — these themes are, interestingly enough, paramount in *Titus Andronicus*, his earliest tragedy. In the play's opening the victorious general Titus does what is right by orthodox Elizabethan standards, putting aside his supporters' claim that he be made emperor and upholding the title of the rightful heir Saturninus. But Saturninus betrays him, and Titus becomes a pariah within Rome, lamenting the execution of two of his sons and the rape and mutilation of his daughter Lavinia. Unable to gain redress from the state, his only recourse is to rebel against the social order he earlier gave up potential kingship to support and murders Tamora and attempts to kill Saturninus.

Moreover, besides being the result of Shakespeare's first attempt to create a tragic protagonist, Titus is the first of Shakespeare's heroes to be ideologically sundered. At the beginning of the play Titus reveals himself dedicated to Rome. Twenty-one sons he has lost in its defense; his patriotism does not allow him to regret their loss in the service of his country. His sense of duty to the accepted patterns of order leads him to renounce the kingship offered by his partisans and offer the crown instead to Saturninus, the elder son of the previous emperor. Titus's adherence to the Roman code of duty and obedience is perhaps dramatized most emphatically when he kills his own son Mutius when the latter opposes Saturninus's decision to make Lavinia his bride. With an almost robotic bent, Titus has functioned all his life as an arm of Rome. An important part of the body politic, he expects the deference, consideration, and loyalty, which — according to his ideology of patriotism — Rome should give him. The rejection of these principles by the brash young emperor Saturninus, his choice of Tamora, Titus' archenemy, as a wife, and his blatant treachery all disrupt the formerly victorious general's sense of position in the social and universal hierarchy. Suddenly the principles that he has lived by, that have formed him, no longer suffice. He has been cast away like a soiled rag. The outer chaos created by Saturninus, Aaron, and Tamora causes inner chaos to erupt into Titus' psyche. As often occurs in Elizabethan drama, the frustration ensuing ideological confusion vents itself in madness. Titus's raison d'etre becomes the destruction of the emperor and the monarch's new family of Tamora and her sons. His thirst for bloody vengeance drives him to oppose the very principles that have formed him. A similar — although not psychotic — reversal of loyalties erupts when Titus' son Lucius, stung by the family's abuse, flees to the Rome's enemies, the Goths, to raise a force to invade his native land.

Intriguingly enough, a similar situation occurs in what is apparently Shakespeare's final tragedy *Coriolanus*, when the prideful Roman general Marcius, because of injustices dealt him, absconds to his enemies, the Volscians, to raise an army to attack Rome. In both plays Shakespeare delves into the dreadful irony of circumstances causing noble persons to betray the states that had nurtured them. Interestingly, in *Titus*, he compares Lucius's foray to that of his later tragedy's hero when Amilius stresses that Lucius "threats in course of this revenge to do / As much as ever Coriolanus did" (IV. iv. 67-68). Early in his career Shakespeare was drawn to portrayals of life's expected reversals, a theme that he would treat jarringly in his final Roman play.

The climactic battles of *Julius Caesar* provide one of the most clearly illustrative examples of the type of chaos presented in *King John*, chaos which in this instance undermines the conspirators and ushers in the era of the power of Lepidus, Octavius, and Antony. The chain of concluding uncontrollable events, compounded by both human error and unpredictable mischance, begins with a strategic blunder committed by Brutus and Cassius. Cassius wishes to wait and draw Antony's and Octavius's troops in, forcing the enemies to weary themselves with trekking and to waste their reserves. Believing that the "people twixt Philippi and this ground" (IV. iii. 203) bear his party little love, Brutus argues that the better course is to march upon Antony's troops and meet them at Philippi lest the opposition add recruits from the area's disgruntled countrymen. Cassius is certainly the more experienced soldier, but falling again into his irrational pattern of giving in to Brutus, Cassius withdraws his argument like an ill-placed rook on a chessboard.

Clearly their opponents see the conspirators' decision as a blunder. As Octavius makes clear, Antony, a battle-tried veteran, had assumed that Brutus and Cassius would not make such a move: "Now, Antony, our hopes are answerèd: / You said the enemy would not come down, / But keep the hills and upper regions. / It proves not so: their battles are at hand; / They mean to warn [attack] us at Philippi here, / Answering before we do demand of them" (V. i. 1-6).

Curiously enough, as the battle nears, Antony and Octavius recapitulate the strategical disagreement of Cassius and Brutus. Antony wishes his younger colleague to lead the left flank of their forces, but Octavius objects: "Upon the right hand I; Keep thou the left (V. i. 18). Although Antony bristles, Octavius has his way. The result is that the two lesser experienced leaders confront each other. Believing Octavius's troops apathetic, Brutus orders his forces to charge them. But Titinius judges the action a battlefield blunder:

> O Cassius, Brutus gave the word too early,
> Who, having some advantage on Octavius,
> Took it too eagerly. His soldiers fell to spoil,
> Whilst we by Antony are all enclosed [V. iii. 5-8].

Soldiers are seen from a distance entering the camp of Cassius. Pindarus, concurring with Titinius, believes them to be Antony's men despoiling the bivouac. The fatal error occurs. Accepting the report and seeing a fire at his camp, Cassius dispatches Titinius toward the scene of apparent mayhem to learn the truth. Pindarus mounts the hill to witness what happens and to report the news to his general. The troops, however, are the jubilant men of Brutus; they swarm about Cassius' messenger, rejoicing. Pindarus interprets their behavior as an attack and so informs Cassius that Antony's men hold the camp. Thereupon Cassius commits suicide.

The episode ushers forth chaotic ironies. Both inexperienced commanders confront each other. The judgments of Cassius, Antony, and Titinius repeatedly underscore the ineptitude of Brutus's battlefield decisions, but in a surprising stroke of irony, he wins—against what seems to be all probability. (This upset adumbrates Antony's later reversal in *Antony and Cleopatra* when, despite the advice of his generals, he achieves a surprise, though momentary, upset of Octavius.) Significantly, however, the text does not tell us what happened during the confrontation between Octavius and Brutus. Did one or the other or both make arrogant blunders? Did one master the other because of wise, split-second judgments? Our lack of knowledge imbues the entire episode with an air of quirkiness, of unpredictability: a concept given immediate recapitulation by Cassius' error-laden decision. Had Pindarus rightly construed the actions of the soldiers—or waited longer to make the report—Cassius would have survived, at least for the moment, and the outcome of the war might have been different. Antony's "Cry havoc and let slip the dogs of war"(III. i. 275)—uttered after the death of Caesar—proves bitterly wry. His determination to avenge Caesar's death and seize power for himself unleashes a torrent of events, the aftermath of which he survives largely by chance. Subtly, the text of *Julius Caesar* underscores *King John*'s world of murky, unforeseeable events. In both plays, rationality, strategy, and cogitation prove defenseless against the onslaught of the chaotic. In the worlds of *King John* and *Julius Caesar*, to borrow Matthew Arnold's famous lines from "Dover Beach," humanity is indeed "as on a darkling plain / Swept with confused alarms of struggle and flight / Where ignorant armies clash by night"(35-37).

One of Shakespeare's most explicit treatments of the theme of chaos which intertwines itself among the events of *King John* occurs in his narrative poem *The Rape of Lucrece*. Published in 1594, this poem could indeed be contemporaneous with the enigmatic history play, generally thought to have been written between 1594-1596. After the heroine's rape, in her lament, in which she rails at Night, Opportunity, and Time, she despairs at her evident helplessness before the dominance of seemingly invincible forces. The lament is too long to be quoted in its entirety, but excerpts such as the following in which Lucrece curses Night communicate a strong sense of Shakespearean dismay at the forces of chaos.

First Lucrece rails against Night:

> O comfort-killing Night, image of hell,
> Dim register and notary of shame,
> Black stage for tragedies and murders fell
> Vast sin-concealing chaos, nurse of blame!

Blind muffled bawd, dark harbor for defame,
Grim cave of death, whisp'ring conspirator
With close-tongued treason and the ravisher! [764-70].

The idea of night as a time for the unleashing of evil was common in Elizabethan culture, given memorable expression in Thomas Nashe's pamphlet *The Terrors of the Night*. Interestingly, Shakespeare identifies night with colossal anarchy, harking back to the classical concept of the primordial chaos, the original darkness from which creation ensued. Realizing the well-nigh intractability of night, Lucrece, its victim, in a kind of witchcraft, calls upon it to punish the sun:

O hateful, vaporous, and foggy Night,
Since thou are guilty of my cureless crime,
Muster thy mists to meet the eastern light,
Make war against the proportioned course of time;
Or if thou wilt permit the sun to climb
          His wonted height, yet ere he go to bed
          Knit poisonous clouds about his golden head [771-77].

Like Webster's Duchess of Malfi, she would curse the world into its first chaos. Traditionally, cursing is the last resource of the helpless; Lear resorts to it after Goneril and Regen's cruelty has driven him into the storm; Webster's Duchess uses to it, of course, during her nightmarish imprisonment.[8] Lucrece seeks revenge against the sun because its light did not appear to shield her from her ravishment, her "cureless crime." She calls upon Night to harass and destroy the sun, hurling the universe back toward chaos, magnifying her misfortune to cosmic proportions. Of course, her lament is based upon a tissue of absurdities. She cannot harm Night nor Day; these great powers are beyond her petty abilities to injure them.

Next she rails against Opportunity:

O Opportunity, thy guilt is great!
'Tis thou that execut'st the traitor's treason;
Thou sets the wolf where he the lamb may get;
Whoever plots the sin, thou 'point'st the season;
'Tis thou that spurn'st at night, at low, at reason;
And in thy shady cell, where none may spy him,
Sits Sin, to seize the souls that wander by him.

Thou makest the vestal violate her oath;
Thou blowest the fire when temperance is thawed;
Thou smother'st honesty, thou murderest troth.
Thou foul abettor, thou notorious bawd,

Thou plantest scandal and displaces laud.
Thou ravisher, thou traitor, thou false thief,
Thy honey turns to gall, thy joy to grief! [776-889].

Next she directs her frenzied animosity toward Time itself:

Misshapen Time, copesmate of ugly Night,
Swift subtle post, carrier of grisly care,
Eater of Youth, false slave to false delight,
Base watch of woes, sin's packhorse, virtue's snare!
   Thou nursest all, and murderest all that are.
   O, hear me then, injurious shifting Time!
Be guilty of my death, since of my crime!

Why hath thy servant Opportunity
Betrayed the hours thou gav'st me to repose,
Canceled my fortunes, and enchained me
To the endless date of never-ending woes [925-36].

Of course, none of her imprecations are effective.

In vain I rail at Opportunity,
At Time, at Tarquin, and uncheerful Night;
in vain I cavil with mine infamy,
In vain I spurn at my confirmed despite.
This helpless smoke of words doth me no right.
   The remedy indeed to do me good
   Is to let forth my foul-defilèd blood [1023-29].

An extremely long list of examples of mischances creating havoc in
Shakespeare's works could be drawn up. To add depth to my thesis, I supply
a few: the crucial storm at sea in *Richard II* which prevents the king's return,
causing his troops to disband, thus tipping the scales in favor of Bolingbroke
and the rebels; Puck's fortuitously encountering Helena and Demetrius in forest and mistaking them for Hermia and Lysander in *A Midsummer Night's
Dream*; the unexpected flood in Richard III, which ends Buckingham's rebellion; the unforeseen collapse of Northumberland's nerve in *Henry IV, Parts
I and II*, which compels him to feign sickness; and Don John's unexpected
flight in *Much Ado About Nothing*, which helps create the happy end.

Concomitant with Shakespeare's concern with chaos is a disquieting
awareness, as expressed by the title of an essay by Montaigne, "That We
Taste Nothing Pure"—that is, we never encounter pure goodness or confront pure evil, but an disturbing, unwieldy fusion of the two. As we have
seen in *King John*, a ravaging flood disrupts Lewis's invasion of England;

Hubert's mercy in sparing Arthur is the prologue to the lad's accidental death; England's political anarchy brings to light the Bastard's hidden nobility. Indeed, throughout his career, Shakespeare was haunted by frequent jumbling of joy and sorrow, good and ill, fortune and misfortune. This concern, amounting to a recurrent obsession, may be illustrated by numerous examples. A few are provided.

For instance, *All's Well That Ends Well* manifests a concern with devastating ironies and the fusions, and the alternations of good and evil theme is underscored by the First Lord's observation: "The web of our life is of a mingled yarn, good and ill together. / Our virtues would be proud if our faults whipped them not; / and our crimes would despair if they were not cherished by our virtues. (IV. iii. 70–73)

Helena, the enterprising heroine, also comments upon the perplexing mixture of good and evil when she decides to substitute herself in Diana's bed so that she might claim the love of her roving husband Bertram:

> Why then to-night
> Let us essay our plot; which, if it speed,
> Is wicked meaning in a lawful deed,
> And lawful meaning in a wicked act,
> Where both not sin, and yet a sinful fact,
> But let's about it [III. vii. 44-48].

Helena's later comment may suggest that all can be resolved and all enigmas be apparent, but, as John Russell Brown has observed, Helena's words do not solve the problem. The complexities trouble our sense of right and wrong: "We may well want to pause and think through the implications of those repetitive and jingling antitheses"(87).

Similarly, Portia, at the conclusion of *The Merchant of Venice*, muses upon relativity when she and Nerissa, nearing Belmont, spy a window glowing, but lighted only by a candle. Nerissa remarks, "When the moon shone, we did not see the candle" (V. i. 92), and Portia speculates upon relative brightness of the candle and the moon. She says

> So doth the greater glory dim the less.
> A substitute shines brightly as a king.
> Until the king be by, and then his state [the substitute's]
> Empties itself, as doth an inland brook
> Into the main of waters [93-97].

Next they hear music drifting from her house. Portia comments, "Nothing is good, I see, without respect. / Methinks it sounds much sweeter than by day" (99-96). Like Emerson in his poem "Each and All," Portia discourses upon her realization that a particular beauty, strength, or virtue may be apparent only on a particular occasion, in particular surroundings.

In *Measure for Measure*, Escalus observes life's stunningly complex interweaving of good and ill: "Well, heaven forgive him, and forgive us all! / Some rise by sin, and some by virtue fall; / Some run from breaks of ice and answer none, /And some condemned for a fault alone" (II. i. 37-40).

In *The Rape of Lucrece*—to return to this poem for the moment—the eponymous heroine, after her ravishment, also speculates upon the dire jumbling of good and ill:

> Why should the worm intrude the maiden bud?
> Or hateful cuckoos hatch in sparrow's nests?
> Or toads infect fair founts with venom mud?
> Or tyrant folly lurk in gentle breasts?
> Or kings be breakers of their own behests?
>   But no perfection is so absolute
>   That some impurity doth not pollute [848-54].

Although nowadays many persons still uphold the power of reason to solve our problems and still have faith that the next act of legislation or the next judicial decision will be preliminary to ushering in Utopia, our own age, with its unremitting social and political turmoil, has been an unhappy witness to the jumbling of good and ill. As sociologist Frank W. Elwell has observed, "There is a reciprocal relationship between social change and social problems. Social change often causes social problems; these problems, in turn often cause further social change. It has often been asserted that that change is accelerating in modern society; it has also been asserted that our social problems appear to be multiplying"(6). Elwell continues by providing a discomforting list of current problems created or accelerated by social change: abuse of the environment; the widening fissure between the rich and the poor; the breakdown of the family; the desiccation of a sense of community; widespread criminal behavior; alcohol and drug misuse; teenage pregnancies; a widespread sense of alienation (6-7). In other words, by and large, modern social change militates against what to Dryden in *Religio Laici* was an overriding goal of human social endeavor: a peaceful society of comfort and repose, "But common quiet is mankind's concern"(450).⁹ Or, to call again upon the terminology of another seventeenth century poet, George Herbert, humanity, by striving to obtain its goals, rests in "repining restlessness" ("The Pulley," 17). Shakespeare would have sympathized with Herbert's wincing view.

I do not suggest that Shakespeare was constantly dogged by concepts of relativity. Yet he deals with them, at times even whimsically, but underlying perhaps all of these treatments is the fear of distinctions blurred, absolutes challenged, ranks overturned, definitions lost — in short, chaos on both the levels of political order and personal harmony — the essence of the world of *King John*.

Of course, Shakespeare's most stunning acknowledgment of relativism's claims is Hamlet's "…for there is nothing either good or bad but thinking makes it so" (II. ii. 249-51).

The world of *King John*, nevertheless, continues to haunt us. Like the original audience we would like to escape from a world of doubt, uncertainty, and chaos to one of order and fulfillment. The Bastard's patriotic closing speech extends a hypothetical ladder for the audience members to climb from the morass by extending the hope of a quasi-Utopian future in which England will always be sovereign, untampled by foreign boots. As rousing as the speech is, a pensive playgoer, upon leaving the theater, may well wonder how inspiring the lines are. Reflecting upon the ironies of the play, our hypothetical spectator may also question if the future generations will be any more successful than that of King John in overcoming greed, treachery, and crime. (We may recall that patterns of order emerging from chaos may be forestalled by further chaos: A rebound of the stock market may be cut short by an unexpected fall.) The Elizabethans, remembering the War of the Roses, may well have shaken their heads in melancholy recognition that all cannot not be right with the world.

King John, of course, cannot be said to embody or illustrate anything like Shakespeare's "view of the world." Certainly other plays, notably the final romances, offer more hopeful prospects for humankind's capabilities. *King John*, nevertheless, presents a Shakespearean view of the world, a troubling perception that Shakespeare struggled with throughout his career.

TWO

One Man's Meat Is Another Man's Poison: Psychetypes and Individual Realities

In his "Epistle to John Hamilton Reynolds," Keats writes, "But I saw too distinct into the core / Of an eternal fierce destruction" (96–97).

These bleak lines occur during a narration in which the poet recalls a pleasant evening at the beach where "the wide sea did weave / An untumultuous fringe of silver foam/ Along the flat brown sand... (90–93). But then meditating upon sea's ferocity, the poet undergoes a mood shift into painful melancholy:

> and tho', to-day
> I've gather'd young spring-leaves, and flowers gay
> Of periwinkle and wild strawberry,
> Still do I that most fierce destruction see, —
> The Shark at savage prey, — the Hawk at pounce, —
> The gentle Robin, like a Pard or Ounce,
> Ravening a worm, — Away, ye horrid moods!
> Moods of one's mind! You know I hate them well.
> You know I'd sooner be a clapping Bell
> To some Kamtschatcan Missionary Church,
> Than with these horrid moods be left i' the lurch — [99–109].

Then the poem's tone changes to uplifting strains.

> Do you get health — and Tom the same — I'll dance
> And from detested moods in new Romance
> Take refuge [110–12].

Interestingly enough, Keats's "eternal fierce destruction" calls to mind "the destructive element" of Conrad's Stein in *Lord Jim.* Marlow, the novel's narrator, seeks counsel regarding Jim, the failed hero, from the aged butterfly collector. Stein advises Marlow that the only way for Jim to regain his sense of fortitude and self-control is to risk losing them by placing himself in another potentially dangerous, ideal-destroying situation. Or, as he says in his not precisely grammatical English, "The way is to the destructive element submit yourself, and with the exertions of your hands and feet in the water make the deep, deep sea keep you up." Later Stein repeats his root idea, "In the destructive element immerse...." (214).

Significantly, both Keats and Conrad, in conjuring up a sense of the forces antithetical to the humanity's happiness, draw upon the dark archetypal associations of the ocean; i.e, its being dangerous, ungovernable, formless, shifting, a place of loss of direction, of incomprehensibility, and of death, a nightmare region "from which all life has emerged and into which it must eventually dissolve" (Bruce-Mitford 34). In their respective works Keats and Conrad confront the essence of chaos and suggest ways of dealing with it. Indeed, how to deal with life's unexpected reversals, its inevitable disappointments, its unfathomable mysteries, its recurring pains, and its senseless tragedies has been an enduring question of the ages.

Much Western philosophy has sought the answer to combating chaos' ravages through what might be called right reason. The recurring hope has been that through learning truth, humankind could subdue its animal nature, order itself into the good society, and find happiness on earth. One of the earliest such thinkers whose work has survived is Plato. To him truth was indivisible and eternal. If those in quest of knowledge persisted on the correct road, all would arrive at the same destination. Hence, the ideal state, the Republic, would be ruled by philosophers—men and women who, having studied until their fifties, would have acquired knowledge and presumably with only minor disagreements would understand the nature of the good society.[10]

The trouble with Plato's idealistic theorizing is that throughout the ages exponents of right reason have not been able to agree on what right reason is. Stoics, epicureans, realists, nominalists, followers of Aquinas, and followers of Sartre have built up rational systems for enduring, controlling, or eliminating life's "eternal fierce destruction," but unfortunately these theories contradict one other. Indeed, some devotees of right reason have constructed systems of "rational ethics" which seem bizarre or downright perverted to common notions of mankind. A case in point is William Godwin, father of Mary Shelley and father-in-law of Percy Bysshe, whose *Inquiry Concerning Political Justice* envisioned the birth of a Utopia founded upon a mass subordination of personal desires and upon mass wishes to act in accord with the universal good. Consequently, inhabitants of Godwin's ideal new order, if offered an either-or choice in such a situation, would readily rescue a dignitary from a burning building and let their children be incinerated. The reason for this astounding choice? The inhabitants' "indisputable" deduction that the dignitary's continued existence is more important than that of their children!

Not only do supporters of all persuasions disagree, but they rigorously suppress or ignore — at times unconsciously — evidence that would knock their prized assumptions into the proverbial cocked hat. People are predisposed to believe what they *want* to believe and adopt numerous techniques to justify their opinions, theories, and values. As Thomas Gilovich, a longtime student of cognitive errors, writes, "People place a premium on being rational and cognitively consistent, and so they are reluctant to simply disregard pertinent evidence in order to see what they expect to see and believe what they expect to believe. Instead people subtly and carefully 'massage' the evidence to make it consistent with their expectations" (53). Among the strategies for mitigating disagreeable evidence are putting a spin on questions asked in statistical surveys, selecting the *correct* authorities for consultation, and digging into evidence only deeply enough to support preconceived opinions. In the words of Gilovich, "Rather than simply ignoring contradictory information, we often examine it particularly closely. The end product of this intense scrutiny is that the contradictory information is either considered too flawed to be relevant, or is redefined into a less damaging category" (55–56). Furthermore, we limit our exposure to possible criticism of our ideas. "It is a fact of social life that we are selectively exposed to information that tends to support our beliefs. Conservatives read conservative periodicals and thus receive support for a conservative political agenda; religious fundamentalists tend to read 'creationist' literature rather than contemporary evolutionary biology...." The following is the upshot. "Because we so often encounter arguments and evidence in support of our beliefs while generally staying clear of information that contradicts them, our beliefs appear to be more sensible and warranted ... than they would if we were exposed to a less biased body of information." Likewise, we limit our friendships to those who share our ideological sphere. "Liberals associate with fellow liberals; exercise enthusiasts affiliate with other athletes.... As a result, when trying to estimate the percentage of people who hold a particular belief, examples of people who believe as we do come to mind more readily than examples of people who believe differently. Our own beliefs thus appear to be quite common" (Gilovich 115).

Perhaps Montaigne — whose mind in so many ways paralleled Shakespeare's—best assessed the cause of wide-ranging and conflicting opinions among intellectual system-builders. In "Of Democritus and Heraclitus," he writes that in attempting to solve a problem, he will take the first solution that pops into his head without bothering to ruminate all possible solutions one could imagine: "all are equally good for me. I never plan to expound them in full for I do not see the whole of anything: neither do those who promise to help us to do so! Everything has a hundred parts and a thousand faces..." (337–38). Because of the limitations of the human mind, Montaigne is troubled by the need to make choices. No matter how carefully one may attempt to explore a given issue, one cannot see all of its aspects. Individual whim and prejudices distort our viewpoints; important bits of knowledge inevitably elude us; our very short-sightedness prevents our seeing other options. No person can be the absolute master or mistress of any given situation. Better to Montaigne — in this mood, at least!— is to choose the first path that happenstance leads us to.

Of course, few of us would want to adopt so cavalier an attitude toward making vital choices. While recognizing the truth of what Montaigne says, most of us would prefer to struggle with all our mental might to discern what we believe are wise avenues of action. But Montaigne does point to a fundamental reason for disagreements among the learned. Humanity's minds cannot grapple successfully with the disarming complexity of life.

We cannot, nevertheless, help but react to the problems which distress us, and indeed we react to them in different ways. Let us return to Keats's melancholy epiphany on the seashore. In his musings calling to mind "eternal fierce destruction," Keats struggles to find a solution, yet he cannot; his mind is captured by a "horrid mood" and he is unable to separate himself from an oppressive awareness of life's ceaseless cruelties. However, wisely knowing that for the moment, he cannot shake his doldrums, Keats recognizes that with time feelings pass. A moment will come when he will not feel oppressed: "I'll dance / And from detested moods in new Romance / Take refuge."

Keats's reaction introduces another reason why humanity faces such difficulty in concluding what is right or good and in adopting unanimously-selected strategies for achieving its goals: differences in personality. People do not react in the same ways to the phenomena of existence. As the saying goes, "One man's meat is another man's poison." This saw, highlighting the relativity of attractions and aversions, may well indicate our approaches to solving humanity's problems. Conrad's Stein and Keats approach the problem of life's destructiveness differently. The melancholy Stein sees the answer in submitting oneself to the destructive element, in risking physical and ideological destruction, in order to survive — a rather theoretical, if not indeed rationalistic approach. Keats, on the other hand, seeks not the intellectualization of experience, but immersion in experience — a plunge into emotions permitting him for the moment to escape his black moods. He endeavors to find relief from melancholy by dancing — throwing himself into rhythm, motions, liberating swells of melody. He also seeks romance, but not necessarily romantic love, even though it is implied. Here Keats's uses of the word "romance," as he often uses it, to mean the exotic, the enchanting, the supernatural, the enthralling — hence, tales of fantasy, chivalry, adventures in "faerie lands," even though possibly at base "forlorn." Keats's central recurring means of escape from melancholy and life's nerve-grating vicissitudes is through sensation. These differences in reacting to life's phenomena call forth Jung's ideas of differing personalities and the possibility of typing them.

Typology, as a general means of characterizing dominant personality traits, was foreshadowed by such theories of the human make-up as that of the four humors. As a modern discipline it has its beginnings in 1921 with Carl Jung's *Psychological Types*. After consultations with many patients, Jung realized that certain faculties, or ways of perceiving and reacting to the world, were stronger in some individuals and weaker in others. From these observations, he developed his theory of the four functions — thinking, feeling, sensation, and intuition.

Of these faculties one, known as the superior function, serves as each person's basic orientation to the world. Another, acts as the individual's secondary means of adaptation. It influences the person powerfully, but not as strongly as the first. The other two faculties play lesser roles in the person's behavior. No human being lacks any of the four. The four functions may be briefly characterized as follows.

Thinking. Reliance upon thought in decision-making. Enjoyment of ideas, theories, abstractions. Vital sense of principles. Liking for regulation. A desire for power, often coupled with a strong drive to reform. Scholarly. Tendency to structure time into clear units. Preference for a well-ordered lifestyle.

Feeling. Emotions central to life, basis for decision-making. Value placed upon intimacy and a sense of belonging. Vulnerability to self-pity, depression, and other negative emotions. Desire to re-experience emotions of the past. Deep sensitivity to problems of others. Emphasis upon friendship, romantic love. Tendency to view life fatalistically. Desire for emotional unity.

Sensation. Experience central to life, basis for decision-making. Enjoyment of variety, newness. Emphasis upon the physical. Assertiveness valued. Self-control admired. Skeptical about thinking, distrust of abstractions. Values sense of being in control, often likes to control others. Action-oriented, desires peak experiences.

Intuition. Personal vision focal point of personality, basis for decision-making. Absorbed in own affairs, indifferent to external world. Imagination valued. Unobservant of surroundings. Highly imaginative. Often eccentric, often excessive. Often charismatic. (Adapted from Malone 241–55.)

This typological scheme and the fundamental interrelationships of the faculties may also be expressed in a convenient chart.

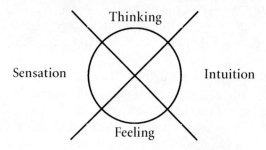

This illustration does not extensively demonstrate the interrelation of the four faculties, but it does show a fundamental pattern. Each function is flanked by the two of the four which can act as the secondary function in a given individual's psyche. For instance, a person whose primary or superior function was intuition would have either thinking or feeling as a secondary function. The secondary function could not be sensation. A predominately thinking person would have intuition or sensation as the main auxiliary orientation, but not feeling.

The function directly opposite each superior function would appear in a given person's psyche as a less powerful, but still influential element. Designated as the inferior function, this trait may be described as "opposite in every way to the superior function," and "the least reliable, least differentiated, and least characteristic function of the personality." The inferior function, however, may affect the individual's psyche profoundly: "The inferior function most often acts as the doorway through which various aspects of the unconscious may meet, encroach upon, or engulf the ego" (Spoto 193).

This fourfold system of typology need not be taken to reduce literary characters to allegorical abstractions or actual persons to oversimplified psychological types in the vein of seventeenth century character sketches or the eighteenth century's infatuation with ruling passions.

Typology provides no easy formula for predicting human behavior. Nor can it be used to predetermine one's occupational effectiveness. Competent physicians, merchants, butchers, teachers, carpenters, social workers, authors can be found among all of the psychological types. Rather than defining human character rigidly, Jungian typology highlights dominant ways of experiencing and reacting to the world's phenomena. Jung himself cautioned against mechanical application of these theories: "these four criteria of types of human behavior are just four viewpoints among many others, like will power, temperament, imagination, memory, and so on. There is nothing dogmatic about them, but their basic nature recommends them as suitable criteria for a classification" (*Man and His Symbols* 61). As Isaiah Berlin commented upon his own typological separation of artists and thinkers into hedgehogs and foxes, "like all distinctions which embody any degree of truth, it offers a point of view from which to look and compare, a starting point for genuine investigation" (2–3). Since Jung's pioneering work, the study of psychetypes has been carried further by Harriet Mann, Richard Smoke, Michael Malone, and others, but Jung's basic theories remain useful analytical tools. Currently they form the basis of the Brigg's Myers Type Indicator Test.[11]

Typology has largely been neglected in literary analysis, having indeed been thrust into the role of the neglected step-sister in preference to Jung's more widely known concept of the archetype. The schema of types can, however, be a useful tool for delving into the lives of writers and into their imaginative creations. Long after the publication of *Psychological Types* in 1921, Jung stressed the two central lessons of his years of researching divergent personalities: "the insight that every judgment made by an individual is conditioned by his personality type and that every point of view is necessarily relative" (*Memories* 207). From Jung's point of view absolute knowledge is an impossibility. Even when we are believing we are being our most rational or feeling that we are certainly right in making a decision, our choice is firmly, indeed often subtly, controlled by our intricate selves.

The unfortunate results of this division within the human psyche was underscored by W. H. Auden in his *For the Time Being, A Christmas Oratorio.* In "The Annunciation" segment, the four faculties themselves address the audience.

> Over the life of Man
> We watch and wait,
> The Four who manage
> His fallen estate:

> We who are four were
> Once but one,
> Before his act of
> Rebellion;
> We were himself when
> His will was free,
> His error became our
> Chance to be [275].

Making use of the Judeo-Christian concept of the Fall, Auden posits a prelapsarian psychological unity, in which the four functions acted in concert. Presumably, in such an ideal condition, one's emotions, reasoning, need for sensation, and inner speculations would have acted together, never conflicting with one another and blurring the grounds for human choice. Although such a wondrous state of psychological coordination is most unlikely to have ever existed, this vital concept illustrates the complete control of our own psyches we would like to have—freedom from rampaging emotions, congruence in thought and feeling, the capability of perceiving truth and adjusting ourselves to it. According to Auden's mythos, humankind's rebellion and subsequent fall forever severed the interconnections of the four faculties. Hence, human beings must wander the earth in psychological confusion, a prey to inner chaos and, as the rest of the poem makes grimly clear, to outer chaos as well.

A sense of quintessential psychological harmony is perhaps latent in all discussions of typology. By using it as a hypothetical yardstick, one may gain a sense of how far from the ideal humankind is in determining and contending with reality. Differences in typology lead to differences in perceptions, choices, and strategies of coping with an ever-shifting chaotic reality.

By taking into account how Shakespeare's characters reflect different typological natures in reaching decisions and in taking action and by understanding these characters as manifestations of Shakespeare's own typological conflicts, we may gain a better idea of how the phenomena of chaos is confronted in his writings and how in turn this recurring conflict shapes his characters. Possibly we shall gain further insight into "the essential" Shakespeare.

Delving, however, into the psychetypology of "a character in a novel, a celebrity, an author, a famous historical person" has its risks, warns Jungian Angelo Spoto, because "typological insights become more and more provisional the further one gets from the lived reality" (56–57). Yet making the attempt is worth the effort, especially since certain typological functions are more evident in some characters than in others. The thinking function is certainly paramount in Shakespeare's Beatrice, whereas, although it appears in Rosalind, defining her as a thinking type would be risky. By concentrating on characters who manifest traits of a given type, we can gain a deeper and more perceptive understanding of fundamental thematic currents which reappear in an author's oeuvre and aid in inform-ing it.

Often in his literary works Shakespeare approached the phenomena of the world primarily through feeling. This tendency is especially marked in the sonnets. Throughout them, in the relationships with the friend and the Dark Lady, feeling is dominant of the four faculties. As the poet's acquaintance with the young nobleman deepens into idealized friendship, the poet's emotional involvement is paramount. He laments when he is separated from the friend, feels abject before his friend, feels stung when the friend is approached by the rival poet(s), and wounded when the friend conducts an affair with the poet's mistress, the Dark Lady.

Likewise, the sonnets involving the Dark Lady revolve on an axis of complex and powerful emotions. The poet feels himself inexplicably attracted to her, while at the same time experiencing remorse and guilt. He feels remorse because the relationship is a dead end, heart-breaking, going nowhere, (evidently he cares far more for her than she does for him). He feels guilt because it is adulterous, demeaning, compromising what he believes is best in himself. The tone of the sonnets range from playful affection (Sonnet 130), to a disillusioned bitterness toward human sexu-ality itself (129), to flashing and at times intense and prolonged bitter hatred toward the Dark Lady herself (152). These latter twenty-seven son-nets call to mind the complex love-hate relationship the Roman poet Cat-ullus found himself involved in with Clodia, a senator's promiscuous wife, whom he celebrated under the deceptively pleasant name of Lesbia, a generic name in classical poetry for a lovely lady. As with his Roman coun-terpart, Shakespeare struggles with an intense attraction to the lady while often — even at the same time — vibrating with contempt for her. Partic-ularly crucial is that the relationship is doubly adulterous; both are mar-ried to others. Without hope of qualification, their intimacy is sinful.

The essential complexity and hopelessness of the situation is suc-cinctly expressed in Sonnet 147.

> My love is as a fever, longing still
> For that which longer nurseth the disease,
> Feeding on that which doth preserve the ill,
> Th' uncertain sickly appetite to please.
> My reason, the physician to my love,

Angry that his prescriptions are not kept,
Hath left me; and I desperate now approve
Desire is death which reason did except.
Past cure I am, now reason is past care.
And frantic-mad with evermore unrest;
My thoughts and discourse are as madmen's are,
At random from the truth vainly expressed;
For I have sworn thee fair and thought thee bright,
Who art as black as hell, as dark as night.

Scholars have sought in vain to identify the Dark Lady. A favorite possibility for nineteenth century biographers of the Bard was Mary Fitton, a rather checkered lady-in-waiting at Elizabeth's court. She had an ill-starred affair with William Herbert, the third Earl of Pembroke, who got her with child but refused to wed her. But Mary Fitton has lost favor during the past century because portraits discovered of her reveal her to have been light-haired. The twentieth century, however, has added its own candidates for the disreputable distinction. G. B. Harrison suggested that the Dark Lady was a brothel keeper, known as "Lucy Negro," perhaps identifiable with one Luce Morgan. Perhaps influenced by Harrison, novelist Anthony Burgess, drawing upon what he identified as a Stratford tradition, proclaimed the Dark Lady to be a black prostitute, a few of which were featured in Elizabethan bordellos. In the 1970s the ever-controversial A. L. Rowse pronounced his own candidate, Emilia Lanier, née Bassano, who had been the mistress of Harry Carey, the first Lord of Hunsdon, Elizabeth's Lord Chamberlain and patron of Shakespeare's acting troop, but the acerbic Cornish scholar could not produce evidence enough to convince all of his many critics. More recently, Jonathan Bate has offered as his possibility for the Dark Lady the wife of John Florio, the tutor of the Earl of Southampton Henry Wriothesley, Shakespeare's patron, and currently the leading candidate to be the young nobleman celebrated in the larger group of sonnets. Bate's suggestion, however, relies upon intricate but intriguing conjectures (546–58).

Whether or not the characters in the sonnets can ever be identified — and indeed whether they are in fact real and not imaginary — is beside the point: the sonnets reveal a predominantly *feeling* orientation toward life.

Yet, as evidenced in Sonnet 147, the rational side of the speaker's psyche is not dead. It has merely withdrawn, and the potentiality exists for its return, for the war between thinking and feeling to resume. In a sense, then this psychomachia can never end. Feeling and thinking — opposing psychic functions — are ever parts of the poet's psyche.

Presumably, of course, the relationship with the Dark Lady did end.

The sonnets provide no clue as to how, when and why. Whether one of them broke off the relationship, whether Shakespeare forgot her, whether he looked back longingly to the days when he and the lady had joyful moments, whether years afterward he wished that the relationship would have continued and indeed blossomed, we can never know. (Nor do the sonnets testify to the nature of the speaker's friendship with his patron after the latter's affair with the poet's mistress.) However the poet's liaison might have ended, we can be sure that the struggle between thinking and feeling continued on the battlefields of the poet's psyche as new reasons for conflict arose.

The question confronts us, though, whether Shakespeare himself can indeed be classified as a feeling type. Malone types the psyches of numerous authors, artists, and celebrities, for instance, categorizing T. S. Eliot, Thomas Jefferson, and Virginia Woolf as a thinking types; Wordsworth, Emily Dickinson, and Thomas Hardy feeling types; Mozart, Mark Twain and Humphrey Bogart as sensation types; and Christina Rosetti, Mark Chagall, and Samuel Taylor Coleridge as intuitives. Interestingly, he does not classify Shakespeare, although he makes numerous references to the dramatist, emphasizing Antony and Othello, two of the poet's characters who are predominantly feeling types.

Shakespeare lacks the system-building, the reliance upon principle, and abstract theorizing associated with the thinking type. For clarification, Berlin's division of persons as hedgehogs and foxes might be consulted. Drawing upon a fragment of verse from Greek poet Archilochus, "The fox knows many things, but the hedgehog knows one big thing," Berlin hypothesizes two fundamental kinds of thinkers— hedgehogs and foxes. Hedgehogs are those "who relate everything to a single central vision, one system, less or more coherent or articulate, in terms of which they understand, think and feel — a single, universal organizing principle in terms of which alone all that they are and say has significance" (7). In contrast, the thought of foxes "is scattered or diffused, moving on many levels, seizing upon the essence of a vast variety of experiences and objects for what they are in themselves, without, consciously or unconsciously, seeking to fit them into, or exclude them from, any one unchanging, all-embracing, sometimes self-contradictory and incomplete, at times fanatical, unitary inner vision"(8). Although foxes could conceivably belong to any psychetype, Berlin's categorization of hedgehogs applies primarily to Jung's thinking types, and Berlin places Shakespeare among the foxes (8).

Although Shakespeare very likely was a feeling type, I, like Malone, hesitate to stamp this label on him. Abiding by Spoto's caution, I suggest that an author's secondary function might well appear in his works and be taken for the primary one. If Shakespeare, for instance, had been a sensation type, his secondary orientation could have been feeling. Conceivably, his feeling aspects could have usurped centrality in his expression of his psyche during artistic creation. Quite simply, we do not know enough about the connection of the creative process with psychetypes to classify with certainty an author's typology, especially in the case of Shakespeare where we lack supplementary evidence such as prefaces to his works, letters, and journal entries. Then, too, we might recall Yeats's theory of the mask; that is, the viability of poets' assuming personas so that they may get in touch with and express hidden, dormant, or opposing sides of their personalities. Whether or not Shakespeare consciously espoused a theory similar to Yeats's, his artistic practice could have followed such a process. All that one can say is that in the sonnets and other works a definite nexus appears between the feeling and sensation sides of Shakespeare's personality, along with a tendency for these to oppose and be opposed by the faculty of thinking. Moreover, Shakespeare was conscious of this opposition and was affected by it. Like Yeats he was troubled by the human psyche's capability of being shattered into opposing factions and yearned for a unity of being.

For instance, in Hamlet's analysis of the causes of his deep friendship with Horatio rises a intense longing for psychological unity.

> Since my dear soul was mistress of her choice
> And could of men distinguish her election,
> Sh' hath sealed thee for her herself, for thou hast been
> As one, in suffering all, that suffers nothing,
> A man that Fortune's buffets and rewards
> Hast ta'en with equal thanks; and blest are those
> Whose blood and judgment are so well commeddled
> That they are not a pipe for Fortune's finger
> To sound what stop she please. Give me that man
> That is not passion's slave, and I will wear him
> In my heart's core, ay, in my heart of heart,
> As I do thee [III. ii. 62–73].

Hamlet, in other words, aspires to the stoic ideal of total control of humankind's wayward emotions, an ideal which, as we have seen, is unrealizable.

This, of course, is but one way a Shakespearean character may seek individuation and selfhood. There are many others, but all such searches take place within a basic thematic framework, which Gary O'Connor astutely outlines.

Every play will reenact the cycle of his [Shakespeare's] own
emotional problems in life: it will begin with an overthrow of
order — it will go on to threaten a total overthrow of all rules
and system, but it will end with the slow recovery of order.
Goethe never stopped re-writing *Faust;* Shakespeare continued
playing through the primal cycle of family life, which itself had
a New Testament parallel: Birth, Crucifixion, Death, Resurrec-
tion. Here was the was basic force field of his universality [27].

In Shakespeare's tragedies in general, chaos overwhelms the protagonist. As we have seen, Brutus, Shakespeare's example of a text-book stoic,
is compelled to kill himself when the cause he struggles so valiantly to preserve appears lost. As we shall see, internal unity is disrupted and fragmented by the individual's inability to comprehend persons of other
psychetypes and the inability to judge and direct human behavior in accord
with any rational scheme of ethics. But, also, as we shall see, emotional
harmony and psychological unity are, in such tragedies as *Othello* and
Timon of Athens, threatened by the emergence of the protagonist's inferior function into the battleground of the consciousness.

In varying degrees, Shakespeare's tragedies reveal an awareness of the
difficulty of obtaining psychological unity. In fact, in the final tragedies,
the destruction of the psyche by the empowerment of the inferior function becomes a disheartening, sinister baseline. *Hamlet* will be examined
as Shakespeare's most complex portrayal of psychetypological discord. In
the romances, we shall see that Shakespeare's artistic psyche attempts to
bypass psychological barriers and reassert at least the illusion of an achiev-
able inner balance. But first we shall take a look at the more stable interrelationship of thought and feeling which occurs in the romantic comedies.

THREE

Thought and Feeling in the Comedies

Recently Jonathan Bate made this crucial observation about the nature of comedy — a point emphatically demonstrated by the Shakespearean variety: "That is one of the reasons why we like comedies: we know that, give or take a few loose ends, they will work out as we would want them to. Which is not something we can say about our own lives" (139).

Fledgling English majors are sometimes surprised when they make their first acquaintance with *Twelfth Night* or *As You Like It.* Most likely introduced to the Bard through high school readings of *Julius Caesar, Macbeth,* or *Hamlet,* having been told that Shakespeare is one of the world's greatest writers and perhaps forced to memorize "philosophical speeches," such as "to be or not to be" or "she should have died hereafter," they sometimes are surprised to learn that Shakespeare developed plots in some ways more in line with a Rodgers and Hammerstein musical like *Oklahoma* or *State Fair* or such delightful Fred Astaire and Ginger Rogers cinematic pastries as *Top Hat* and *Follow the Fleet* than with the dramas presenting the dark musings of Hamlet and the dangerous ambition of Macbeth.

The comparison of Shakespeare's comedies with twentieth century musicals is apt. In fact, some literary textbooks refer to Shakespeare's lighter productions as "romantic comedies." For, as with the Rodgers and Hammerstein musical and the Astaire-Rogers flick, romance between male and female is the linchpin of *Two Gentlemen of Verona, Loves Labor's Lost, As You Like It,* and other plays included in the comedies section of an anthology of Shakespeare's work.[12]

Quite clearly, Shakespeare delighted in plays using the old formula of boy meets girl, boy almost loses girl, boy eventually wins girl, and avidly penned such works himself. In general, a Shakespearean comedy features one or more sets of young lovers for whom the course of true love does not run smooth. Often they are momentarily prevented from speaking their wedding vows by blocking characters—those who oppose the wished-for unions and do all in their power to prevent them from taking place. At times the blocking characters are members of the older generation—parents like old Baptista in *The Taming of the Shrew* or Sylvia's father, the Duke, in *Two Gentlemen of Verona*—who wish for the heroine to wed someone else. The blocking character may be a rival suitor who has the father's approval. On the other hand, the blocking characters may not be involved in the immediate romantic perplexity but act from self-interested concerns, thus causing the lovers' separation as when Duke Frederick banishes Rosalind from his court in *As You Like It* and removes her from proximity to Orlando (Ironically, however, the villainous Frederick provides the fine opportunity for the mutually-attracted pair to come together in the forest of Arden). Or another character may unintentionally function as a blocking character. Olivia in *Twelfth Night* has captured the eye of Orsino and thus deters Viola's attempts to interest him. At times the wooers themselves may block their own romantic opportunities as when the King of Navarre in *Love's Labors Lost* swears that for three years he shall study and not view a distracting member of the opposite gender!

In addition to this basic scheme, a number of frequently recurring character types, plot devices, and themes recur, helping to define the style of comedy that intrigued Shakespeare. Bumbling clowns and witty court fools animate the plots. Evil, though present, is muted, so that the audience members do not sit on the edges of their chairs, alarmed at what may happen to a sprightly Shakespearean heroine, but is ever ready to enjoy the play's essential lightheartedness. A Mediterranean setting, cross-dressed heroines, and repartee may often enliven the tale. The plot may also involve a shift from the constrictive environs of the court to the fields and woods of nature and a paradoxically vital return to the civilized world of social stratification and protocol.

Of course, the comedy ends happily. The proper lovers are paired together. Hostilities and enmities are forgotten and forgiven. Almost all of the characters are united in a newly-born concord, often symbolized by a forthcoming wedding feast, to which all are invited. (Not even rejected suitors or formerly irate fathers are refused a place at the table!) By and large the conclusions promise happy marriages.[13] Hence, Bate's judgment that these comedies appeal to us because the events work out as we wish them to—a boon not consistently provided us by life.

Bate's view needs stressing. For the last thirty years at least, a trend has developed amid academics and theatrical personnel to magnify hitherto unnoticed personal flaws. Major character defects now abound in those who were previously seen as fortunate lovers; virtuous behavior is called in doubt, and subtle notes of the sinister and grotesque are now combined into fully developed chords.

To be sure, the worlds of the comedies are not Edens. Even the forest of Arden in *As You Like It* is unsettled by a winter wind! In the world of the court in the same play, Duke Frederick has usurped his brother's right, taking over the estate. Oliver denies Orlando his inheritance. In *Twelfth Night* the helpful sailor Antonio is arrested because he has ventured into enemy territory to aid Sebastian. In *Love's Labour's Lost.* festivities are forestalled when news of the death of the King of France arrives.

Not only are the worlds of the comedies darkened by shadows, but at times the lovers themselves act less than worthily. Albeit he is under the influence of the magic juice, Lysander's words to Hermia — once he has switched his romantic allegiance to Helena — are bitter, cruel. At times Benedick and Beatrice's verbal sparrings drip with an acidity that smarts. And the unhappy fortunes of Shylock in *The Merchant of Venice* have caused not a few critics to judge that the play veers too close to tragedy to be an unadulterated comedy.

True, if readers wish to look for somber implications and sinister undercurrents in the comedies, they will not be disappointed. Grim implications exist — we would scarcely have an enjoyable play without them. But in general these darker implications are subsumed by the prevailing comic spirit, the overriding sense of things working out as we would want them to. Few viewers of a spirited performance of *Much Ado About Nothing* would seriously question whether Benedick and Beatrice are headed for the divorce court on the assumption that they have little more than their verbal games to unite them. Nor do we question whether in *Two Gentlemen of Verona* Sylvia's and Valentine's long-sought marriage will have a rocky start because shortly before the play's conclusion the hero had offered step aside so that Proteus, his best friend, might wed her (Proteus who had also attempted to rape Sylvia!). Even in *The Merchant of Venice* care is taken so that Shylock's controversial downfall may not overwhelm the audience: It occurs at the end of what is now considered the fourth act. The remainder of the play attempts to direct our attention away from him as the couples return to Belmont and unravel their temporarily complicated relationships.

Much of the appeal of a Shakespearean comedy, then, results from its offering the reader a holiday from reality. Such a statement may seem to deny these works' claim to a serious reader's attention, for it finds their essence in an unabashed "escapism," certainly a pejorative term to many readers.

But such escapism need not be decried. Other serious readers besides Bate have found these comedies of lasting value. In his bitter "City Without Walls," an unflinching dissection of twentieth century life, W. H. Auden underscores the following situation as a mark of the modern world's decadence:

> If few now applaud a play that ends
> with warmth and pardon the word to all,
> as, blessed, unbamboozled, the bridal pairs,
> rustic and oppidan, in a ring-dance,
> image the stars at their stately bransles [*Collected Poems,* 564].

The value that so many intelligent readers of these plays have found is perhaps difficult to couch. Certainly central to the comedies' appeal to all levels of readers and theatergoers is that, in the words of Bate, "they will work out as we would want them to." But besides fulfilling our need for vicarious success, these plays remind us of such often unfulfilled goals as justice, social concord, and marital harmony — lessons in human potentialities that we can ill afford to neglect. Then, too, the essential escapism of the plots of Shakespearean comedy do not preclude in them the presence of wise observations upon the foibles, faults, follies — and indeed the joys of humankind! Thus if one wishes to find justifications for these plays beyond their immediate value of producing pleasure, one may readily do so.

But as the plays stand, they spread the joys of comedy. As such they provide a playground for the human psyche's feeling function, for it is this orientation that primarily seeks expression in these plays, finds itself threatened, and ultimately triumphs. Romantic love is one of the prime means through which this function attempts to project itself into the exterior world of actuality and realize itself. But let us not forget that that these plays also place a high value upon friendship. As we recollect these plays, more than likely we first recall the engaging pairs of lovers — Valentine and Sylvia, Rosalind and Orlando, Beatrice and Benedick, Petruchio and Katherine. But often these characters share the stage with devoted pairs of heterosexual friends — Benedick and Claudio, Rosalind and Celia, Antonio and Bassanio, Portia and Nerissa, the Queen of France and Rosaline, Helena and Hermia.[14] Serving as the background to these attention-getting lovers and friends are often subsidiary lovers and friends; for instance, Berowne's fellows and the Queen of France's ladies add romantic color to the background of *Love's Labour's Lost,* while Bottom's cohorts add to the conviviality, sprightliness and fun of *A Midsummer Night's Dream.* At the ends of these plays the feeling functions are indeed realized; the impulses toward love and friendship survive their challenges and intensify, and the characters gain objects of their attentions. Hence, the festive endings in which all — even former foes — are united.

Despite whatever personal problems Shakespeare was having at the time he penned these plays — whether a strained marriage with Anne Hathaway or a tumultuous relationship with the Dark Lady — he was able to muster enough psychic energy to project and embody his strong feeling impulse in the comic works he penned.

To assume that during this process his rational function lay dormant would be absurd. The rational impulse is embodied — not so much in its systematizing as in its critical aspect — in a variety of characters, but in the feeling-sensation world of the comedies its role is less evident. Many of Shakespeare's comic heroes, of course, are feeling types — Orlando, Orsino, Bassanio, even Posthumous and Leontes, if we wish to reach into the tragi-comedies. But some important thinking types appear. Interestingly enough, the two major thinking types among Shakespeare's comic heroes expend their mental energies in attempting to prove and justify the importance of love — Berowne of *Love's Labour's Lost* and Benedick of *Much Ado About Nothing*. A first impression of Berowne, however, may argue that he is at core a feeling or a sensation type. At the play's very beginning, he convincingly asserts the folly of the King's wish for himself, Berowne, and their friends to sequester themselves for three years amid books and with a meager diet while avoiding female companionship altogether. Berowne indeed may seem a sharer of Keats's view "O for a Life of Sensations rather than of Thoughts!" But the King's remark is telling: "How well he's read, to reason against reading!" (I. i. 94). Delighting in exercising his mind, Berowne enjoys paradoxes, quibbles, and arguments. Indeed it is because of the rude side of his intellectual feistiness and his acidic barbs and humiliating quips that Roseline sentences him to a year of penance by requiring him to entertain the sick and dying with his wit. (Or as she says it, "To weed this wormwood from your fruitful brain" [V. ii. 837])." In fact, his spirited criticism of the king's idealized asceticism displays the thinking type's delight in argument and in victory in debates. Nevertheless, he accedes to the monarch's wishes. Although a champion of the natural joys of loving ladies, Berowne is not a connoisseur of the flesh. In reality, his attitude toward love is double-sided, in fact ambivalent. We later learn that he has not only been a mocker of love, but, at least for portions of his life, an apostate from it as well. When the thoughts of Rosaline occupy him, he remarks that Cupid is punishing him "for my neglect / Of his almighty dreadful little might" (III. i. 200–201). In essence, he both celebrates and is wary of man's capacity to love. He is aware of *amor*'s pitfalls as well as its joys.

Perhaps Berowne's ready acceptance of his monarch's outrageous demand indicates that part of this intellectually agile courtier wishes to wall himself away from involvement with the opposite sex. However, after the Queen of France and her ladies arrive and Rosaline entices his eye, he struggles within himself, wrestling with whether or not to disregard his vow to the king and pursue the entrancing dark-eyed heroine. Looking at himself from a rationalistic perspective, he sees himself as inconstant and foolish — in short, ridiculous.

> And I, forsooth, in love! I that have been Love's whip,
> A very beadle to a humorous sigh,
> A critic, nay, a night-watch constable,
> A domineering pedant o'er the boy,
> Than whom no mortal so magnificent!
> This wimpled, whining, purblind, wayward boy....
> And I to be a corporal of his field
> And wear his colors like a tumbler's hoop!
> What? I love, I sue, I seek a wife?
> A woman, that is like a German clock,
> Still a-repairing, ever out of frame,
> And never going aright, being a watch,
> But being watched that it may still go right?
> Nay, to be perjured, which is worst of all;
> And, among three, to love the worst of all —
> A whitely wanton with a velvet brow,
> With two pitch-balls stuck in her face for eyes;
> Ay, and, by heaven, one that will do the deed
> Though Argus were her eunuch and her guard.
> And I to sigh for her, to watch for her,
> To pray for her! Go to, it is a plague
> That Cupid will impose for my neglect
> Of his almighty dreadful little might.
> Well, I will love, write, sigh, pray, sue, groan.
> Some men must love milady, and some Joan [III. i. 172–77, 185–203].

Nevertheless, when it becomes evident that he and his fellows are incapable of abiding by their abstemious credo, Berowne uses reason, if not, in fact, common sense, to justify their apostasy.

> Sweet lords, sweet lovers, O, let us embrace!
> As true we are as flesh and blood can be.
> The sea will ebb and flow, heaven show his face;
> Young blood doth not obey an old decree,

We cannot cross the cause why we were born;
Therefore of all hands must we be forsworn [IV. iii. 210–15].

Yet, ever a thinking type, Berowne realizes the naturalness of sexual desire and the need for love are natural. (He does not even consider the possibility of a vow of lifelong chastity!) In the first section of the play he is caught between two limited rationalistic perspectives: 1) to be in love is foolish, humiliating, if not dangerous; 2) to be in love is joyful, rewarding, if not necessary for a man's fulfillment. A bit later in the play he reconciles the two views by deciding to favor the delights of love when he argues that he and his follows should break their vow to abstain for three years from the company of women. Berowne's mental process might be stated as a syllogism.

1. All men must love.

2. I am a man.

3. I must love.

Two conflicting "rational perspectives" are then fused in an kind of alliance: Although love is / may be / can be foolish, humiliating, and dangerous, it also is natural and is / may be / can be joyful and in fact ennobling. (However, the alliance of these perspectives is, potentially unstable. As we shall we in the cognitive processes of Hamlet, they split apart!)

Similarly, once he can no longer deny his deepening love for Beatrice, Benedick — one of Shakespeare's carefully drawn thinking types—calls upon his wits to justify the reasonableness of love. Duped by his friends into believing that a heartsick Beatrice languishes for him, Benedick is jolted by the rebellion of his previously governed feeling side. Almost without reflection, he decides to requite her love, but still he must justify to himself his *volte face.* He is troubled by the thought that his fellows will tease him once they learn that the confirmed bachelor has become a lover. He seeks to prepare a justification to be presented to them — as well as, very likely, justifying his action to himself: "But doth not the appetite alter? A man loves the meat in his youth that he cannot endure in his age. Shall quips and sentences and these paper bullets of brain awe a man from the career of his humor? No, the world must be peopled" (II. iii. 234–38). He challenges the probable jests and witticisms with what to him is a powerful generalization. Implied by his *sententia* are that the generative force in nature is prepotent and should not be denied and that marriage and subsequent childbirth are woven into the Almighty's overriding plan.

(Berowne's "the cause why we were born" and woe to those who would circumvent divine ordinance!) Yet the effort he invests in the generalization indicates that he is trying to convince himself of the rightness of his change of course as well as erect a shield against witty barbs of others: "When I said I would die a bachelor, I did not think I should live till I were married" (238–39). This statement rings with self-deception. Never in the play has he voiced a belief that he should not marry because of the likelihood of a soldier's death. Probably, however, he has speculated upon the possibility that death might take him before he finds a bride, but suddenly — not wanting to admit, even to himself, that he has changed his mind — he magnifies this fear into the major reason he has not married. Like Berowne, Benedick — when he loves — must argue with himself, put things into perspective, and justify his course of action not only to others but to himself.

Such different lovers are feeling types like Orlando, Orsino, and Bassanio who need no justification for love! Although at times these men are daunted by difficulties, their bent is to pursue spontaneously and enthusiastically the ladies who charm their eyes and invade their hearts. And in the plays these romantic heroes generally are triumphant and justified in their choices!

However, in these happy comedies, another aspect of the author's rational analytic side is not absent or asleep; the need to question, doubt, mistrust, even mock romantic love recurringly opposes the air of festivity. One does not have to venture far through the pages of the comedies to find skeptical or even cynical comments on love. At times they are whimsical, innocuous; at others they present a troubling accompaniment to the play's overriding comedy.

A variety of examples follows.

In *A Midsummer Night's Dream* Puck, preparing to enjoy the irrational behavior wrought among the two pairs of lovers by the misapplied flower juice, remarks to Oberon, "Shall we their fond pageant see?/ Lord, what fools these mortals be!" (III. ii. 114–15), his sly implication being that lovers, whether under the influence of magic or not, are fools.

In the same play, Bottom remarks to the ensorcelled Titania about their "relationship": "And yet, to say the truth, reason and love keep little company together nowadays— the more the pity that some honest neighbors will not make them friends" (III. i. 138–41).

In *As You Like It*, amid her playful needling of Orlando, Rosalind, disguised as Ganymede, often skeptically comments on love. For instance, after Orlando insists that he will love Rosalind "forever and a day," she responds, "Say, 'a day' without the 'ever.' No, No, Orlando, men are April when they woo, December when they wed. Maids are May when they are maids, but the sky changes when they are wives" (IV. i. 137–42). Although her strictures about romantic love tend to be couched in banter, at times are exaggerated, and are often whimsical, they disturb us, nevertheless, with an unsettling reverberation. They call to mind actual difficulties the search for romantic love may encounter in the world outside the playhouse.

Of course, the same play contains Jaque's unflattering description of "the lover / Sighing like furnace, with a woeful ballad / Made to his mistress's eyebrow" (II. vii. 146–48).

Then, too, Shakespearean characters like Puck and Feste seem to stand aside from love, indeed, appear incapable of experiencing it. Yet they view it wryly, if not with muted cynicism. (For example, Feste's cryptic but disturbing concluding song of *Twelfth Night*, chronicling in the downward spiral of a drunken husband.) Once a libertine, Jacques may be said to have joined their ranks in that while maintaining a detached attitude toward ladies, he at times casts verbal darts toward lovers. Touchstone, too, shares their cynicism, as when he mocks Orlando's inept romantic verse, yet he hardly can be said to stand aside from love — or lust, in his case! He seeks to mislead the simple shepherdess Audrey into a "quickie" marriage to fulfill his immediate needs for pleasure. Indeed, looked at without the spectacles of comedy, we would find him atrocious. He not only causes Audrey to break up with her rural fiancé William, but lies to her, feigning love while planning to ditch her eventually. But, of course, Shakespeare urges us to wear us the spectacles of comedy.

His treatment of Touchstone, then, may offer a paradigm of his recurrent handling of the rational impulse to question and analyze, romantic love, indeed, to strip away illusions. Touchstone both stands aside from and mocks romantic/erotic experience while at the same time actively engages in its pursuit. In the comedies in general this potentially disruptive skeptical proclivity is subsumed in the overriding comic spirit of boy meets girl, boy almost loses girl, boy happily wins girl. But like the Fenris wolf of Norse mythology, cynicism is restrained but ever in danger of breaking its chains and escaping in the forefront of the play. In essence, this is what happens in Shakespeare's dark or problem comedies—*All's Well that Ends Well*, *Measure for Measure*, and *Troilus and Cressida*. Critics have long noticed an unsettling, even a bitter, tone in these supposed comedies—a franker portrayal of sex, starkly cynical comments about romantic attraction, and problematical portrayals of humanity's hope to achieve happiness through love and marriage.

But in the comedies proper the rational and feeling functions are wed, as the heroines and heroes discover the right (or reasonable) person for a spouse, look forward to or celebrate a wedding, and thereby recapture something of the preplasarian unity of being that Auden hypothesized.

Whatever his personal problems, Shakespeare was able to keep the rational cynical side of his psyche restrained in the comedies. And it is well that he does so, for by becoming unleashed it threatens beliefs in the joys, harmony, and solidity that a happy marriage may present. In the tragedies, the sniggering, mocking demon of doubt at times escapes.

FOUR

Antony and Cleopatra and *Troilus and Cressida:* Lovers and Other Strangers

Unfortunately, we do not always listen well, and one of the reasons we don't is our tendency to assume that everyone must be or should be like us, that if we speak the same language, we mean the same things. That's not true. We don't always speak the same language, though we may use the same words. Words like "right," "good," "moral," "goal" or "future" can mean very different things to different people. In our efforts to communicate, we resort to analogies, examples, to inflection and volume, to "body language." And still we may throw up our bands, sighing, "You'll never understand me. Let's face it, we're in two different worlds. Either you're crazy or I'm crazy." The truth is probably that neither of us is crazy; the problem is that we assume we ought to be *alike*, that in the same situation our experience, our way of perceiving and reacting, will be shared by another person. If not, there's something the matter with one or us. Not necessarily so…. Far too many people are deemed eccentric who are functioning well within the normal boundaries of their particular type. A "neurotic" may be "neurotic" only insofar as we misunderstand his or her typology or choose to define that typology as variant and therefore aberrant [2–3].

In these observations, Michael Malone, one of the first scholars to discuss psychetypology and literature, dissects central interpersonal problems that arise from the differences in psychetypes. Often we trust in the hope that by "holding a dialogue" with those whose viewpoints differ from ours, conflicts may be mitigated and mutual comprehension and tolerance will flower. While few would deny the importance of attempting to understand others and their points of view or would deride the capability of empathy to improve human relationships, the theory of psychetypology indicates that achieving such understanding is not always easy; in fact, at times doing so may be impossible.

In terms of the pattern of chaos running through the works of Shakespeare, external discord begets discord within human psyches, which, in large part because of the characters' typological differences, creates further chaos in the external world by their attempts to resolve the conflict which produce further internal discord. This chaotic pattern evinces itself with unsettling clarity in two plays concerning the opposition of thinking and feeling types resulting from conflicts involving passionate love, *Troilus and Cressida* and *Antony and Cleopatra*. The plays are provocatively similar; both feature lovers willing to risk much to consummate their desires, disruptive conflicts between the lovers, and opposition from thinking types who seek to disprove the value of such ardent love or disregard such passion in the pursuit of "rational goals." In both plays the chaotic pattern produces disastrous consequences. However, in *Antony and Cleopatra* the difficulties stem from the inability to resolve opposing points of view; likewise, *Troilus and Cressida* is founded upon this conflict, but also questions explicitly the very existence of ultimate values. The plays will be discussed initially in reverse order of their composition.

Troilus and Cressida (ca. 1601), the earlier drama, was written as Shakespeare was completing his final "pure" comedies—*As You Like It* and *Twelfth Night*—and beginning his concentration upon the so-called problem comedies (which *Troilus* is often classed as) and the tragedies. Indeed, it contains many similarities in terms of imagery and thematic darkness to *Hamlet*, written at roughly the same time. *Antony and Cleopatra* (ca. 1606–1607) was penned near the close of the tragic period. In fact, with its emphasis upon reconciliation and redemptive love, this drama seems to herald the romances. Considering the first last, however, will enable us to see more clearly a subliminal pattern which informs many of the plays, for the central thrust of this study is to examine important thematic patterns in the drama rather than chart the development of "Shakespeare's philosophy." Each of these plays, moreover, presents in basically pure forms conflicts involving feeling and thinking types, which reappear in other plays.

Many of the misunderstandings and conflicts in *Antony and Cleopatra* results from the opposition of thinking and feeling types. This opposition gives depth to the struggle involving Antony and Cleopatra and their opponent Octavius, and emerges in Enobarbus's problematic relationship with Antony.

To begin with, Antony and Cleopatra are clearly feeling types.[15] Their involvement with each other is central to their lives. Both reveal a readiness to act principally upon emotion; Cleopatra, for instance, shows this when she berates and strikes the messenger bearing news of Antony's marriage and Antony when he impulsively marries Octavia. Antony's emotion is underscored when he suddenly decides to fight by sea at Actium and when, without deliberation, he forwards treasure to Enobarbus, who has deserted him. The importance of feeling in the two lovers' lives is presented perhaps most emphatically in the moments before their deaths. Each upholds the love of the other as an incomparable gem. Despite Cleopatra's repeated trickery, her near betrayal of him, and the lie that provokes his suicide, Antony dies while kissing her and advising her about whom to trust. Likewise, despite her bargaining with Caesar, Cleopatra, once she learns of her proposed punishment, turns all thoughts to Antony and a possible Elysian reunion. "Husband, I come!" (V. ii. 287) she cries, before applying the asp. Despite their selfishness, crudities, and indeed volatile relationship, their romantic-erotic bond remains. Almost the epitome of the feeling type, Cleopatra sees death as a doorway to their reunion.

Octavius, their antagonist, is their opposite psychological type: a thinker. As critics have often observed, he is decidedly rational, in fact logical to the point of cruelty. Not that all thinking types are cruel; far from it. But Octavius fosters a cold efficiency without regard for sentiment, honor, or human life. A diabolical practicality characterizes his treatment of those of who have deserted Antony — they are placed on the front lines. Thus Antony will be infuriated at seeing his own troops advancing against him, and the deserters themselves, untrustworthy followers, will more likely be slain than Octavius' original soldiers. His rationality again arises in his treatment of Antony's challenge to single combat. Honor might have guided a feeling type to accept the proposition. A sensation type might have been provoked by the dare. But not the calculating Octavius. Why should he? His army is winning. Why should he chance life and victory for what to him is mere chivalric extravaganza? "Let the old ruffian know / I have many other ways to die; meantime / Laugh at his challenge" (IV. i. 4–6). Throughout the play Octavius emphasizes order and rationality, which will bear fruit in his "universal peace" (IV. vi. 5). Frequently thinking types are impelled to connect their ambitions with principles and abstractions.

Observing the world from a thinking type's viewpoint, Octavius cannot comprehend Antony's reckless love for "his Egyptian dish" (II. vi. 126). Before the war between him and Antony erupts, he criticizes Lepidus' willingness to excuse their fellow ruler.

You are too indulgent. Let's grant it is not
Amiss to tumble on the bed of Ptolemy,
To give a kingdom for a mirth, to sit
And keep the turn of tippling with a slave,
To reel the streets at noon, and stand the buffet
With knaves that smell of sweat. Say this becomes him —
As his composure must be rare indeed
Whom these things cannot blemish — yet must Antony
No way excuse his foils, when we do bear
So great weight in his lightness [I. iv. 16–25].

He concludes his judgment by stressing that Antony is "to be chid /
As we rate boys, who, being mature in knowledge, / Pawn their experience to their present pleasure, / And so rebel to judgment" (I. iv. 30–33).
Similarly, Antony does not sympathize with Octavius' subordination of the
personal nor the future emperor's dedication to schemes of universal gov-
ernment.

Despite his years as a politician, Antony rejects the political world with
its rewards of power and honor. "The nobleness of life / Is to do thus" (I.
i. 36–37), he exclaims as he embraces or kisses Cleopatra. Cleopatra den-
igrates Octavius' success calling it "the luck of Caesar, which the gods give
men / To excuse their after wrath" (V. ii. 286–87). She also has little sympathy with the thinking type's dedication to order. After Antony returns
to Rome to confront Octavius about several political crises, she remarks
to Charmion, "He shall have every day a several greeting [from her]/
I'll unpeople Egypt" (I. v. 80–81). Hyperbole indeed, but her extravagant
decree underscores her willingness to value her relationship with Antony
over the welfare of her citizens.

The conflict between the royal lovers and their Roman-minded adversary intensifies because of each side's inability to comprehend the other's
behavior.

The opposition of thinking and feeling types is again developed in
the relationship of Enobarbus, the play's second important thinking type,
with Antony. As may easily be seen, Enobarbus is relatively unemotional,
does not worship physical pleasures, and is not given to amorous
whirligigs. He enjoys using his reason. He delights in calling attention to
truths other men hide or ignore. For instance, when Antony and Octavius
celebrate the concord that the former's marriage to Octavia should bring,
Enobarbus remarks, "Or, if you borrow one another's love for the instant,
you may, when you hear no more words of Pompey, return it again. You
shall have time to wrangle in when you have nothing else to do" (II. ii.
109–11). Similarly, in the fortune-telling scene, his cynicism interjects a

withering observation amid the other characters' jocularity: "Mine, and most of our fortunes tonight, shall be — drunk to bed" (I. ii. 47–48). Throughout the play he casts darts of reason at the canards, the illusions that others prize. Enobarbus, moreover, prides himself as the voice of rationality. When Antony, irked by one of his companion's astute witticisms, orders him to be silent, Enobarbus exclaims, "That truth should be silent I had almost forgot" (II. i. 114–15).

Enobarbus, almost an obsessive rationalist, must seek the truth of situations and fit the phenomena of life into patterns. This propensity, however, amid the chaotic ironies of the play's subcreated world, causes his ruin. When Antony's errors begin to damage his and his followers' fortunes, Enobarbus attempts to come to terms with the problem rationally. To preserve his safety, he is tempted to desert his lord, yet he cannot abscond with the ease of many of Antony's retainers. As a result he must struggle to see Antony's behavior from a perspective that justifies desertion. A sensation type, tending to judge situations upon their own individual merits rather than in the light of principle, might simply leave. But Enobarbus inwardly wrestles to view Antony as a fool who irresponsibly squanders his fortunes.

He first makes this attempt after Antony's humiliating flight from Actium. When Cleopatra asks whether she or Antony has caused the debacle, Enobarbus replies, "Antony only, that would make his will / Lord of his reason" (III. xiii. 3–4). Later he says, "Caesar thou hast subdued / His judgment too" (III. xiii. 36–37), and then stresses, "The loyalty well held to fools does make / Our faith mere folly" (III. xiii. 42–43). Enobarbus, the rationalist, reduces the complexities of Antony's involvement with Cleopatra to unadulterated folly. Disinclined to value romantic love, Enobarbus cannot comprehend the feeling type's almost compulsive need for emotion's heights, for intimacy's depths— qualities which render Antony's love more complex and more sympathetic than a dotard's lustful infatuation with a trollop nearly half his age. Enobarbus cannot recognize even a gram of worth in the relationship.

Still he cannot leave Antony; the recalcitrant sense of loyalty, which he would squelch, binds him. In one of the play's supreme ironies, Enobarbus reports Cleopatra's traitorous dickering with Thidias to Antony, who angrily prevents her siding with Caesar. Yet when Antony forgives her and vows to continue the fight, Enobarbus concludes, "A diminution in our captain's brain / Restores his heart" (III. xiii. 199–200). Thereafter he himself deserts.

Enobarbus does not find security or happiness. He soon becomes aware of Caesar's treatment of deserters. When Antony sends his treasure,

Enobarbus realizes that his view of Antony as fool is incomplete. Noble qualities dwell in Antony. Guilt-ridden, grappling with confusion as to what is real, unable to fit the chaotic vicissitudes of life into a pattern, Enobarbus turns anger upon himself.

> O Antony
> Nobler than my revolt is infamous,
> Forgive me in thine own particular,
> But let the world rank me in register
> A master-leaver and a fugitive [IV. ix. 21–25].

Again, exemplifying Montaigne's opinion that we experience difficulty in perceiving the entirety of any situation, Enobarbus is partially correct. Antony's behavior did cause others to desert, as Antony himself realizes (IV. v. 14–18). Antony is both a foolish and a noble master. With his need to simplify complexities, Enobarbus cannot grasp the perplexing dualities in Antony. He seeks the simple way out of his dilemma by blaming himself as an ingrate, a traitor. He places too great a burden of guilt upon his shoulders; his heart as well as his life breaks. In a sense, he is immersed in Stein's "destructive element" and drowns.

Antony and Cleopatra is one of the first literary works to investigate differences between psychological types as Jungian psychotherapy has come to understand them. Moreover, it reveals a remarkable awareness that human beings judge and respond to the phenomena of life differently. It also suggests that confusion and psychological chaos occur in part because we cannot always or fully enter imaginatively into the skins of others and see the world from their vantage points.

Shakespeare's *Troilus and Cressida*, in many ways *Antony and Cleopatra*'s sister play, is difficult to classify. Tending toward both comedy and tragedy, it has conveniently been placed among the problem plays. Even here difficulties in classification arise. For one thing, it verges far more closely to the tragic than its fellow problem plays *Measure for Measure* and *All's Well That Ends Well*, which, however much they may reveal a similar dark spirit, have their major conflicts within the boundaries of conventional romantic comedy with its concluding marriages. Christopher Flannery has aptly described the critical uneasiness *Troilus* so often generates:

> It is the common, if not universal, reaction to *Troilus and Cressida*, to feel that it is dramatically fragmented, that it lacks dramatic unity and completeness, and that as a result it is somehow dissatisfying or perplexing, even unpleasant [151].

Few, however, would deny the play's fascination. Generations of readers have found themselves drawn to its unsettling plot. The Royal Shakespeare Company's recent production, featuring Joseph Fiennes as Troilus, Victoria Hamilton as Cressida, Clive Francis as Pandarus, and Philip Voss as Ulysses, demonstrates that *Troilus and Cressida* appeals to current audiences and strikes a sensitive nervous chord in the human psyche. Like *Antony and Cleopatra*, *Troilus and Cressida* gains much of its power and import from its baseline proposition that the human personality is quite intractable to being molded into a coherent psychological pattern. Like its successor, *Troilus and Cressida* gives attention to feeling types, but whereas in the characters of Antony and Cleopatra feeling was the primary function, in the personality of Cressida, the sensation aspects receive almost equal orchestration. In real people one orientation is said to predominate, but with literary characters, as Spoto cautions, deciding upon distinct classifications can difficult. Such a problematic character is Cressida. Hence, I hesitate to choose between the options by labeling her primary function either feeling or sensation. Rather, in dealing with her psychetypology, I shall discuss the nexus of feeling and sensation functions in her psyche.

Even though he is clearly more of a feeling type, Troilus has a secondary orientation of sensation. Much of the discord experienced by the lovers in the play results not from the opposition of thinking types but from conflicts between the feeling-oriented lovers themselves. But as we shall see, psychetypological difficulties also affect the play's thinking types.[16]

The play's very first scene stresses the predominance of feeling as Troilus' mode of functioning. He immediately decides that he will disarm rather than venture forth to battle. He is overcome by love and melancholy: "Why should I war without the walls of Troy, / That find such cruel battle here within?" (I. i. 23). He cries to Pandarus, "I tell thee I am mad / In Cressid's love" (I. i. 53–54). So intense is his desire for Pandarus' niece and so acute his frustration that he declares "Each Trojan that is master of his heart,/ Let him to field; Troilus, alas, hath none ['no heart to fight with']" (I. i. 4–5).

Shakespeare thus impresses upon the audience Troilus' central need for romantic experience. Along with his youth and naiveté, this need has produced sharp unrest, so much so that for the moment he cannot function in his accustomed military role. Like other feeling types, Troilus is deeply engaged by the romantic intensity of the emotional level he desires to ascend to.

Troilus's proclivity to live his life by what he feels is seen in the well-known debate with Hector over the advisability of returning Helen to Menelaus. Drawing upon logic and concepts of natural law and universal order, Hector stresses the folly of retaining Helen. Quite simply, she is not worth the Grecian and Trojan lives spent to keep her in Paris's arms.

"What's aught but as 'tis valued?" (II. ii. 52) argues Troilus. The younger man propounds that value resides in the subjective view of the valuer. To Troilus, gold would be valued not because of its rarity or its color, but because human beings have decided that it is valuable. Neither keeping Helen within Troy's walls nor returning her to her husband can logically be shown to be better. The question of whether to return her can be determined only subjectively.

Arguing further, Troilus, perhaps unwittingly, exposes the *modus operandi* of his thinking:

> I take today a wife, and my election
> Is led on in the conduct of the will —
> My will enkindled by mine eyes and ears,
> Two traded pilots twixt the dangerous shores
> Of will and judgment [II. ii. 61–65].

Troilus argues that although a wife may be chosen subjectively, one is still obligated to keep her — a view inconsistent with his basic premise. Yet in so arguing, he exposes cognitive dissonance in his own mental processes. Erecting this discussion's background is the common Renaissance tripartite division of the mind into will, reason, and appetite — a paradigm wherein the human psyche is seen as a battleground on which reason and appetite struggle for control of the will, which, of course, mandates conduct. Individual Elizabethan writers came up with numerous variations upon this theme, but central to this concept was the view that reason should guide the will away from unwholesome appetites. Troilus, in contrast, sees his eyes and ears — agents of appetite — as guiding forces between will and reason. Perhaps unwittingly he underscores his departure from much basic humanistic thought, yet he characterizes his mode of thought and behavior and subliminally prepares the audience for the disaster his search for romance creates.

His sensation-seeking side is underscored immediately before his tryst with Cressida:

> I am giddy; expectation whirls me round.
> Th' imaginary relish is so sweet
> That it enchants my sense. What will it be
> When that the watery palate tastes indeed

> Love's thrice repurèd nectar? Death, I fear me,
> Swooning destruction, or some joy too fine,
> Too subtle-potent, tuned too sharp in sweetness
> For the capacity of my ruder powers.
> I fear it much; and I do fear besides
> That I shall lose distinction in my joys,
> As doth a battle, when they charge on heaps
> The enemy flying [III. ii. 16–28].

Oscar James Campbell's oft-cited use of this passage to suggest that Troilus is an experienced epicure of the flesh is certainly off-center (211–212). The play clarifies Troilus' youth, naiveté, idealism. He is indeed a neophyte wooer. The passage, however, points to the centrality of sensation and sexuality to Shakespeare's protagonist. The expectation of lying with Cressida makes him "giddy"; the prospect whirls him about. He sees sexual consummation with Cressida as a exquisite delight, a kind of rare liqueur of love. He fears that the delight shall be so intense that he shall lose distinction in his joys. Troilus is not yet Campbell's arch libertine, yet he might have become such a one had he undergone several disillusioning affairs.

Cressida also reveals a feeling and sensation orientation. After surveying much criticism of Cressida's character, James O'Rourke underscored a recent critical trend to part with the established view of her as a downright wanton and to defend her character and choices (139–40). Certainly her character is more complex than earlier critics believed. It certain ways it is ambiguous. And theories of psychetypology can explain a significant measure of her behavior.

Her initial soliloquy, right after Pandarus' departure, opens, as it were, a window to the feeling and sensation aspects of her psyche. After revealing that she is fascinated by Troilus, she continues

> Yet hold I off. Women are angels, wooing;
> Things won are done, joy's soul lies in the doing,
> That she beloved knows naught that knows not this:
> Men prize the thing ungained more than it is.
> That she was never yet that ever knew
> Love got so sweet as when desire did sue.
> Therefore this maxim out of love I teach:
> Achievement is command; ungained, beseech.
> Then though my heart's content firm love doth bear,
> Nothing of that shall from mine eyes appear [1. ii. 288–97].

Although some lines may suggest the maneuverings of a practiced courtesan, the speech as a whole indicates a fundamental naiveté. Her basic intention is clear: She plans to play hard to get. For in her view, the essence of romantic joy for a woman is being pursued: "Things won are done, joy's soul lies in the doing." Once a woman bestows her affections upon a man, he begins to lose interest. A certain lack of clarity exists as to how she plans to conduct her relationship. Does she intend it to be a teasing friendship? Does she desire to maintain a basic aloofness, allowing herself to admired from afar, imitating, in effect, Dante's Beatrice and Petrarch's Laura? We are uncertain. Perhaps Cressida herself is unsure. Possibly her intentions regarding Troilus are still inchoate.

What is clear is that her approach to Troilus's maneuverings derives from feeling and sensation. As she puts it, "joy's soul lies in the doing." She expects to gain supreme pleasure from being sought upon a pedestal. She overlooks a likely danger to her plans: That Troilus might indeed tire of unavailing pursuit. She confesses a "firm love" for him, yet gives little detailed thought as to how to sustain it, basking in the assurance that by not giving into Troilus's entreaties, she will remain the object of his longings. She also fails to consider how long such an arrangement might be continued. She seems not to suspect that her "firm love" under these conditions might be rejected.

The desire for sensation at this juncture in her life is foremost in her mind. A thinking type, similarly attracted, would not so naively paint a romantic portrait, but would very likely consider varying ways of conducting the possible romance or of declining the offer.

When Cressida finally meets Troilus, her attitude toward the possible affair has undergone a striking metamorphosis. No longer does she appear to be a manipulator, scheming to trap Troilus in her web. Gone is her resolution to bask in the sunlight of being sought. Her impulse is to declare her love, to place herself in a torrent of emotion arising from involvement with Troilus. She readily admits her love for him. When the puzzled Troilus questions why she was so hard to be won, she replies, "Hard to seem won; but I was won, my lord, / With the first glance that ever — pardon me; / If I confess much, you will play the tyrant" (III. ii. 116–18). In an ironic reversal, Cressida admits that she has been worshiping him from afar. Reversed as well is her attitude toward mastery in a male-female relationship. Earlier she had expressed discomfort with male dominance. Now she speedily declares that her admission has placed her in his power. She tries to compensate for her verbal fumble by claiming that she loved him but not so much that she could not control it. Immediately her emotions eddy about. She informs him that she has just lied about having been able to control her feelings and then tries to explain her immediate feelings: "My thoughts were like unbridled children, grown /

Too headstrong for their mother. See, we fools! / Why have I blabbed? Who shall be true to us, / When we are so unsecret to ourselves?" (III. ii. 121–24).

To be sure, hypocrisy coils itself about her words. She does not confess her central reason for being standoffish. But much, however, of what she says is sincere! Her entire speech is not a skillfully-wrought verbal net employed to catch an unsuspecting Troilus. To a large extent, Cressida is saying what she feels and acting out what she feels. True to the feeling type, what she feels to be right dominates her approach. Earlier she had felt playing "distant" was right; now confessing her infatuation seems the correct course. Indeed, spontaneously, after Troilus pledges his truthfulness, she professes her sincerity, vowing that if she proves untrue, all faithless women shall be described as "'As false as Cressid" (III. ii. 195). To feel, to experience — these are central currents in her psyche.

Her feeling and sensation orientation, moreover, leads her to her betrayal of Troilus. After meeting with him, Cressida, having abandoned her resolve not to surrender, gives herself to him sexually. Several times, during the scene before she departs from Troy, the question of her truthfulness unpleasantly rises. Twice she is hurt, indignant that Troilus raises it. The third time she questions whether Troilus believes that she will be tempted, "Do you think I will?" (IV. iv. 92), Troilus edges back from the awkward verbal exchange, speaking in generalities about temptation. She then raises the question of whether he will be true and Troilus declares his steadfastness. The scene closes, then, having emphasized the emotional insecurity of each lover. (Indeed, fear of each other's possible betrayal is evident throughout their courtship and is very likely another reason for Cressida's initial standoffishness, but the scene concludes with each lover's dedication to remaining true.)

The next scene, therefore, is all the more surprising. It, of course, is the notorious kissing episode in which Cressida freely bestows kisses upon assembled Greek leaders— a segment of the text often used to prove the heroine's wantonness. O'Rourke defends her by asserting that "she uses her wit as best she can to fend off a stylized gang rape" (154). No one can deny that this motive might not in part produce this moment of dalliance, but a logical stratagem is not the sole reason. Her behavior can be explained to a large extent by her feeling and sensation orientation.

An important consideration of the scene is that Cressida does not immediately speak. She enters with Diomede. The Greek leaders approach; she is then kissed in turn by Agamemnon, Nestor, Achilles, and Patroclus. Her silence leaves a great deal to interpretation. One can only speculate how the scene was originally performed. But the most likely reason for

Cressida's silence is her uncertainty upon entering the Greek camp. She does not know how indeed she may be accepted; whether she will be spurned, honored, or even molested. She becomes compliant, even submissive, until she is kissed a second time by Patroclus. Two changes then take place in her mind. She realizes that she is accepted, and her sensation side comes to the fore. She finds herself enjoying the attention, reveling in again being sought. The unexpectedness, the newness of the situation thrills her. Immediately, by entering into the "kissing game," she reverses roles. She becomes dominant, in control when she refuses a kiss to Menelaus and even quips about his cuckoldry. Cressida relishes the kissing game, which in fact, allows her momentarily to enjoy the kind of dominance she had hoped to maintain over Troilus. Ulysses remarks upon her wantonness:

> Fie, fie upon her!
> There's language in her eye, her cheek, her lip,
> Nay, her foot speaks; her wanton spirits look out
> At every joint and motive of her body [IV. v. 55–58].

The words of Ulysses need not be understood to certify that Cressida is totally corrupt. However, they do call attention to her Protean sensation-seeking and call into question her ability to remain steadfast to Troilus.

The judgment of Ulysses becomes prophetic. We next encounter Cressida as Troilus does, when he journeys with Ulysses to see her and discovers her with Diomede. Along with the protagonist, we discover that she has already begun a relationship with her escort to the Grecian camp. But nature of the relationship is still unclear. Clearly, Diomede demands her full attention and continued sexual compliance. Cressida whets his interest yet struggles to remain aloof, at times chiding him, at times stroking him with words. Their quarrel soon concerns the sleeve Troilus had given her. Diomede demands it as a token of her love. She refuses to surrender it, then complies. How are we to understand Cressida's behavior? Are her complicated dealings with Diomede — as Thersites alleges — simply a whore's trick to sharpen the warrior's appetite? Or does she sincerely care for Troilus? The answer is not simple, nor is it meant to be. Her concluding words suggest truth in both possibilities:

> Troilus, farewell! One eye yet looks on thee,
> But with my heart the other eye doth see.
> Ah, poor our sex! The fault in us I find:
> The error of our eye directs our mind.
> What error leads must err. O, then conclude:
> Minds swayed by eyes are full of turpitude [V. ii. 110–41].

Her words indicate a conflict between the feeling and sensation modes of behavior. Part of her yearns for the love of Troilus and the emotional intensity granted by that experience. Another part is enticed by the newness of Diomede and the potential excitement and emotional involvement that he offers. As Patrick Cruttwell long ago commented, Cressida is intended to be ambiguous (23–24). We are to share Troilus's startled reaction, "This is and is not Cressid." (V. ii. 150). Shakespeare's treatment of his female protagonist is not unlike that of Marvell's of Chloe in "The Gallery," in which the speaker explores the complexity of Chloe's personality by seeing her as a series of portraits in the gallery of his mind — pictures of her as a murderess, as Aurora, as Venus. The portrait the speaker prefers most is that of her as a shepherdess. We are left with ambiguity as to which portrait — if any — most nearly represents the lady. Shakespeare provides us with differing portraits of Cressida. When she disappears from the stage with the lines quoted above, we wonder whether we have seen and understand the real Cressida. Nor does she understand herself, nor feel competent to manage her life. With the fatalistic propensity that Malone associates with feeling types (157–58), she concludes with a sense of ineluctability, "Minds swayed by eyes are full of turpitude," and stresses her feeling of being led down error's path. The feeling and sensation sides of her personality are in conflict. She is uncertain how to navigate a course through her troubled psyche. Perhaps circumstances provide the prevailing winds. She heads for the port of Diomede.

If the rapid disintegration of their affair produces confusion in Cressida, it creates an almost suicidal frenzy in Troilus. Feeling types are particularly vulnerable to romantic disappointment. As Malone makes the point, "The failure of romanticism is disenchantment; that, to a feeling type, may entail an absolute collapse of one's personal identity. When innocence, when faith, when honor is lost, 'Chaos is come.' Suffering such loss, Shakespeare's Othello and his Anthony [sic] kill themselves…" (157). Pandarus astutely realizes this potential danger to his young friend's psyche: "The young prince will go mad. A plague upon Antenor!" (IV. ii. 77–78). Since his rational side is not as developed as his emotional side, Troilus is unable to view his romantic plight with a vital measure of objectivity. He thrusts himself into the battle with the Greeks in a wild effort to kill Diomede, takes foolish risks, and even battles with Diomede and Ajax at the same time. A brush stroke of black comedy appears in the picture when Diomede captures Troilus' horse as a prize for Cressida. Although he is not slain by Achilles, as his counterpart is in Chaucer's redaction of the tale, for Troilus the tumultuous afternoon comes to a head with the death of Hector. Troilus fatalistically sees in his brother's death the mirror images of his devastation and of the devastation of Troy: the "sure destruction" managed by the gods (V. x. 9).

Troilus and Cressida — the play's prime representatives of the sensation and feelings types — are victims of their psyches. To discomfiting extent their psychetypologies become a kind of quasi-fatalism, limiting their choices and producing discord and mayhem. We might recall Jung's lesson "that every judgment made by an individual is conditioned by his personality type...." Similar patterns of self-limiting psychetypes may be observed, however, in characters who embody other psychic faculties, particularly the representatives of the thinking type — Ulysses, Nestor, and Thersites. These characters, in varying ways, seek to control reality by understanding it. Each of these men, however, fails.

Ulysses is vital to the play's design. His dominant faculty is rationality. Interestingly, Bethel believes his character harkens back intermittently to the allegorized wisdom of the morality plays (122). Ulysses is the planner, the arranger, indeed the schemer, maneuvering Ajax, Achilles, and others to obtain his ends. He understands the foibles and failures of mankind, and is able to utilize these defects. His speech praising universal order and warning against appetite — the "universal wolf: (I. iii. 120) — points to the thinking type's need for territoriality, ranking and labeling. Although he may not believe in all the cosmic implications of the Elizabethan world picture, he admires the well-oiled working of a rational plan. The disorder of the Greek camp, he stresses, ironically creates the strength of Troy. If an arranged, orderly attack were made on Priam's city, Troy would fall.

To accomplish this end, he attempts to bring Achilles back into the war by setting up Ajax as a rival hero to be awarded with Greek applause. Yet his labors go for naught; they are checkmated by a reversal, recalling the chaotic world of *King John*. When it seems that he is on the brink of success, when Achilles begins to eye killing Hector as a means of regaining his prestige, a letter comes from Hecuba urging Achilles again to abstain from battle for the sake of her daughter Polyxena's love and the mighty warrior capitulates. Yet Ulysses's goal is achieved by the intervention of the unexpected, by chaos, when Hector kills Patroclus, Achilles' male lover. Wrath and grief drive Achilles to the battlefield. Hector is killed and clouds of forthcoming disaster hang over Troy.

Ulysses's object is achieved in spite of the failure of his efforts to gain it. His plotting, weighing events and analyzing personalities have been in vain. Like the complex worlds of *King John* and *Antony and Cleopatra*, the world of *Troilus and Cressida* proves unamenable to rational formulation. Chance and chaos render the efforts to understand and control events largely ineffective, as happenings rearrange themselves about the "strange attractor" of Patroclus's death. The bedlam on the battlefield presents a grotesque counterimage of the heavenly order that appeals to Ulysses' categorizing intellect.

Nestor — another prominent thinking type in the play — similarly demonstrates the danger of reliance on the intellect. In furthering the designs of Ulysses, Nestor shares in his fellow warrior's successful defeat. He mirrors his more enterprising companion's ineffectuality.

Thersites — the play's last remaining thinking type — also represents a degree of failure with his temperamental mode's manner of apprehending the world. Like Ulysses, he finds importance in order, but not the order of the cosmos or of tactical plans. The order that tantalizes Thersites is the order of the lowest possible level of human conduct. He is obsessed with proving that all is "wars and lechery; nothing else holds fashion" (V. ii. 198–99). He reduces the Trojan war to a squabble over a whore, rechristens Menelaus as a "cuckold," and interprets, as we have seen, Cressida's complex interaction with Diomede as a whore's tricks. Of course, to an unsettling extent he is correct in his estimations of human behavior. Helen is adulterous, Ajax a pompous fool, Diomede an opportunistic lecher. But Thersites goes too far. He misses the good that appears in some of the characters; for instance, Troilus' devotion to Cressida. Struggling with his disillusionment concerning Cressida, Troilus begins to share Thersites' proclivity for reducing human behavior to its lowest possible denominator when, for instance, he proclaims that Cressida's falsehood stains all mothers. Ulysses replies with common sense: "What hath she done, Prince, that can soil our mothers?" (V. ii. 137). Such a rejoinder could well be applied to Thersites with his proclivity to reduce all human behavior to wars and lechery.

The psychetypology of one more vital character in the play needs discussion, that of Hector. Here, the path seems to lead to a critical quagmire, for Hector is difficult to analyze. His initial appearance in the play, at the debate about whether to return Helen to the Greeks, is baffling because of his *volte face*, which makes his character seem inconsistent at best or at worst poorly conceived.[17] Hector begins the scene by staunchly arguing for Helen's return, yet, having made his case, crosses to the side of Troilus and Paris and vows to keep her for the honor of Troy. During the debate Hector seems an undisputed thinking type. He appeals to reason, to theories of natural law, to a system of universal order calling to mind that propounded by Ulysses. He chides Troilus for being emotional: "Or is your blood / So madly hot that no discourse of reason, / Nor fear of bad success in a bad cause, / Can qualify the same?" (II. ii. 115–17).

Later he accuses both Troilus and Paris of arguing "superficially" like "young men, whom Aristotle thought / Unfit to hear moral philosophy" (165–67). Afterward he declares that he will side with his brothers because the keeping of Helen is tied to "our joint and several dignities" (II. ii. 193). In other words, he upholds Troilus' insistence on heroism and honor. "Honor" to Hector is not simply a Machiavellian stratagem to publicize the might of Troy. It is a romantic, chivalric ideal rooted in his character. Indeed, it drives him to his death. Despite the warnings of Andromache, Cassandra, and Hecuba — all of whom experience oracular insights — Hector goes to the battlefield, having vowed to combat certain Greeks and feeling the need to be true to these pledges. He begins the play as a partisan of logic, but subsequently becomes as idealistic and misguided as Troilus.

Hector's inconsistency has troubled critics, especially his *volte face* during the debate. Graham Bradshaw tried to restore the clarity of Shakespeare's portrayal of Hector by arguing that Hector is not as noble as he appears. Instead of being a spokesperson for reason and moral order, Hector uses these concepts in an impressive bit of grandstanding, intending all along to keep Helen and maintain the war. Bradshaw writes, "We might wonder how any attentive critic could resist the conclusion that the Hector-problem is properly resolved by seeing through him — as a hollow man who needs to be admired as Cressida needs to be desired" (138). Bradshaw's commentary calls attention to a possible, less appealing side of Hector, but still his theory may not adequately explain the warrior's about face, particularly his long, spirited argument to return Helen.

I suggest that Hector's behavior during the debate cannot be fully explained by character motivation as we normally understand the term. Too often critics fail to recall a dramatic convention which S. L. Bethel long ago named depersonalization, which "results from the simplest form of episodic intensification, where the writer has so concentrated on the content of a speech, as apparently to have ignored the speaker's identity" (109). In other words, the dramatic personages speak out of character or about events of which they could have no knowledge. Hector's speech on surrendering Helen is a sharp example of depersonalization. His *volte face* is not in character. It is as though two personalities are awkwardly fused in him. Or, to describe the phenomenon in terms of this study, Hector seems an ungainly fusion of thinking and feeling functions.

According to Jung's theories, thinking and feeling are polar opposites. As we have seen, this view does not mean that feeling types never think, nor that thinking types never feel. But the dominance of one function in a person precludes the other as a secondary trait. A thinking type could have intuition and sensation as secondary traits, but not feeling. It is as though Shakespeare unconsciously created an illogical, but symbolically powerful fusion of these two traits in Hector — a fusion which has ramifications for the work's thematic design, for it suggests the impossibility of unifying these opposing faculties into psychological concord.

Of course, in pointing out the typological aspects of these characters, I am not suggesting that Shakespeare arrived at Jung's theory of typology centuries before Jung or that the dramatist drew up any formal typological system of his own. If pressed about the motivations of his characters, Shakespeare might well have fallen upon Aristotelian ethics or astrology for explanations. What I do suggest is that Shakespeare, through his knowledge of human nature, creates characters in *Troilus and Cressida* who illustrate the workings of the basic Jungian functions and that conversely, the theory sheds light on the play.

In *Troilus* certain characters show the functions in bold relief. This does not dehumanize them into the dullest of allegorical abstractions, but it does highlight the particular workings and difficulties of the types. The play indicates the insufficiency of each psychological function as a sole or major means of ordering human behavior. People, of course, may draw upon all of their four functions in acting out their wishes. But no one can use them all at one time to regulate conduct. Or, to express these ideas alternatively, it is as though in the play Shakespeare is illustrating the workings of an individual human psyche writ large in which the functions fight for influence or perhaps dominance, yet, as Auden suggests in *For the Time Being*, humankind's misfortune is that the functions can never work in tandem. Everyone is in some sense unbalanced. Hector, with his inability to maintain consistency, becomes a paradigm for major conflicts besetting the events of the play, for his contradictions suggest the impossibility of unifying opposing faculties into psychological concord. Auden's prelapsarian Eden of emotional unity again proves to be a wispy dream.

In presenting characters who may be taken to illustrate the workings of an individual human psyche, the play verges toward allegory, but cannot be classed as allegory. Perhaps the best term to apply to it is the one D. A. Nuttall supplied to *The Tempest*, that of "pre-allegorical": that level of psychic function in which one senses a significance in phenomena but cannot label that significance. As Nuttall wrote of Prospero's island — and indeed of the world of the play as a whole — "it shimmers between subjectivity and objectivity, presents itself differently to different eyes, yet it will not keep still long enough for one to affix an allegorical label" (159).

Failures at self-fashioning abound in *Troilus and Cressida*. Cressida fails in her apparent attempt to be a Petrarchan-blessed damsel; Agamemnon to be an effective leader; Troilus to be a chivalric lover. One of the most bitterly satirical attempts at self-fashioning is that of Achilles, who wishes to create himself (or perhaps re-create himself) in the image of what we understand as his Homeric prototype by slaying Hector. During their first battlefield encounter, the out-of-practice Achilles flees and must return with his henchmen to complete the task.[18]

Shakespeare, then, portrays the potential inner hell caused by conflicting psychetypes. To paraphrase Troilus, one wars within himself and thus cannot fight with others. Shakespeare realizes that such conflict is intolerable, yet feels that escaping totally from it is impossible. He realizes, however, the importance of the human need to continue trying to master some form of inner control.

Problems with self-control, of course, are universal. What gives those of the Renaissance their particular poignance and tension is the breakup of the medieval world with its ordered system of values. But the era's particular slant given to the problem need not obscure for us central undercurrents. Looking at Shakespeare's plays through this psychetypological lens can add to our understanding of his works and their treatments of a central problem of their age and of any age. In summary, Shakespeare ventures into the realm of inner psychological chaos in order to arrive at some understanding of the psychological workings of humanity; moreover, he realizes the difficulty of controlling the self, but affirms the need to do so.

Placed side by side, *Antony and Cleopatra* and *Troilus and Cressida* reveal intriguing similarities and equally intriguing differences. Each play calls attention to the problems thinking and feeling types face in interacting with each other and in fashioning a concept of the self. However, the dominant psychetypological note in *Antony and Cleopatra* is the confusion and bafflement produced by the inability of characters of contrasting psychetypes to comprehend each other. In *Troilus and Cressida,* on the other hand, the emphasis falls upon the inability of individual psychetypes to fashion themselves. Although in *Antony and Cleopatra* Enobarbus fails in his quest for individuation, Octavius succeeds. Owing his success to his ruthless rationalism, he removes his opponents from the international chessboard, establishes an empire, and becomes an emperor. Antony and Cleopatra, although they lose the complicated quest for power, in a sense complete themselves. Antony dies affirming his love for Cleopatra and before her death Cleopatra cries, "Husband, I come!" In avowing their devotion before their deaths, they free themselves from the flux of chance and from emotional permutations; they achieve a paradoxical fleeting permanence, a kind of momentary apotheosis. In *Troilus and Cressida,* the process of self-fashioning, of individuation, fails dismally. Both plays emphasize the same human dilemmas and perplexities. Reading them one after the other is like looking at a hill from the north and then the south. One views the same mound, but intriguingly different features capture the observer's attention. Placing them side by side, we see a pattern or reproduction but not resolution of similar conflicts.

Neither play, then, presents Shakespeare's final word on the problems under consideration. What can be said is that at crucial junctures in his career Shakespeare felt the need to explore and highlight significantly the relationships of feeling and thinking to the human psyche. *Troilus and Cressida* came roughly mid-way in Shakespeare's career. Ahead lay some of his greatest works—*Othello, King Lear, and Macbeth.* In *Antony and Cleopatra*, as noted, he would return to the depiction of thinking and feeling types with even more subtlety. Beyond that work lay the final romances, works in which he still strove to understand the human psyche, its contradictory drives, and the need to reconcile them. The *Troilus and Cressida* world of psychological chaos often subtly becomes part of the backdrop of these later works.

Since this chapter deals with thinking-feeling conflicts in tragedies dealing with romantic love, a few words about *Romeo and Juliet* are almost obligatory. Both Romeo and Juliet are without doubt feeling types, feeling types of the nth degree. Passion, affection, closeness—these are their personal hallmarks. Their interrelationships become so intense that they cannot consider life without each other. Believing that Juliet is dead, Romeo becomes frantic, unreasonable, homicidal, and then suicidal. Not without a warning, he kills the relatively blameless Paris, who believes the young Montague has come to despoil Juliet's grave. Then Romeo swallows the poison bought from the apothecary for the exact purpose of committing suicide. Upon waking and discovering his body, Juliet, without hesitation, kills herself with his knife.

Their tragedies result not from the conflict of the functions of feeling and thinking, but from the very underdevelopment of their thinking functions. More so than even Antony and Cleopatra and Troilus and Cressida, Romeo and Juliet lack any capacity to look at themselves critically, to see any possible shoals in their planned course. Hence, they become the prey of chaotic unexpected events.

The thinking function appears primarily in two characters. The mocking, rational spirit of Puck, Feste, Jaques, and Touchstone reincarnates itself in the jesting Mercutio. Friar Lawrence, however, is able to view Romeo and Juliet's extreme attachment from a rational vantage point and offers thoughtful, but neglected, counsel:

These violent delights have violent ends
And in their triumph die, like fire and powder,
Which as they kiss consume. The sweetest honey
Is loathsome in his own deliciousness,
And in the taste confounds the appetite.
Therefore love moderately. Long love doth so;
Too swift arrives as tardy as too slow [II. vi. 9–15].

Whether he himself is a thinking type is another matter. Despite his mature awareness, he allows himself to be sucked into the rush of events, so that he not only abets the lovers but becomes an instrument of their tragedy. The satirical Mercutio, however, does not have the final word. Friar Lawrence's advice points to a potentially noble course the mutual attraction might have taken. Although some critics have derided Romeo and Juliet as abjectly foolish and even errant sinners (for instance, Battenhouse, 102–29), this opinion is surely incorrect. The very structure, tone, and poetry of the play convinces us of something essentially noble in their love. Their tragedy results in large part because their undeveloped rational faculties are unable to help them deal with their unexpected and powerful torrents of emotions.

Although the conflicts of thinking-feeling are not manifested in *Romeo and Juliet* in the same fashion they are in the other two plays considered in this chapter, the application of psychetypological theory to Shakespeare's tale of the "star-crossed" lovers illustrates another way this recurrent conflict is manifested in Shakespeare's oeuvre and also offers insights into the personalities of the characters.

A beckoning question raised by all of these plays needs to be addressed. Shakespeare, as noted earlier, was obsessed by life's chaotic intermingling of good and evil, in particular the capability for a good act to have evil consequences and vice versa. Do these plays offer any hope of unscrambling the mixtures? In other words, do they affirm the relativity or objectivity of values? As we have seen, the debate in *Troilus and Cressida* is cut short by Hector's unexpected *volte face*. He neither retreats from his position nor affirms Troilus's. We must look to the drama's subsequent action for an answer.

On the surface, Hector's point of view may seem to be justified. Troilus bitterly discovers that his idealized Cressida is not worth his valuing. Her instability, her insecurities, indeed her feeling and sensation orientation itself, leads her to desert him, proving the she is not the woman he has valued her as and idealized her to be. Likewise, Achilles is revealed to be unworthy of his reputation. In his confrontation with Hector, he flees, and upon realizing that he is out of shape, and returns with his henchmen to butcher the Trojan champion.[19]

But do these examples justify Hector's view that values are objective? Not necessarily so. The play does not offer us morally a unadulterated character to evince the reality of objective values. Some readers may offer Hector as the Shakespearean ideal of the soldier, but his *volte face* blows smoke in our eyes as we attempt to evaluate his conduct. His depersonalization, while fulfilling an immediate dramaturgic purpose, obscures our picture of him. Moreover, certain flaws mar his portrait. He seems heedless of caution during the final day on the battlefield and downright foolhardy when he removes his helmet while he is still outside the walls of Troy. His *volte face* from what he apparently upholds as the side of reason in the debate on value makes him appear insincere and hypocritical, even misguided by Troilus. One may still honor him, but must do so by downplaying his less noble qualities. One may disqualify him as an ideal by recognizing his lesser qualities. In other words, in evaluating Hector, we find ourselves again confronted with the dilemma of relying upon subjective assessments of the character's worth. The dispute isn't whether or not Hector has noble or less than nobles qualities. Opinions clash on what they are and what weight to give them. In attempting to decide on Hector's worth, our wished-for agreement is forestalled by our own psychetypologies. To repeat Jung's two central lessons derived from his study of psychological types, "the insight that every judgment made by an individual is conditioned by his personality type and that every point of view is necessarily relative." So, in a sense, readers, like the characters, are drawn into and victimized by the chaotic world of *Troilus and Cressida*.

By excluding any character who unambiguously has ascertainable value, *Troilus and Cressida* may seem to tip the scales to Troilus's view—for the lack of a competing example. But then the lack of such an example could be seen as not concluding but leaving the debate open.

Does *Antony and Cleopatra* present a final clarification of the issue? I doubt that it does. Are we to be for the lovers or to condemn them? Criticism has never reached accord. Essays and books have been written energetically supporting each side. The best answer is to suggest that Shakespeare's attitude toward his pair of volatile lovers is contradictory and paradoxical. To be sure, their conduct creates much evil: Antony's neglect of his governmental duties, his unfaithfulness to Fulvia, his desertion of Octavia, his recklessness at Actium, among other derelictions, must be placed in the pot along with Cleopatra's selfish manipulations, her cruelty to the messenger, and her final trickery which actuates Antony's suicide as evidence of the disruptive and destructive consequences of their turbulent relationship. Yet we cannot help admiring the bond that unites them, in spite of their mutual-distrusts, mutual-recriminations, and desertions of each other. Do their avowals of love at their deaths tip the scales of judgment on the side of their love?

We cannot be sure. We may recall the Misfit's words at the conclusion of Flannery O'Connor's "A Good Man is Hard to Find." After having killed the self-centered grandmother who had experienced a rush of emotion in the fleeting moments before he pulled the trigger, O'Connor's asylum escapee remarks, "She would of been a good woman ... if it had been somebody there to shoot her every minute of her life"(153). We may well wish to adapt the statement thus: "Antony and Cleopatra would have been the sincerest of lovers if death had been threatening them every minute of their lives." We suspect that had Antony's fortunes altered before his grotesquely comic suicide and had Octavius been defeated, Antony and Cleopatra's relationship would have been as turbulent as ever.

The play, of course, clearly demonstrates that Cleopatra plans to live on after Antony's death. Although she sincerely grieves his suicide, she considers surrendering to Octavius and keeps her squirreled away fortune hidden from the conqueror until her steward Seleucus betrays its existence. Only after she learns that she will be mocked by being paraded through Rome in Octavius's triumph does she decide to join Antony in death.

But does the intensity of their love at the point of death, their need to affirm it at this crucial moment, indicate that their apparent mutual adoration is at base, false and hollow? The undeniable sincerity of their avowals would undercut such a judgment. At best, we can say that their mutual love is married by selfishness, insincerity, and cruelty as well as glorified by the intensity and endurance of their devotion. Again we are faced with the impossibility of trying to label something that is not easily labeled.

Likewise, in the political realm, the play provides no simple categorization of value. Like the Bastard in *King John*, Octavius, an unscrupulous self-seeker, takes vital steps that create good for the masses. Octavius wins the war and initiates long-lasting peace in the Mediterranean. But he does so by treachery, betrayal and cruelty. Even in our cynical, scandal-ridden age, many of us would prefer to have politicians that are morally upright. We would like to believe that good deeds are produced by good rulers. But the victories of Octavius pull us up short, forcing us to face the unpleasant reality that the political world is dishearteningly complicated.

In the constantly mutating world of *Antony and Cleopatra* nothing can be taken for granted. After Antony's death Cleopatra emblazons him extravagantly:

> His legs bestrid the ocean; his reared arm
> Crested the world; his voice was propertied
> As all the tunèd spheres, and that to friends;
> But when he meant to quail and shake the orb,
> He was rattling thunder. For his bounty
> There was no winter in 't; an autumn 'twas
> That grew more by the reaping. His delights
> Were dolphinlike; they showed his back above
> The element they lived in. In his livery
> Walked crowns and crownets; realms and islands were
> As plates dropped from his pocket [V. ii 81–91].

But, uncertain of the validity of her claims, she asks Dollabella, "Think you there was or might be such a man /As this I dreamt of?"(92–93).

His answer is sympathetic, but frank: "Gentle madam, no"(93). Her view of Antony, as expressed to Dollabella, is a kind of self-induced mirage, a self-deluding will-o-the-wisp. Certainly we are to agree that her praise is excessive, but is it entirely misapplied? After Antony sends his treasure, Enobarbus stresses his former master's nobility: "O Antony, / Thou mine of bounty, how wouldst thou have paid / My better service, when my turpitude/ Thou dost so crown with gold!" (IV. viii. 32–35). Before his death Enobarbus declares, "O Antony, nobler than my revolt is infamous...." (IV ix. 21–22). Enobarbus founds his testimony of Antony's nobility of spirit, generosity, and forgiveness upon a concrete act — the sending of the treasure, lending some substance to Cleopatra's praise of her lover's bounty. But where can the line be drawn between Cleopatra's fictitious, bountiful Antony and Enobarbus's factually-founded, but also idealistic, view of Antony? Obviously the answer is unclear: margins dissolve, definitions blur, and abstractions totter. A similar difficulty in definition can be applied to Cleopatra's worth. Although she is conniving, hot-tempered, potentially traitorous, Antony nears death wishing "Of many thousand kisses the poor last / [to] lay upon thy lips" (IV. xv. 21–22).

G. Wilson Knight pointed out that imagery of shifting and changing circumstances formed a thematic baseline for *Antony and Cleopatra*.[20] A few examples follow:

In the play's beginning, when Cleopatra chides Antony for being more concerned with the world's affairs than with her, he responds, "Let Rome in the Tiber melt and the wide arch / Of the ranged empire fall!" (I. i. 35–36). Later, when he discovers Cleopatra dickering with Thidias, Octavius's emissary, and her possible betrayal of him, Antony cries, "Authority melts from me of late!" (III. xiii. 91). Upon Antony's death,

Cleopatra cries, "The crown o' th' earth doth melt! (IV. xv. 65). When she prepares to join Antony in death, she says, "Husband, I come! / Now to that name my courage prove my title!/ I am fire and air; my other elements / I give to baser life" (V. ii. 287–290).

Before killing himself Antony reviews his tangled fortunes by comparing himself to the Protean clouds.

> Sometimes we see a cloud that's dragonish,
> A vapor sometimes like a bear or lion,
> A towered citadel, a pendent rock,
> A forkèd mountain, or blue promontory
> With trees upon 't that nod unto the world
> And mock our eyes with air. Thou hast seen these signs;
> They are black vesper's pageants....
> That which is now a horse, even with a thought
> The rack dislimms and makes it indistinct
> As water is in water [IV. xiv. 2–11].

This recurrent imagery indicates a world of shifts and changes, where labels are ineffective and opposites join only to separate again. In such a world objective value seems impossible. The very psychetypologies of the characters, their subjectivities, defeat efforts to create a rationally-based concord. Do the subcreated worlds of *Troilus and Cressida* and Antony *and Cleopatra*— and indeed the Shakespearean corpus as a whole — deny the existence of objective values? The answer is not easy to formulate. Graham Bradshaw, however, has provided us with provocative possibility. In attempting to describe what Shakespeare might have believed about humanity's need to find objective values, Bradshaw writes, "'There are, or may be, no objective values, but the need to endow life with value and significance is an objective fact about human nature'"(37). Such a concept seems to lie in the background of Shakespeare's concern with values in a number of instances in his plays. But this view should not be understood as an iron-clad maxim the poet readily recited when perplexed about ethics. The view recurs throughout the plays, disintegrates, and reforms itself, assuming other dramatic emphases and thematic implications. For as we shall see, Shakespeare is not ultimately comfortable with this stance. Like the world outside him, his mind is in flux.

The world of *Antony and Cleopatra* both affirms and denies values. It is world that perturbs us because of its chaos, a world very similar to that of *King John*, a world that daunts us with its confusions, reversals, and treacheries. We shrink from it. To borrow words from *King Lear*, we fear, "O, that way madness lies" (III. iv. 21).

FIVE

"Stay, We Must Not Lose Our Senses": The Emergence of the Inferior Function

In the first act of Gilbert and Sullivan's *The Pirates of Penzance,* young Frederic, the unfortunate former "pirate 'prentice," who has just found Mabel, his true love, breaks from the rapturous caroling of his joys when he recollects that his fiancée's multitude of beauteous sisters are endangered by his late comrades, the Pirates of Penzance. Warning the ladies, he sings

> Stay, we must not lose our senses;
> Men who stick at no offenses
> Will anon be here.
> Piracy their dreadful trade is;
> Pray you, get you hence, young ladies,
> While the coast is clear.

The girls' chorus repeats the stanza, beginning with "No, we must not lose our senses" and continuing with appropriate modifications. Alas, before they can withdraw, they are seized by the returning pirates.

Of course, in the topsy-turvy world of Gilbert and Sullivan the girls' danger is treated humorously as the pirates wish to marry them. The scene's purpose is to amuse and produce chuckles, not to make the spines of the audience taut with suspense. But, surprisingly enough, the lines play upon one of humanity's oldest and most troubling anxieties. Frederic fears (and the ladies share his fear) that they will all lose control of themselves and therefore fall into the pirates' clutches. Because ladies are never raped or murdered in the world of comic opera, Gilbert and Sullivan can play with the dread of emerging panic, render it comic and provide their audience a momentary but pleasing catharsis of this deep, prevalent fear.

The fear of losing control becoming in some measure helpless shows itself in many ways, from stage fright, the dreaded return of a panic attack, to the obsessive compulsive's fear of going berserk and committing a vile act, to the lucid psychotic's apprehension about possibly recurring insanity. The kind of "losing one's senses" that typology mainly concerns itself with is the threat to the ego caused by the intimidating emergence of the inferior function into consciousness. We might recall that the inferior functions are the least developed of the four in individuals' psyches. As Jung himself defined them, "These functions may properly be called *inferior* in a psychological but not psychopathological sense, since they are in no way morbid but merely backward as compared with the favored function" (*Types* 450). Normally in the psyche the four functions coexist in reasonable harmony. While it may manifest itself in the consciousness, the inferior function largely remains unconscious. However, in certain circumstances, when the psyche in upset, the inferior function seeks to emerge into the consciousness and, in essence, take it over. The individual psyche's divisions into categories of "the good and the bad, the familiar and the unfamiliar, the known and the unknown" (Spoto 77) begins crumbling. Thus what Jungian Marie-Louise von Franz calls "the great conflict" begins. According to Spoto, "Such a person sooner or later will have to contend with the feeling of being particularly separate or divided from himself or herself, a psychological problem that is the modern equivalent of being cast out of the Garden of Eden for the second time" (77). The consciousness then will confront the task of dealing with this exiled portion of the personality. "Failing that, the individual will regress to earlier, more nondifferentiated stages of development. The inferior function, in its most animalistic or barbaric form, then can and will take over" (78). Such persons find their sense of reality turned upside down. These troubled persons then may project their "inner shadows" upon other individuals, viewing them with hostility and seeing them as embodiments of evil. As Spoto stresses this deterioration, "the person soon fails to be able to tell the difference between friend and foe, contending with the ever present adversary he or she always seems to be finding. In the extreme, the world itself becomes a Machiavellian nightmare from which the person cannot awake" (89). In severe cases, persons so inclined encounter a psychotic breakdown (81).

Drawing upon an analogy developed by Jung and von Franz, Spoto likens the psyche to a room with four doors, stating "that whatever is behind the first three doors that one opens, consciousness can handle more or less on its own terms; but the fourth door is often experienced as a trap-door leading to parts and places as yet unknown. The contents behind the fourth door are often then beyond the ego's normal scope of integration" (86–87). Nevertheless, the hope of Jungian theory is to bring the essence of "the inferior function to consciousness." This process "makes further development possible"(Jung *Types* 451).

The threatening emergence of the inferior function is a disturbing undercurrent in the tribulations of Shakespeare's tragic heroes. This chapter shall investigate the interior function of Shakespeare's characters by concentrating on his tragic period and by examining this conflict in *Othello*, *Timon of Athens*, and *Coriolanus* and in Angelo of the so-called problem play *Measure for Measure*. Again we shall see this conflict between the thinking and feeling functions and note variations of this discord in such characters as Richard II and Lady Macbeth.

However, a word of caution should be offered. In delving into the "inner psychology" of these characters, we should caution ourselves not to treat them as though they are actual clinical cases. Always a risky enterprise, this method has more chance of success when applied to the characters of realistic fiction such as Tolstoy's Anna Karenina and Flaubert's Charles and Emma Bovary. The underlying conviction of such literature is that fictional characters should be portrayed "scientifically"—that is, they should be as realistic as possible in accord with the author's own acute observations on human behavior and psychological theory. Writers then should include no improbabilities—no sudden character reversals from bad to good, no unmotivated actions. Hence, writers of realistic fiction are more likely to portray more accurately such psychological ailments as clinical depression, schizophrenia, and Korsakov's psychosis than their early modern counterparts.

How different were the literary goals of writers of the English Renaissance! Shakespeare, Jonson, Dekker, Marlowe and Middleton had never heard of the realistic criteria of the brothers Goncourt or of Zola. Their plays abound with type characters, sudden personality reversals, seemingly unmotivated actions and behaviors actuated by the most elementary of incentives, for instance, lust or greed. The situation is not that Elizabethan and Jacobean dramatists *never* created realistic characters. Quite clearly their own observations of human behavior were among the ingredients that went into their creative blending cauldrons, but the creation of realistic characters happened as if by accident. Neither Shakespeare nor Marlowe believed that his worth as a writer depended upon his ability to create fictional characters as real as persons one might meet in the tavern or in the apothecary's shop.[21] Hence, it would be amiss to categorize such characters as hysterics, manic-depressives, or psychopaths unless such labeling is indeed warranted. Rather, in most cases, it would be more accurate to say that certain characters suggest a behavioral pattern similar to clinical depression rather than saying that they are afflicted with it.

On the other hand, the relatively "fluid" personalities of many Elizabethan-Jacobean dramas lend themselves readily to psychetypological analysis. The abrupt reversals of personalities and emotional shifts of these characters can be understood to manifest the emotional flows and psychetypological conflicts that are ordinarily suppressed and concealed in everyday life as well as in realistic characters.

Thus, without labeling Othello, Timon, and Coriolanus as schizoid, hysteric, or obsessive personality types, I will attempt to illustrate the psychetypological struggles of these characters while maintaining that these interior battles are illustrative of those taking place in the psyches of actual persons.

Another important basis for our discussion must be established. Some years ago Manfred Weidhorn pointed out a fundamental pattern in tragedies, one especially applicable to Shakespeare's. "What happens to the traditional tragic hero is nothing less than the humiliating and disastrous dissolution of the self" (304). Because of their own *hamartias* and the machinations of evil persons, tragic figures experience a painful sense of separation from themselves, a loss of identity. These tragic figures, even though on the brink of death, gain "an understanding at the end" entailing "a recapture of identity through adversity and sorrow, a redemption of sorts not granted to those marching anonymously to the gas chamber"(304). In Shakespearean tragedy, moreover, Weidhorn observes, this pattern of psychological transformation may be charted by the labels and names applied to the tragic heroes either by themselves or others. Noting the appellations and the designations applied to Cleopatra, for instance, Weidhorn writes

> The change in Cleopatra's titles—from "Royal Egypt,"
> "Empress" to "wife"— are symbolic of changes in her character.
> The affair with Antony went to such depths as ultimately to
> push her out of her role of enchantress and royal intriguer into
> a passionate commitment to one other human being [306].

This pattern of loss of identity and a temporary regaining of it before death is fundamental to Shakespearean tragedy. However, the depth, pain, and significance of such a painful dissociation from the self can be sharply illuminated by drawing upon our studies of typology.

In Shakespeare's tragedies the thinking-feeling nexus becomes central to the protagonist's interior disintegration. This point is seen in *Oth-*

ello. Malone repeatedly categorizes Shakespeare's tragic Moor as a feeling type (34, 150–51, 157), and I see no reason to disagree. Like other feeling types, Othello places a high value upon romantic attachment; his love for Desdemona becomes dominant in his life. Other evidence of his basically feeling-centered nature can be offered. In her classic Jungian reading of the play, Maud Bodkin, noting Othello's exuberance in matters martial as well as matrimonial, characterizes him as "a symbol of faith in human values of love and war, romantically conceived" (214).

These concepts are melded together in the epithet he bestows upon Desdemona upon her arrival at Cypress: "O my fair warrior!"(II. i. 78). The designation may seem puzzling because Desdemona, in her teens, sheltered, inexperienced and female, seems anything but martial. But we must recall that she has just ventured through storm-threatened waters to be in Cypress with her husband — an act of astounding courage to Othello. No wonder he identifies her as a warrior! But at the same time, we find Othello's projection of his anima upon her — that, is the archetype of the ideal female which lies ready in the heterosexual male's mind to be activated whenever he encounters a woman in the exterior world matching the ideal image in his psyche.[22] In doing so, Othello's psyche betrays a complex mental maneuver. A warrior himself, Othello prizes her courage and dubs her a warrior — in a sense he incorporates her into himself, or makes her into a second self, a second Othello. Hence, Othello views his love for Desdemona in terms of a soul union — a connection of inner spirits transcending sexual attraction but grounded in it. The lovers, although maintaining discrete identities, become intangible parts of each other. The concept of lovers developing a spiritual union has a long and venerable history in European erotic verse, frequently featured throughout the late Middle Ages in the Petrarchan "heart transplant image," in which the lover has the lady's heart in his chest and she has his in hers. This ideal of soul mates, moreover, was prevalent in Renaissance literature. In his love poetry Donne repeatedly embraced it, as when in the "The Sun Rising" the two lovers become each other's world, in "A Valediction: Forbidding Mourning" when the distanced lovers are compared to the two feet of a compass (separate but joined), and in "The Ecstasy" when the lover's soul and his lady's soul commingle in an out-of-body rhapsody.

This sense of soul-union with Desdemona at this moment is so complete that Othello views it as the pinnacle of his life.

> If it were now to die
> 'Twere now to be most happy, for I fear
> My soul hath her content so absolute

> That not another comfort like to this
> Succeeds in unknown fate [II. i. 188–92].

But as Malone observes, such exuberant romanticism has its concomitant dangers. For one, it is vulnerable to disillusionment.

> The failure of romanticism is disenchantment; that, to a feeling
> type, may entail an absolute collapse of one's personal identity.
> When innocence, when faith, when honor is lost, "Chaos is
> come." Suffering such loss, Shakespeare's Othello and his
> Anthony [sic] kill themselves… [157].

Othello's anguish throbs even more acutely because of his sense of isolation from his past. Psychetypological theory teaches us that not all persons perceive the passage of time alike. Some persons are continuous; that is, each day is a new link in the chain of their existence. Consequently, yesterday is a part of every today. Continuous types revel in memory; they luxuriate in a sense that the present is developing flower-like from the seeds of the past. To such persons past and present are parts of a vital ongoing sense of wholeness. To discontinuous types, however, each day marks a fresh beginning. Past events are irrelevant. Reveling in memory seems useless. Each day offers a new slate to be written on. Feeling types tend to be continuous in their perceptions of time. In their romantic lives, they enjoy celebrating anniversaries, returning to familiar restaurants, gathering keepsakes and making use of other techniques to assure themselves that their love relationships are parts of an on-going, developing whole. When Iago casts doubt upon Desdemona's faithfulness, he is in effect invalidating Othello's past, stamping "cancel" on what has been.[23] No longer capable of seeing Desdemona as he has been able to, isolated from past moments, Othello finds himself cast into an interior "destructive element" that his feeling psychetype is particularly vulnerable to.

No longer able to find direction in his psyche, his ideological assumptions torn apart, Othello, in an eruption of passion, laments "I had been happy if the general camp, / Pioners and all, had tasted her sweet body, / So I had nothing known" (III. iii. 361–63).

In this wild moment, he declares that he would have preferred her lying with every soldier in his camp as long as he would not have known of her promiscuity to his learning of her unfaithfulness with one man! For such dreaded knowledge whirls his past from him like a dried October leaf.

His well-known farewell speech follows.

> Farewell the tranquil mind! Farewell content!
> Farewell the plumèd troops and the big wars

That makes ambition virtue! O farewell!
Farewell the neighing steed and the shrill trump.
The spirit-stirring drum, th' ear-piercing fife,
The royal banner, and all quality,
Pride, pomp, and circumstance of glorious war!
And O, you mortal engines, whose rude throats
Th' immortal Jove's dread clamors counterfeit,
Farewell! Othello's occupation's gone (III. iii. 363–73).

His sense that his past has been obliterated is so crucial that he feels himself separated not only from Desdemona but from his very occupation, his very image of himself as a man of action and split-second battlefield grandeur. Keats's "eternal fierce destruction" has moved inward: Othello finds himself upon an internal sea of turbulent emotions. His conviction, emerging at this moment, is that he cannot function as he had before. In sense, he has become the damned ghost of his former self.

A sensation type most likely would have acted differently in a similar predicament. While deeply stung initially by a wife's infidelity (or presumed infidelity), a sensation type — generally discontinuous in the perception of time — would have been more able to gain a sense of distance from the unhappy events. Such a man would have sooner or later come to feel that the past *has* passed and that nothing can be done about it. " True," he might tell himself, "I made a bad choice in selecting her as my wife. But that's over now. Tomorrow's a new day. I've plenty of years ahead of me to enjoy. I'll start looking for a new spouse."

Othello cannot let go of his past with Desdemona — it is too important to him. To let go would be to rob himself of a vital part of himself! This conviction drives its roots through his being and entangles his past military career. It is also gone. Too often readers assume that Othello has a stunted intelligence, that he is gullible. Ray Fearon, who mastered the role of Othello for the Royal Shakespeare Company's 1999 season at Stratford-Upon-Avon, criticizes such interpretations.

> I don't think Othello should be played as gullible, he isn't.
> Doubt about the person you love is in everybody, and Othello
> tries to resist jealousy until the very end. This man swears alle-
> giance to hate and murder, throws away love — but he takes
> three acts to kill Desdemona: he tries to hate her but can't
> because, unlike Iago, he's not made like that. Every time he faces
> Desdemona he crumbles [Jays 5].

Othello is insecure and troubled, but he is not foolish. His resistance to Iago's insinuations and deceptions, though eventually overcome, is formidable. "Villain, be sure thou prove my love a whore! Be sure of it!" (III. iii. 376–77), he cries at one point, threatening Iago if he is lying. Othello's love for Desdemona is so completely a part of his psyche that he cannot excise it. Before he kills her, he must kiss her. When he realizes that she was "falsely murdered," the burden of knowledge is too great for him to bear. He must destroy himself.

The upheaval in his psyche causes his loss of identity. After bidding farewell to the military profession, he experiences a diminution of his sense of selfhood until, after Desdemona's death, he speaks of himself as follows: "That's he that was Othello. Here I am" (V. ii. 292).

Certainly Othello's feeling psychetype makes him vulnerable to Iago's mental onslaughts. But another factor plays a bitter role in his psychological disintegration: the emergence into his psyche of his inferior function, which is thinking. This inner psychological invasion is symbolically dramatized by the machinations of Iago, for Iago is essentially a thinking type. Malone, however, classes him as a discontinuous sensation type, mainly because of the ancient's delight in manipulating and controlling others, a common activity of some sensation types (34, 182). True, Iago manifests aspects of this psychetype, but he is lacking in others. For instance, the festivity celebrating the storm's vanquishing of the Turks does not excite him as an opportunity for friendship and merriment; rather he seizes upon it as a lump of clay to be molded whichever way may please him to further his machinations. His interest in sex is minimal; his marriage to Emilia is not joyous. He never expresses feelings of intimacy with her, and lards his speech with jibes against women. Emilia's bitter disparagement of men likewise convinces us that their marriage is not praised by the angels.[24] To sum up, Iago simply lacks the delight of immersing himself in the thrill of experiences—a hallmark of the sensation type.

Iago may be seen as a thinking type. He delights in theories, speculations, plans. He enjoys matching wits with others and proving the superiority of his own by deceiving others—whether the person be Roderigo, Cassio or Othello, all of whom fail to see his sadistic nature while trusting him. Moreover, he devotes energy to proving his theories. Critics have long suggested that he believes his accusations of the sexual fallibilities of Othello, Desdemona and Cassio to be true and suspects that adultery between Othello's wife and the Moor's lieutenant has indeed occurred or is likely to occur. Bitterly he strips away what he believes is the cheap veneer of Othello's and Desdemona's love:

> These Moors are changeable in their wills....The food that to
> him now is as luscious as locusts [fruits] shall be to him shortly

as bitter as coloquintida. She must change for youth; when she
is sated with his body, she will find the error of her choice. She
must have change, she must [I. ii. 349–54].

To Iago, to believe that love exists between Othello and Desdemona
is sheer folly. Both members of the self-deceived pair are, to him, victims
of their own dream worlds. Othello is merely a lusty old Moor, drawn by
desire to a younger woman. Desdemona is simply an illusion-addled girl,
an especially lustful girl, who will quite readily prove untrue to Othello in
her compulsive quest for sexual variety. Of course, one could argue that
since the lines quoted above are addressed to Roderigo, Iago is knowingly
fabricating a falsehood to deceive the gullible Venetian, but when his dupe
is not near, Iago continues his cynical comments about the sexuality of
others. When he views Desdemona and Cassio greeting each other soon
after their arrivals at Cypress and notes their kissing, he suspects that a
volatile attraction draws them.[25] Later, when alone, he says, "That Cassio
loves her, I do well believe 't;/ That she loves him, 'tis apt and of great
credit" (II. i. 287–88). To support the view that Iago devalues sex and is
bitterly cynical toward those who (to him) seem to experience love, we
might recall his characterizations of Othello as "an old black ram / ... tup-
ping [covering] your white ewe" (I. i. 90–91) and "a Barbary horse" (114)
covering Desdemona. We might also recall his bitter description of Desdemona and Othello experiencing intercourse as "making the beast with
two backs" (120). Deep within Iago is an animus against love and a cynicism which seeks to reduce romance to what he believes is its lowest common denominator: bestial sexuality. In these bitter categorizations we
discover the thinking type's proclivity to fit the phenomena of life into a
seeming coherent pattern. He is intellectually a cousin to Thersites in
Troilus and Cressida. Both are acid-minded intellectuals who compulsively
seek to deglorify humanity and to fit all apparently noble behavior into a
paradigm of greed, selfishness, cruelty, and lust.

In essence, Iago infects Othello with his cynicism. In his essay "The
Othello Music"— one of the finest pieces ever written on the play— G.
Wilson Knight points out the prevalence of poison imagery in the text. A
few examples will suffice. Regarding Brabantio, Iago charges Roderigo "to
poison his delight" (I. i. 70). Most significantly, poisoning represents Iago's
growing power over Othello's psyche. After Othello's falls into a trance,
the gloating Iago jeers, "Work on / My medicine work!" (IV. i. 43–44).
Poison is a particularly apt metaphor for this maligned process. Like poison throughout a body, cynicism spreads throughout Othello's psyche; as
poison destroys tissue, turning what was healthy flesh into diseased mat-

ter, so Iago's bitterness works its sinister alchemy upon Othello's romantic idealism. As poison threatens life, so Iago's pessimism threatens the health of Othello's personality. Or, in terms of this study, he awakens Othello's inferior function of thinking and allies it with joy-destroying negativism.[26] In accord with common phenomenology of the inferior function's invasion of the psyche, Othello begins projecting his inner shadow outward on others—particularly Cassio, Emilia and Desdemona—convincing himself that they are brimming with baseness and treachery.

Significantly, Iago compares the power of an unsettling idea to the spread of poison.

> The Moor already changes with my poison.
> Dangerous conceits [ideas] are in their natures poisons
> Which at the first are scarce found to distaste,
> But with a little act upon the blood
> Burn like the mines of sulfur (III. iii. 341–45).

Iago's dangerous disruption of Othello's psychic stability is compared to what would become in Jungian terms the emergence of the thinking function.

Not many lines later Othello himself couches his dilemma in terms of the thinking orientation. He says, "I think my wife be honest and think she is not; / I think that thou art just and think thou art not" (400–401).

Interestingly, the verb chosen in this passage is "think," not "feel." *The Oxford English Dictionary*'s earliest recorded usage of the verb "feel," used to mean "to entertain a certain sentiment, be in a particular frame of mind," is 1340. (577). Presumably Shakespeare could have written "I feel that my wife be honest and feel she is not!" Had he done so, the lines both in his age and ours would have had a different impact. According to Jungian thought, both feeling and thinking are judging functions—that is, they are used to determine reality. Had the lines been written to stress the feeling function, they would indicate a strong emotional certitude in Othello's heart that Desdemona was both true and false, a very unlikely state for a normal psyche. Of course, as written they convey an entirely different mental process, as if on some level of consciousness Shakespeare was aware of the typological disparity between thinking and feeling as means of reckoning reality. Interestingly enough, Othello seeks the truth of Desdemona's nature by not looking into his own heart or trusting his own feelings. "I'll have some proof!" (402) he utters, drawing upon the thinking function's prime tool for determining reality.

As Knight also points out, as Othello's psyche alters because of Iago's cynicism, the Moor's very language changes. Othello's "romantic" avowals, couched in magnificence, ornateness and occurring in the earlier portions of the play, are to Knight, "the most Miltonic thing in Shakespeare" (104). As the Moor's mind becomes poisoned against Desdemona, his language begins resembling Iago's. It becomes bitter, scornful, vibrant, teeming with grotesque imagery — such as that of fire and brimstone, toads, monkeys, goats (116–17). One can understand the impact of this unsettling conversion by comparing the "fair warrior" passage quoted above with the following:

> O curse of marriage,
> That we can call these delicate creatures ours
> And not their appetites! I had rather be a toad
> And live upon the vapor of a dungeon
> Than keep a corner in the thing I love
> For others' uses [III. iii. 284–289].

The cynical guise of the thinking function has won, but only momentarily; the feeling function has not been obliterated. A few lines later, when Desdemona enters, Othello beholds her beauty and experiences a rush of feeling, an emotionally-wrought conviction that she *is* the Desdemona he has known and that cannot be an adulteress: "If she be false, O, then heaven mocks itself! / I'll not believe it!" No proof shown to the rational function produces this effusion. Rather, the feeling function again possesses his ego. Implied by the line is the Renaissance belief in the Platonic doctrine that a beautiful body houses a beautiful soul! Heaven would not deride itself by placing a corrupt spirit in a comely body. The sentiment comes to him not through a review of Platonic thought, but the momentary upsurge of the judging province of feeling — also momentary, for the critical, cynical guise of the thinking function again replaces it. An inner war within Othello has erupted, as faith-inspired feeling is in conflict with thinking-inspired cynicism. We might recall Fearon's observation that Othello struggles not to lose faith in her. But faith tends too lose ground before the onslaught of the pounding rational function. Cynicism spreads outward: He comes to see Cassio as a false friend and an adulterer; Emilia as a bawd; Desdemona as a strumpet. His molten-hot suspicions reveal themselves disarmingly in the scene in which he treats Emilia as a procuress and Desdemona as her prostitute. The cynicism intensifies until he murders his wife.

In commenting upon the text's repeated linkages of Iago with the devil, Bodkin astutely observes that "If we attempt to define the devil in psychological terms, regarding him as an archetype, a persistent or recurrent mode of apprehension, we may say that the devil is our tendency to represent in personal form the forces within and without us that threaten our supreme values"(217). She observes that as Othello falls more and more under Iago's sway, the Moor's "sense of devil in all around him becomes acute. Desdemona has become 'a fair devil'; he feels 'a young and sweating devil' in her hand. The cry 'O devil' breaks out among his incoherent words of raving"(217). In other words, Othello finds himself, in Spoto's terms, in a "Machiavellian nightmare."

Like Blanche and Constance in *King John*, Othello finds himself being psychologically torn asunder. But unlike him, they are primarily tortured by external circumstances. On some level, however, he probably experiences a sense of helplessness and frustration before seemingly insuperable circumstances sources similar to Lucrece's when she berates unconquerable forces.

> In vain I rail at Opportunity,
> At Time, at Tarquin, and uncheerful Night
> in vain I cavil with mine infamy,
> In vain I spurn at my confirmed despite.
> This helpless smoke of words doth me no right. [1023-27]

Like her, he seeks escape from turmoil through violence. Whereas she commits suicide, he vents his frustration by ordering Cassio's death and by murdering Desdemona.

But the dark libidinal energies of Othello's psyche do not have the final victory. After he learns that Desdemona was indeed faithful, his feeling function asserts itself and his love for her reclaims his ego. Numerous critics have seen Iago as the victor, conceding that something was corrupt about Othello's love. But such a view simplifies his inner war. Faith and cynicism, not love and lack of love, are in conflict. True, cynicism and hatred triumph, but again only momentarily. Among the telling facts is that Othello can no longer live with himself; he seeks death. Before killing himself, he reaffirm his love for Desdemona: "I kissed thee ere I killed thee. No way but this, / Killing myself, to die upon a kiss" (V. ii. 69–70). His falling upon the bed beside her evokes the archetype of the ill-fated lovers such as Ovid's Pyramus and Thisbe, Tristan and Isolde, Shakespeare's Romeo and Juliet and Malory's Lancelot and Guenevere. They are denied lasting joy in this life, but are somehow united spiritually in death, with underlying suggestions of reunion beyond this world.

One, of course, should not treat Othello's psychetypological struggle as a textbook study. A psychologist would be ill-advised to use it as mirror for patients to see exact representations of their own thinking and feeling conflicts. Taking its cue from the dramatic prototype of the madness of Hercules,[27] Othello's psychological metamorphosis is dramatized not with the techniques of realism but in accord with the conventions of Elizabethan and Jacobean drama such as the sudden character reversal, the structure of the morality play and motivations based on Elizabethan theories of humors. Indeed, the entire play is more like a surrealistic painting in motion rather than a realistic drama by writers such as Ibsen, Chekov, and Shaw. Iago is more an embodiment of hatred and cynicism rather a realistically portrayed sociopath; Desdemona enters as a spunky, individualistic girl ready to defy her society's patriarchal organization for the man she has chosen, but, as the plot moves forward, she becomes more and more a blessed damozel, an incarnation of the idealized or light anima; Othello's switch from idealizing husband to raging cynic occurs within minutes. Shakespeare does not present a clinical study, but a dramatization of a basic but disturbing psychological pattern.

Nor, of course, in the absence of primary documents, can typological criticism venture to ascertain what internal circumstances provoked Shakespeare to pen the tragedy of the Moor of Venice. We can, however, discern in the play a schema similar to that of the Dark Lady sonnets, the thwarted need to idealize the love object, the revulsion from the lady because of unfaithfulness (actual in the sonnets), and consequent bitterness and anger. Certainly the mind that created "For I have sworn thee fair and thought thee bright, / Who art as black as hell, as dark as night" could empathize with Othello's negative "O curse of marriage! / That we can call these delicate creatures ours /And not their appetites!" (III. iii. 284–5). What particular circumstances caused these feelings of bitter disillusionment to reemerge when he took up the pen to write *Othello* we cannot say. We can speculate that Shakespeare was still smarting because of his unhappy liaison with the Dark Lady — or that some circumstance opened the old wound. Or we can surmise that after the reestablishment of his relationship with his wife Anne, some circumstance caused Shakespeare to suspect her fidelity. All we can do about discovering particular causes is to speculate on them. But the psychodynamic pattern is undeniable; it recurs in the sonnets and in the tragedies.

Nor can we say with certainty what Othello's affirmation of love before his death means. Did Shakespeare, during the composition of the play, experience a reawakened faith in married love? Did he feel an artistic compulsion to satisfy his audience by ending the play on an upbeat note? Does Othello's kissing Desdemona just before he dies merely indicate a hope that such undying love may exist? Despite creating the frightening jungle of Othello's mind, did Shakespeare maintain an unqualified faith in love all along? What can be stated is that *Othello* evinces a pattern of idealization and disillusionment which Shakespeare had trouble eradicating from his psyche.

In "The House that Jack Built," a compelling episode of the classic TV series *The Avengers,* Mrs. Emma Peel finds herself in a automated mansion from which there is apparently no escape. Lost in a maze, she discovers herself in a bizarre room with a whirring mechanism; she runs through a doorway to find herself in an identical room with an identical whirring mechanism. Her tension and dismay mounting, she again bolts through a doorway, only to find herself again in an identical room with an identical whirring mechanism. (Interestingly enough, the episode was one of the few from the series that was resurrected for the 1998 movie remake starring Ralph Fiennes, Uma Thurman, and Sean Connery.)

Let us return to Spoto's comparison of the psyche to a room with four doors which represent the four functions, with a trapdoor that leads to the inferior function. But we might add a fifth door, a kind of escape hatch in the ceiling, through which the ego hopes to escape the conflict. The ego leaps through the escape hatch only to find itself in a similar room (the entry having vanished) with three doors and a new beckoning escape hatch above. The frantic action is repeated. "The House That Jack Built" is memorable because it represents the normally cool, intellectual Emma Peel approaching panic; it embodies our fears of losing control, of falling into hysteria and helplessness, of becoming the victim of psychological obliteration. The pattern is all the more disturbing because we (along with Mrs. Peel) cannot escape it. For whatever reasons Shakespeare felt compelled to relive the pattern of conflict between the dominant feeling function being threatened by the thinking function or visa versa. Again we find the pattern of reduplication without (or with minimal) resolution.

Timon of Athens offers us an intriguing analogue to *Othello.* The unsettling story of the predominant feeling function being threatened by the emergence of the inferior thinking function, occurs again but, in a sense, on a more grand level. For unlike Othello, Timon is a lover of mankind in general. A naive idealist and a relentless philanthropist, he assumes that all persons are essentially equally worthy of awards. Without discriminating, he lavishes vital capital on a host of servants and friends, largely composed of sycophants. To his servant Lucillius he provides the needed funds to undertake a much desired marriage. He rewards the Poet and Painter. He has already established such "friends" as Lucullus, Lucius, and Sempronius in affluence. His bountiful benevolence as well as his predominantly feeling orientation is highlighted in the following conclusion to a speech given to his friends.

> We are born to do benefits; and what better or properer can we
> call our own than the riches of our friends? O, what a precious
> comfort 'tis to have so many, like brothers, commanding one
> another's fortunes! O, joy's e'en made away ere 't can be born!
> Mine eyes cannot hold out water, methinks. To forget their
> faults, I drink to you [I. ii. 101–07].

True to the feeling type, Timon values concord, closeness, and mutually exchanged gifts. The conviction that his "friends" share his sentiments
brings tears to his eyes, which he seeks to control by a toast, an act which,
nevertheless, attempts to confirm the cause of the joy clouding his eyes.
But the lines also reveal Timon's naiveté. He blithely assumes that he and
his companions have a fraternity of mutual love and admiration. He pre-
supposes that they, like him, see wealth as a liquid benefit to be poured
from one person's goblet to another's. He fails to consider humankind's
selfishness and greed.

The plot develops along the clear lines of a fable. Despite warning
from his loyal steward Flavius, Timon gives away so much gold that he
himself is threatened with poverty. When his servants seek money from
his "fraternity of friends" for him they encounter refusals and outright pre-
varications. Stung by his financial ruin and the brazen neglect by those he
had benefited, Timon finds himself in psychological turmoil. Fierce waves
of bitterness, disillusionment, and hatred for humanity supplant his former placidity. Accompanying this psychogenic upheaval, his hitherto dis-
regarded inferior thinking function surges fiercely into his consciousness
with bitter results. Like Othello, he begins projecting his shadow upon
others. Having learned of the ingratitude and selfishness humanity is capable of, he becomes obsessed with *proving* that his newly-minted view of
humankind is real and universally applicable. At one point he concludes,
"All's obliquy; / There's nothing level in our cursèd natures / But direct
villainy" (IV. iii. 18–20).

Later, his propensity for "proving" the rightness of his misanthropy
rises to the fore when he confronts the thieves:

> I'll example you with thievery
> The sun's a thief, and with his great attraction
> Robs the vast sea. The moon's an arrant thief,
> And her pale fire she snatches from the sun.
> The sea's a thief, whose liquid surge resolves
> The moon into salt tears. The earth's a thief,
> That feeds and breeds by a composture stol'n
> From general excrement. Each thing's a thief [IV. iii. 440–47].

Although to moderns Timon's argument may seem to be made of false analogies, to Shakespeare and his fellow Elizabethans these comparisons carried unsteadying force. Habituated to seeing the cosmos as a mirror of the little world of man (for instance, comets foretelling the deaths of kings), early moderns would have sensed a disarming relevance in Timon's comparisons. Quite possibly, they might have reasoned — if only for the nonce — if so much "thievery" exists throughout the world of nature, then it must dominate the heart of man! Adopting a didactic mission, Timon wishes to teach the brigands that, in essence, they are no different from anyone else. Rogues and villains are the rank and file of humanity. What is the impulse behind his rabid preaching? Certainly vengeance is one of the foremost motives. Bereft of wealth, influence, and power, Timon cannot harm his adversaries. They are beyond his reach except for brutal physical attack which he is disinclined to (except, of course, for his outbreak during the mock feast to which he invites his hypocritical friends). What he can do is gain vicarious power over his enemies in the kingdom of his own mind by revealing them for what they are. Hence, he gains a sense of superiority. But his internal campaign of vengeance does not stop with Lucullus, Lucius, and Sempronius, but expands to include all of humanity. By a kind of mental witchery, a fanatic means of classification, he wishes, like Thersites, to transfer all of humanity into a category of subhuman ingrates. He is also reacting to his disillusionment. His philanthropic love, once embracing all of humanity, now seeks to blacken all humankind.

How accurate is his new assessment of humankind? Clearly Shakespeare reveals that Timon has become an extremist. He forgets his loyal servant Flaminius, who was stung by the ingratitude of Lucullus. But more significantly, he forgets the kindness of his faithful steward Flavius, who comes, bringing money, hoping to join him in his self-imposed exile.

The scene in which Timon encounters his former steward is well-worth examining for the light it sheds upon the emergence of the rational, pigeonholing function in the psyche of the grim protagonist. When Flavius identifies himself as "An honest poor servant of yours" (IV. ii. 480), Timon reacts to this challenge to his newly-forged misanthropy by denying that Flavius ever was virtuous: "Then I know thee not. / I never had honest men about me, I; all / I kept were knaves to serve meat to villains" (IV. iii. 481–483). The surprised Flavius responds by weeping. Nevertheless, he offers Timon money, further challenging his former master's new opinion of humankind. After being momentarily nonplused by this irrefutable evidence of generosity, Timon experiences fleetingly a rebirth of his former love of humanity and of Flavius in particular. He says, "One honest man — ... / How fain would I have hated all mankind, / And thou redeem'st thyself! But all, save thee, I fell with curses" (502, 504–506). A part of Timon gladly welcomes Flavius' loyalty, but another part resents its challenge to his new intellectual stance; hence, his dismissal of the rest of mankind. A few lines later, however, Timon again tries to reclassify Flavius as a villain: "But tell me true —/For I must ever doubt, though ne'er so sure —/Is not thy kindness subtle, covetous/ A usurping kindness, and, as rich men deal gifts, / Expecting in return twenty for one?" (511–15). Timon does not wish to relinquish his newfound stance. Quite simply, it provides him with too much satisfaction — born of pride, inverted prestige, and vengeance.

But steadily vowing his love for and loyalty to Timon, Flavius continues to challenge Timon's bitter template of human nature. Timon relents and offers him gold, but with the qualification that Flavius use it to build a dwelling far from humanity and nourish within his breast a misanthropy similar to Timon's. But Flavius' response is to offer to live with Timon and comfort him. Thus again he challenges Timon's wholesale condemnation of mankind. Instead of relenting in his bitterness, of embracing his former steward in friendship, Timon reacts with a tongue-lashing: "If thou hat'st curses, / Stay not; fly, whilst thou art blest and free. / Ne'er see thou man, and let me ne'er see thee" (499–501). Timon refuses to fully consider contradictory evidence, indeed dismisses it and refuses to accept its validity. Here we might recall Gilovich's observation that we often seek to minimize or otherwise render innocuous those prickly contradictions which tend to undercut our prized assumptions.

Timon, nevertheless, in his bitter criticism of humankind, is on target. The Flaviuses and Flaminiuses are painfully few. In the subcreated world of the drama, humanity is by and large materialistic, hypocritical, self-seeking and treacherous.

Along with the emergence of Timon's thinking function, another psychogenic transmutation occurs within him — the switch from extroversion to introversion. In the play's beginning Timon is clearly an extrovert who gains a sense of self-worth by directing his psychic energy outward, by establishing what he believes are mutually-satisfying relationships with others. Once disenchantment possesses him, he begins to withdraw from society and from friendships, moving his attention to his festering inner sore of disillusionment and bitterness. His inner withdrawal is paralleled by a physical withdrawal from Athens: He removes himself from human beings, isolates himself in a forest cave, feeds upon roots and adopts a semi-bestial existence.

But the acerbic Timon, dying alone in the wilderness, does not have the final word. Shakespeare skillfully counterpoints Timon's mistreatment by Athens with the Athenian's ill-treatment of Alcibiades. Banished for seeking leniency in a death sentence of a friend, the general is also betrayed by his fellows. Instead of withdrawing into his own shell of bitterness, Alcibiades assumes another course. He gathers an army and brings Athens to its knees, promising a better order.

We are inclined to applaud Alcibiades, judging his course the proper one. Yet his heroism does not cancel Timon's actions nor his judgments of humanity. To a disturbing extent, Shakespeare identifies with Timon and shares his antipathy. The triumph of Alcibiades does not disprove the rationale for Timon's bitterness nor atone for his treatment.

Timon is right — but only to a certain extent. The honesty and loyalty of Flaminius and Flavius belie his wholesale cynicism regarding mankind, but examples of ingrates within the play abound. Timon has exchanged one lopsided view of reality for another. Early in the play he naively assumes that all men are good, that people are what they seem, that he is truly beloved. The predominance of his feeling function misleads him into living in a fantasy world; the emerging dominance of his thinking function also causes inner upheaval and misapprehension of reality. His fortunes, then, call to mind Montaigne's judgment that we never see reality in its entirety. Timon fails to function wisely both as a philanthropist and as an outcast because he cannot construct an enduring or accurate conception of human nature. Examples of just and unjust persons exist, but Timon's troubled psyche prevents him from arranging these examples into an indisputable rational pattern. Indeed, however, stepping back from the play, we may question whether trying to reach a definitive conclusion as to the goodness or badness of human nature is in fact possible. Like Timon, we would prefer absolutes. They are easier to live with than uncertainties, but the very complexity of the human species makes them impossible. Too many variations appear in the human personality; indisputable definitions of good and evil are impossible to construct; persons whom we deem evil perform noble actions, and those we judge noble perform ignoble deeds. Indeed, reaching a consensus as to the nature and extent of humankind's proclivities toward virtue and vice, we may wonder, may be as impossible as the first step upon Norse mythology's rainbow bridge. Like Timon, nevertheless, we continue to try to fashion abstractions so that we might live more comfortably, but chaotic reality continues to furnish us with unwieldy exceptions.

Like Montaigne, Shakespeare, in this play, seems acutely aware of the difficulty of delineating human nature: Hence the courses of Timon and Alcibiades counterpoint each other, but do not cancel each other out. On a first reading, one could, of course, decide that Alcibiades' heroism, in bringing an self-centered Athens to its knees in punishment for its sins, belies Timon's rejection of humanity. But Alcibiades is not established as a norm; he is, as we have seen, outweighed by examples of evasive, self-seeking, and treacherous humankind. Likewise, one could assume that Shakespeare prefers the constructive aggression of Alcibiades to the bitterness and withdrawal of Timon, but the play's conclusion undercuts even this simple paradigm. No words reproving Timon or disapproving of his assessment of humankind are uttered by the remaining characters. His death is somber, lamented. His own bitter epitaph is disturbing, indeed haunting:

> Here lies a wretched corpse, of wretched soul bereft.
> Seek not my name. A plague consume you wicked
>   caitiffs left!
> Here lie I, Timon, who, alive, all living men did
>   hate.
> Pass by and curse thy fill, but pass and stay not
> here thy gait [V. iv. 70–73].

Shakespeare discomforts us by suggesting that, as extreme as Timon's recourse was, he was started in a direction that, given his psychetypology and the evil in humankind, he could not have avoided. Damned by his altering psychetypology, Timon encounters a no-win, no-exit predicament. His death is indeed merciful.

The problem play or dark comedy *Measure for Measure* likewise furnishes us an intense conflict between thinking and feeling ways of perceiving reality, but with an intriguing variation. Angelo—the character in which the psychetypological struggle is most forcefully embodied—is a thinking type and struggles to suppress the feeling currents of his personality.

Given to a puritanical temperament, Angelo has a reputation for lacking emotion. The whimsical Lucio sums up what he assumes is the young man's character: "Some report a seamaid spawned him; some that he was begot between two stockfishes. But it is certain that when he makes water his urine is congealed ice; that I know to be true. And he is a motion unregenative; that's infallible" (III. ii. 105–09). Of course, Lucio's remarks are intended to be humorous; in fact they point to Lucio's own rascality and proclivity to "extend" the truth, but they also underscore Angelo's obsessive rationality and suppression of his sexuality.

Temporarily promoted to power by the Duke, Angelo rigorously takes on his mission of cleansing Vienna of sexual vices. In doing so he reveals

not only the thinking type's proclivity for intellectualization of phenomena, for patterns, for order, and for regulation, but also the often dangerous corollary to his mode of perception — the compulsion to overgeneralize
by dividing humanity into blacks and whites. When Claudio and Juliette
are brought before him for judgment because they have had intercourse
before having an official wedding ceremony, he decides to make an example of the unfortunate young man and orders his execution.[28] When the
sage Escalus protests that Angelo himself must have on occasion felt such
desires, Angelo curtly rebuffs him, "'Tis one thing to be tempted, Escalus,
/ Another thing to fall" (II. i. 17–18). He has no difficulty dividing humanity into doves and ravens. Those who succumb to temptation are evil and
deserve punishment. The sexually remiss of Vienna — without exception —
are to feel the whip of justice.

His simplistic paradigm of human nature begins to crumble when
Isabella, Claudio's sister, pleads for her brother's life. Intrigued by her
beauty, unexpectedly fascinated by her, Angelo finds himself struggling
with his long-shelved sexuality.

> What's this? What's this? Is this her fault or mine?
> The tempter or the tempted, who sins most, ha?
> Not she, nor doth she tempt; but it is I
> That, lying by the violet in the sun,
> Do, as the carrion does, not as the flower,
> Corrupt with virtuous season. Can it be
> That modesty may more betray our sense
> Than woman's lightness? Having waste ground enough,
> Shall we desire to raze the sanctuary
> And pitch our evils there? O fie, fie, fie!
> What dost thou, or what art thou, Angelo?
> Dost thou desire her foully for those things
> That make her good? O, let her brother live!
> Thieves for their robbery have authority
> When judges steal themselves. What, do I love her,
> That I desire to hear her speak again
> And feast upon her eyes? What is't I dream on
> O cunning enemy that, to catch a saint,
> With saints dost bait thy hook! Most dangerous
> Is that temptation that doth goad us on
> To sin in loving virtue. Never could the strumpet,
> With all her double vigor — art and nature —
> Once stir my temper; but this virtuous maid
> Subdues me quite. Ever till now,
> When men were fond, I smiled and wondered how [II. ii. 169–94].

Once the dam suppressing Angelo's emotions breaks, it cannot be easily repaired. Overcome by lust, Angelo seeks to force Isabella to his bed by blackmail, by promising to free her brother if she will have intercourse with him. Angelo's descent into spiritual darkness is unnerving to us. Instead of maintaining his standards, he becomes conniving, false and treacherous. He even plans to renege on his word should Isabella in fact lie with him, lest her newly-released but enraged brother seek him out for vengeance. Angelo becomes monstrous.

His emotional metamorphosis, however, may disturb some readers as implausible. True, many a would-be saint has fallen to temptations of Venus, but to pass abruptly from rigorous morality to contriving homicide would strike many as most unlikely. Again we must remind ourselves of fundamental Elizabethan dramaturgy. In delineating Angelo, Shakespeare is not offering us a psychological case study, but creating a symbolic portrait of a spiritual odyssey, an interior journey from light to darkness and then (hopefully) to a subdued but steady afterglow. Certainly many a person has fallen from moods of loftly idealism, dedication to rectitude and love of humanity to anger, bitterness, and vengeance (whether or not the darkened feelings pass into action.) In the words of the Bible, we all are sinners. In this sense Angelo represents an eternal troubling cavern in human nature.

But in terms of this study Angelo's dilemma represents potential difficulties of attempting to unify the feeling and thinking currents of the human psyche into a smoothly flowing stream. The deputy's psychological throes suggest that Shakespeare was aware of the possibility of what von Franz would call "the great conflict."

Angelo's opposite, the rigorously chaste Isabella, likewise manifests intriguing psychetypological implications—but of another order. She is essentially a feeling type. Her dedication to a nun's life is based upon an emotional orientation to life. Her insistence that the vows of the order are too lenient suggest she unconsciously wishes to intensify her religious devotion until it obliterates all other emotions. She calls to mind Flaubert's Emma Bovary who, during her girlhood in a convent, luxuriated in reveries of sainthood and even fantasies of suffering martyrdom.

Isabella's critics, particularly those of the twentieth century, have long faulted her for not saving her brother's life by acceding to Angelo's demands. After all, according to this view, saving one person's life is more important than preserving another's chastity. She has been accused of being a hypocrit, an insensitive prude, and an rigid disciplinarian. Her defenders, on the other hand, have underscored the sincerity of her religious ideals. To be sure, Isabella is vexed by a daunting theological problem:

Whether one can indeed commit a sin while planning to ask forgiveness and indeed be forgiven. In other words, can one cry, "Forgive me, Lord!" then stab a business rival, and hope for salvation? This quandary — in various forms— disturbed medieval and Renaissance thinkers. Sinning while hoping to be forgiven is the central reason Dante's Guido de Montefeltro suffers hellfire. Persuaded by Pope Bonifice VIII that he would receive papal absolution, Guido helped the pontiff overthrow his enemies, the Colonnas, but after death the crafty Guido learned the frightful consequences of such a theologically-dubious maneuver. In *Hamlet,* Claudius suffers a variation of this theological dilemma. He would receive absolution from the sin of murdering his brother, but questions whether his prayers will be granted because he still enjoys the profit of the murder. Unable to resolve this spiritual dilemma, he struggles ineffectually to pray, but at length breaks off the attempt to win redemption: "My words fly up, my thoughts remain below. / Words without thoughts never to heaven go" (III. iii. 97–98).

Isabella faces a similar quandary. No one can doubt the sincerity of her longing to save Claudio. She hastens from the convent which she has entered as a novice, abases herself by pleading before Angelo and tries— even begs— to reason with him. But the deputy proves obdurate in his humiliating demand. She is well aware of reasons for acceding to Angelo's desires. No one will know of her fornication and her brother will live.

But along with her theologically-based scruples, Isabella refuses to comply, simply because she *feels* doing so is wrong. Her reactions to the request are intense; she refers to her proposed sexual capitulation in emotionally charged language. To her it is "abhorred pollution" (II. iv. 184), an act that "I abhor to name" (III. i. 102). Significantly, not once does she ever debate with herself whether or not to comply. Her aversion to such coitus rooted in her being; her possible compliance is, to her, without qualification, evil. Claudio, when he hears of her decision, at first seems willing to accept her choice, but, then, as his fear of impending death again intensifies, he begins to temporize, weighing pros and cons, rationalizing his wild desire to live. He declares, "Sure it is no sin, / Or of the deadly seven it is least" (III. i. 111–12). Later he adds of Angelo, "If it were damnable, he being so wise, / Why would he for the momentary trick / Be perdurably fined?" (114–17). When he requests forthright that she save him by surrendering her body, Isabella reacts with an outburst, "O you beast! / O faithless coward! O dishonest wretch! / Wilt thou be made a man out of my vice?" (138–40).

Her conviction that compliance would be "abhorred pollution" also underscores her feeling orientation. To her, submission would be a transgression, reverberating through all her being. Even her past of devotion to God and of dedication to ideals would be canceled by her intercourse with Angelo. Here again we might recall the feeling type's continuous sense of time. Past and present are always part of an ever-flowing continuum. Breaking her vow of chastity would create a muddy backflow upon her past. A discontinuous type, we might recall, would be more likely to compartmentalize experience, to commit the breach and keep from brooding about it simply because the event has passed. A sensation type — temperamentally more given to situation ethics — might have more easily agreed with Claudio's casuistry and lain with Angelo. But not the feeling-oriented Isabella!

Claudio's character is not explored deeply enough in the text to permit us to label his psychetype. But the confrontation between brother and sister illustrates the difficulty of communication between persons of differing orientations. Willing to explore different courses, to question the received theology, Claudio can broach the unpleasant possibility of Isabella's compliance as an alternative. But Isabella cannot follow him along that path. Her brother seems to be changing into another person. She cannot allow herself even to share his speculations or much less see value in them.

Nevertheless, something of her thinking side may be said to emerge in Claudio's counter-arguments to her objections to coitus. Or, perhaps more accurately, Claudio's attempts to persuade her may be said to correspond to the awakened speculations and furtive reasonings within her own psyche. Here we may see the makings of a "great conflict" in Isabella, but her feeling-oriented psyche — at least for the moment — is too strong to allow the invasion and dominance of the inferior function. In Isabella we again see Shakespeare's sensitivity to the conflict between thinking and feeling aspects of the psyche and awareness of Malone's view that we each live in different worlds.

Also worth remarking upon is that *Measure*'s sister problem play, *All's Well That Ends Well*, likewise calls attention to a predominantly feeling-oriented heroine, Helena, whose devotion to the callow Bertram drives her to recurrent chicanery to gain her unwilling husband's love.

A compelling variation on the recurrent pattern of the dominant feeling orientation of a Shakespearean protagonist being confronted by the rising thinking function appears in *Richard II*. Without doubt the melancholy monarch primarily perceives the world by feeling. Emotional heights are central needs of his psyche, and he enjoys arranging events that will nourish this need. For example, at the beginning of the drama he purposely delays until the last moment before dropping the scepter to stop the trial by combat involving Bolingbroke and Mowbray so that he may gain the pleasure of ending the conflict dramatically at a peak moment. Moreover, soon afterward we learn that the king and his council have already decided to exile both accusers rather than letting them fight until the death of one. Hence, Richard's allowing the conflict's preliminaries to proceed can be seen as a complex charade that allows him to revel in the emotions produced by his appearing to be decisive, powerful, and godlike. (Such behavior also argues for a strong sensation-seeking component in his psyche.) True to the feeling type, he relishes friendships, even though his chosen companions— Bushy, Bagot, Greene, and the Earl of Wiltshire — are unwise choices. Also, the capacity to experience romantic love is strong in Richard. Although the play suggests that to some extent he has been neglecting Queen Anne, the pair's tearful parting before his imprisonment underscores their mutual devotion.

Once power is wrested from his grasp and he becomes Bolingbroke's victim, Richard continues to indulge his dominant feeling orientation by masochistically, even self-pityingly, wallowing in his humiliation and loss of power and prestige. For instance, his rhetorical extravagances, such as comparing himself and his arch foe to the descending and rising buckets in a well, and his histrionic behavior, such as calling for a mirror so that he may study his face, allow him to objectify and call attention to his inner ferment.

Strangely enough, during his turmoil, Richard seems to be unaware of his profound psychogenic need to manifest his grief objectively so that he may revel in it until Bolingbroke astutely couches the truth. Then he readily agrees.

> 'Tis very true, my grief lies all within;
> And these external manners of laments
> Are merely shadows to the unseen grief
> That swells with silence in the tortured soul.
> There lies the substance; and I thank thee, King.
> For thy great bounty, that not only giv'st
> Me cause to wail, but teachest me the way
> How to lament the cause [IV. i. 296–303].

Along with this channeling of his feeling function into sentimental masochism, Richard's psyche undergoes another far-reaching change: the emergence of his thinking function. Previous to his being deposed, Richard seems never or rarely to have confronted agonizing questions regarding humankind's lot, such as the meaning of suffering and the nature of personal identity. Like Lear, buoyed aloft by flatterers, aggrandized by his own ego, and absorbed in himself, he has never looked critically at himself nor undertaken philosophical quests. Like Lear's suffering, his begets introspection and speculation.

To a large extent, the rise of his thinking faculty into his consciousness begins after his return from Ireland and with his realization that many of his apparently loyal forces have disbanded or gone over to Bolingbroke's side. "For God's sake, let us sit upon the ground / And tell sad stories of the death of kings" (III. ii. 155–56). Thus begins the famous passage in which Richard, aware of his impending defeat, perversely gains inner sustenance and a sense of philosophical direction by comparing his misfortunes with those of predecessors. His speculating and questioning thereafter increases until his final scene when, imprisoned at Pomfret castle, he speculates upon his destiny, his identity, and the nature of God. At this point the dominance of his thinking function has not passed into the bitter cynicism and misanthropy of Timon. (But such indeed might have been the upshot had he not been murdered.)

Perhaps Shakespeare's most haunting portrayal of the conflict between thinking and feeling in a human psyche is the psychological degeneration of Lady Macbeth. Quite clearly she wishes to suppress her capacities to experience pity and sympathy and to replace them with a ruthless rationalism and dedication to power. She even calls upon the powers of darkness to aid her:

> Make thick my blood;
> Stop up th' access and passage to remorse,
> That no compunctious visiting of nature
> Shake my fell purpose, nor keep peace between
> Th' effect and it! [I. v. 43–47].

Although her portrait is not etched clearly enough for us to without qualification, label her a thinking or a feeling type, we find in her psychomachia a clear effort of the rational function to suppress, if not blot out, its emotive counterpart. Of course, the task proves impossible. Lady Macbeth's embattled sympathies assert themselves in her consciousness with a vengeance. Her madness ensues.

Other instances in Shakespeare's plays reveal similar conflicts between thinking and feeling modes of perceiving reality. We have already — in another contexts — noted the plights of Enobarbus, in which the inferior function of feeling attempts to subdue his consciousness, and of Troilus, in which the reverse is true. After his disillusionment his rational side begins rising to the fore in the form of cynicism. He reveals a tendency to become more like Thersites and Timon.

This discussion of the "great conflict" brought on by the emergence of the inferior function into the consciousness ought not to be concluded without consideration of one of Shakespeare's most disquieting portrayals of psychogenic disintegration: *Coriolanus*. In this play, it is the rise of emotions which dooms Rome's super patriot. But, for all its power and relevance to our discussion, the drama does not fit smoothly into the paradigm at hand. It is tempting to declare Coriolanus a thinking type, but the label has trouble sticking. To be sure, he reveals the thinking type's penchant for classifying, and labeling. To him, the plebeians are almost without exception lazy, cowardly, greedy, and base, while on the other hand he holds his own class, the patricians, to be courageous, noble, heroic, and deserving of honor and privilege. However, he lacks the thinking type's customary love of reasoning, questioning, and attempting to prove a point. Rather than being at base intellectual, his mind seems to a receptacle for received ideas from those of his class. He seems incapable of questioning the patrician arrogance and fanatic patriotism drummed into his head by his iron-willed mother Volumnia.

His personality does, however, reveal a marked repression of emotion. In one of the finest essays written on the play, Katherine Stockholder observes this tragic hero's savage capability of suppressing his emotions as he seeks to fulfill his idealized course as a champion of Rome. Only rarely, in the ordinary course of his life, does he allow his emotional side to blossom forth in his psyche. For instance, after his victory over the Volscians at Corioles, he recalls once being aided by a poor man of the city while lodging there. He saw the man amid prisoners and was on the cusp of releasing him when "Aufidius was within my view, / And wrath overwhelmed my pity" (I. ix. 84–85). Instead of freeing his former host, he charges after his arch enemy. Nevertheless, he urges Cominius and Lartius to release the prisoner, but when asked for the man's name, Coriolanus cannot recall it, then asks for wine, his momentary humanitarianism wisping away. A deficiency of what may be termed nobler emotions is marked in his personality.

But Coriolanus is far from emotionless. Pride, rage, contempt, vengeance seethe in his psyche. At crucial movements, especially when his self-image is threatened, they well dangerously into his consciousness, sparking violent verbal abuse and savage rage. A case in point occurs when, provoked by the unscrupulous tribunes, Coriolanus reviles the Roman mob they represent — and does so at the very moment when he needs the approval of the populace so that he may become a consul.

A grotesque childishness manifests itself in Coriolanus's pathological rages. On several occasions the text invites us to identify the Roman's hero's behavior with that of a child as when Aufidius cuttingly calls him a "boy of tears" (V. vi. 105). Perhaps the most telling instance of this is when Coriolanus' emotional rampages are symbolically linked with those of his son, the young Marcius. Valeria tells the anecdote of the young boy's attempting to catch a butterfly. Upset by the insect's attempts to escape, or perhaps by his falling, he savagely attacks it, tearing it with his teeth.

Like father, like son, the text seems to tell us. Young Marcius is a Coriolanus in miniature. When confronted with frustration, both vent their wrath uncontrollably.

His enemies are well aware of this trait. The Tribunes use it to provoke him into tongue-lashing the plebeians at the very moment he needs their approval, and Aufidius employs it to provoke Coriolanus's anger against the Volscians when the Roman general is surrounded by them. As a result, the mob tears Coriolanus to pieces.

Although Coriolanus cannot be indisputably labeled a thinking type, his character and downfall again reveal Shakespeare's interest in "the great conflict" generated when the psyche is called upon to deal with unaccustomed or recalcitrant feelings and emotions. The play suggests that the human psyche is a most dangerous forest.

Indeed, Shakespeare's awareness of this dangerous recurring conflict and his recurrent bent toward portraying it add substantial depth to his understanding of human nature and the religio-philosophic dimensions of his tragedies. In essence, the presence of the great conflict in these characters dovetails with the Judeo-Christian view that humanity is deeply flawed. This view in turn suggests that barring some scientific discovery which will reorder the human psyche, humankind must face inner limitations, and Utopia must remain a pipe dream. In dramatizing these conflicts, Shakespeare adds troubling depth to the saw about one being one's own worst enemy.

SIX

Hamlet in Hell:
Psychetypological Chaos

Now and then Shakespeare includes in his texts a line or two that encapsulates what we have come to think as of themes of a work of literature. There are several of them in *Hamlet*. One of the most relevant to the design of the play is the Player King's response when the Player Queen assures him that after his death she will not seek a second husband. He replies, "Our wills and fates do so contrary run / That our devices still are overthrown; / Our thoughts are ours, their ends none of their own" (III. ii. 209–11).

Chilling words perhaps, for they blow the trumpet of challenge to facile optimists, social engineers, planners and propagandists of all persuasions. The Player King suggests that whatever humans beings may do to provide their various dream castles with firm foundations, the unexpected, the uninvited, the undesired — indeed, chaos— might well scatter the edifice's bricks and mortar.

A second comment in the play dovetails grimly with this one, the poignant following words of Ophelia uttered during her madness: "Well, God 'ild you! They say the owl was a baker's daughter. Lord, we know what we are, but know not what we may be. God be at your table!" (IV. v. 42–44). Ophelia's lines underscore the helplessness of the individual to maintain identity in a mingling rush of outer and inner anarchy. Her words refer to the folk tale fate of a baker's daughter who, in differing versions, either stingily gave a beseeching Christ a small loaf of bread or who mocked her mother for providing bread to him. The daughter's punishment was her transformation into an owl. In this paradoxically meaningful gibber, Ophelia stresses her own inability to maintain her identity amid the increasingly volatile whirls of psychogenic chaos.

Like the world of *King John*, the world of *Hamlet* is a subcreation in which chaos reigns. Horatio's closing description to the ambassadors, with perhaps a modification or two, could well be used as an epigraph for the history play.

> So shall you hear
> Of carnal, bloody, and unnatural acts,
> Of accidental judgments, casual slaughters,
> Of deaths put on by cunning and forced cause,
> And, in this upshot, purposes mistook
> Fall'n on th' inventors heads [V. 2. 382–87].

Plans and purposes backfire throughout *Hamlet*. Claudius plots one murder, one murder only, to gain for himself the woman he loves and the scepter he craves, yet, because of a strange attractor — the unforeseen intervention of his brother's restless spirit — Claudius becomes entangled in a chain of consequences which pits him in a no-quarter struggle with his nephew. This conflict causes, among other things, the death of the woman for whom he committed the murder. Hamlet, on the other hand, conceives a well-constructed plan to prove the ghost's truthfulness, but in obtaining the longed-for proof, he inevitably betrays his suspicions to his enemy. Polonius incautiously hides behind the arras, and cries out and thus welcomes his own death. Hamlet's wild killing of the egotistical adviser sets the dominos tumbling that lead to the madness and death of Ophelia, the woman he loves, and to the vengeful retaliation of Laertes.

In such a world of reverberating mischances, the individual's need to fashion and maintain a sense of social and personal identity is severely handicapped. It is a world in which although bakers' daughters do not literally become owls, fair young Ophelias can become incurably insane. It is also a world in which seemingly ideal Renaissance princes can become baffled neurasthenics.

Hamlet's inner division is quite evident. But other major characters are divided as well. The King's psyche is sundered by his crime. His desire to maintain his Queen and throne — both acquired by murder — wars with his guilt. He seeks absolution through prayer, but cannot muster the fortitude to do what he must to gain redemption: cast aside both queen and scepter. Despite his good intention, he remains divided, or, as he puts it, "My words fly up, my thoughts remain below. / Words without thoughts never to heaven go" (III. iii. 96–96). Indeed, his contradictory impulses add humanity to his portrayal and raise him from the lot of nondescript villains (Labriola 130).

Likewise, the queen is painfully cleft by her conflicting loyalties to her husband and to her son. (After Hamlet upbraids her in her bedroom and reveals the murder to her, she neither betrays her son to the king nor, as in some versions of the tale, aids Hamlet in his vengeance.) In her madness, Ophelia becomes, as the King puts it, "Divided from herself and her fair judgment / Without the which we are pictures or mere beasts" (IV. v. 87–88). The murder of her father by the man she loves proves the catalyst which disrupts her mind. The very subcreated world of *Hamlet* is one in which divisions abound, categories mix, the basic guidelines of society wax distorted. By marrying his brother's wife, Claudius has blurred the very distinctions among family members as Hamlet implies when he calls Claudius his "mother." The King corrects him, "Thy loving father, Hamlet." The sarcastic prince replies, "My mother. Father and mother is man and wife, man and wife is one flesh and so, my mother" (IV. iii. 55–57). One could list examples of division beyond the brink of fatigue.

The world of *Hamlet* and its primary characters become dysfunctional because on many levels—sociological, psychological, spiritual. In such a world, unity of being becomes crucial for mental equilibrium and effective action. Interestingly enough, one of the reasons Hamlet values Horatio is the latter's apparent self-control. Or, as the prince himself expresses his feelings,

> Since my dear soul was mistress of her choice
> And could of men distinguish her election,
> Sh' hath sealed thee for herself, for thou hast been
> As one, in suffering all, that suffers nothing,
> A man that Fortune's buffets and rewards
> Hast ta'en with equal thanks; and blest are those
> Whose blood and judgment are so well commeddled
> That they are not a pipe for Fortune's finger
> To sound what stop she please. Give me that man
> That is not passion's slave, and I will wear him
> In my heart's core, ay, in my heart of heart
> As I do thee [III. ii. 62–73].

Significantly, what Hamlet values as the unity of self is in accord with the goal of Stoicism, one of the ancient philosophies resurrected by the Renaissance. The classical stoics taught that persons should shun pleasure and make themselves impervious to fortune's blows. They believed pleasures should be shunned, because their sources could be removed, causing those deprived to suffer and despair. Ideally, the sources of pleasure — wealth, property, lavish furnishings— should be avoided as though diseased. Or, if the temptation to enjoy them proves too strong, the stoic should enjoy them moderately, rationally — that is, by not valuing them as indispensable items and by being willing, should the time come, to part with them. Persons should look at their possessions, cautions Epictetus, as a guest regards the furnishings of a room at an inn — objects to be used and enjoyed for the time being, then left to the possession of others. One should not even become too attached to a spouse or a child lest the deaths of these persons provoke despair. One should also expect disasters and misfortunes; in fact, one should become inured to their inevitability so that when they arrive, there will be no or minimal distress and sorrow.

By and large, the Renaissance did not adopt the classical stoic's strategy of forswearing pleasures, but rather opted for the ability to endure adversity, or to muster, in Hemingway's famous phrase from *A Farewell to Arms*, "grace under pressure."

Hamlet's valuing of stoicism leads us then to a consideration of his psychetypology, for this philosophy appeals primarily to the intellect. Coleridge long ago put us on the right track toward understanding Hamlet's makeup:

> Shakespeare's mode of conceiving characters out of his own intellectual and moral faculties, by conceiving any one intellectual or moral faculty in morbid excess and then placing himself, thus mutilated and diseased, under the circumstances. This we shall have repeated occasion to re-state and enforce. In Hamlet I conceive him to have wished to exemplify the moral necessity of a due balance between our attention to outward objects and our meditation upon inward thoughts— a due balance between the real and the imaginary world. In Hamlet this balance does not exist — his thoughts, images, and fancy [being] far more vivid than his perceptions, and his very perceptions instantly passing thro' the medium of his contemplations, and acquiring as they pass a form and color not naturally their own. Hence great, enormous, intellectual activity, and a consequent proportionate aversion to real action, with all its symptoms and accompanying qualities [Raysor, Vol. 1. 34].

Coleridge's comments direct our attention toward two possible identifications of Hamlet's primary function. In this passage and elsewhere, Coleridge underscores the prince's propensity for ratiocination. Hamlet repeatedly analyzes, questions, deliberates. Clearly, thinking is a dominant strain in his enigmatic personality. Later, in the same series of lecture notes, Coleridge stresses Hamlet's psychological dependency upon abstractions, generalizations, and principles— a salient characteristic of the thinking type: "Hamlet's running into long reasonings [while waiting for the ghost] carrying off the impatience and uneasy feelings of expectation by running away from the *particular* in[to] the *general*. This aversion to personal, individual concerns, and escape into generalizations and general reasonings a most important characteristic" (36).

William Hazlitt, at almost the same time, emphasized Hamlet's thinking orientation: "He is the prince of philosophical speculators; and because he cannot have his revenge perfect, according to the most refined idea his wish can form, he declines it altogether.... It is not from any want of attachment to his father or of abhorrence of his murder that Hamlet is thus dilatory, but it is more to his taste to indulge his imagination in reflecting upon the enormity of the crime and refining on his schemes of vengeance, than to put them into immediate practice. His ruling passion is to think, not to act: and any vague pretext that flatters this propensity instantly diverts him from his previous purposes" (234–345).

Coleridge's assumption that a well-ordered personality must possess a "due balance between the real and the imaginary world" and his judgment that in "Hamlet this balance does not exist" invites us to entertain another possibility as to the Prince's dominant trait. Coleridge also suggests intuition: "[Hamlet's] thoughts, images, and fancy [being] far more vivid than his perceptions, and his very perceptions instantly passing thro' the medium of his contemplations, and acquiring as they pass a form and color not naturally their own" (34). To Coleridge Hamlet becomes lost in his own inner world of speculation and thus his connection with the commonplace, the exterior, and the personal are atrophied. Interestingly enough, Malone classifies Hamlet as intuitive, stressing this trait as the cause of the prince's procrastination (205).[29] As was the case with Cressida, this complex character defies precise classification. What is clear is that the thinking and intuitive sides of his personality are profoundly interlaced. A glance at the psychetypological chart indicates that in the Jungian scheme, thinking and intuition are side by side. Therefore, a person whose basic function is thinking may have intuition as a secondary function; conversely, one whose dominant trait is intuition may have it bolstered by the secondary function of thinking. Trying to decide which of these two traits is dominant in Hamlet is useless; both affect his behavior profoundly.

Likewise, it is evident that his feeling and sensation sides are not as developed as his thinking and intuitive aspects. In fact, Hamlet seems to have marked difficulty in expressing his feelings. Perhaps is this nowhere more manifest than in his complex relationship with Ophelia. A discussion of their mutual attraction, however, demands caution. So much of their involvement prior to the play's beginning remains unstated and unimplied;

attempting to characterize it is rather like trying to draw a figure by inter-connecting prearranged dots when a good number of the dots are missing.

Nevertheless, some basic formulations can be advanced. Kenneth Branagh and Rebecca West notwithstanding, the play presents no evidence that before the drama's opening lines Hamlet and Ophelia copulated.[30] Moreover, it is hard to imagine them caught up in the tumultuous emo-tions of Romeo and Juliet, impelling the pair to seek immediate marriage while casting parental objections in a dust bin. Clearly, however, Hamlet and Ophelia's relationship has gone beyond the friendship stage. Hamlet has offered her favors, presents which she returns to him in the famous nunnery scene. He, moreover, has informed her of his love in the missive which Polonius has obtained. Indeed, giving some attention to it may well shed valuable light on its author and his relationship to the addressee. It begins with "To the celestial and my soul's idol, the most beautified Ophe-lia" (II. ii. 109–10). Almost immediately Polonius interjects his criticism of Hamlet's diction: "That's an ill phrase, a vile phrase; 'beautified' is a vile phrase" (111–12). Although Polonius's attempts to be a literary dicta-tor are pompous, Shakespeare's witty sword cuts both ways. Hamlet's words are extravagantly Petrarchan, calling to mind Sir John Davies' gulling sonnets which burlesque the well-used literary tradition. But Shakespeare is not finished with his satirical rendition of Hamlet's roman-tic overtures. Several lines later Polonius reads a patch of doggerel from the letter: Doubt thou the stars are fire, / Doubt that the sun doth move, Doubt truth to be a liar, / But never doubt I love (116–19).

Hamlet is indeed an inept wooer: He himself realizes his lack of romantic suaveness. Polonius continues reading, "O dear Ophelia, I am ill at these numbers. I have not the art to reckon my groans. But that I love thee best, O most best, believe it. Adieu" (120–22). These are not the words of a Lothario nor of a man brimming with confidence in his abil-ity to charm a member of the opposite sex. His tentative, awkward verses are followed by this abrupt admission of his poetic ineptitude. Having thus far failed in communicating his feelings, he blurts out his admission.

We have no sure knowledge of how Ophelia received his declaration of love other than to say she did not discourage him. Polonius remarks of the prince's further "solicitings." But we receive the impression that the burgeoning romance was forestalled, temporarily at least, by Claudius's Machiavellian move to gain the throne. Even before the play's beginning, depression has dogged Hamlet since his father's death. The ghost's reve-lation intensifies his festering feelings, compounding them with indigna-tion. The desire for vengeance, hatred, and other emotions are difficult to manage. Wrestling with inner turmoil, he has withdrawn from Ophelia.

Some readers have faulted Ophelia for not giving him emotional and spiritual support during this crisis. But the text provides no evidence that he sought these psychological balms from her. The next episode involving the pair which we see is his entry into her chamber as he feigns madness by grasping her wrist and holding her as he studies her face, then, after emitting a sigh, leaves her. Clearly he has not taken her into his confidence. Very likely their relationship had not reached the stage where he would have done so without reservation.

Nor is Ophelia one to inspire such confidence. Despite Helena Bonham Carter's attempt to provide us with a liberated Ophelia in Zeffirelli's production featuring Mel Gibson as the melancholy prince, Shakespeare's Ophelia is a restrained, repressed, fledgling woman, dominated by her brother and father. Very few modern girls—and I suspect very few Elizabethan girls—would be so pliant as she. When her father and brother double team, as it were, to persuade her to no longer encourage the prince's attentions, her response to Polonius is "I shall obey, my lord" (I. iii. 137). No irony bristles in her reply. Later we learn that she has been totally compliant, filling Polonius in on the details of her romance with Hamlet and even supplying her father with Hamlet's letter. Like her apprentice wooer, Ophelia is not skilled in expressing her feelings. At the time of their abortive romance's rupture, their relationship had not probably advanced much beyond Hamlet's unpracticed love letter.

Not only does Hamlet's relationship with Ophelia seem plagued with obfuscated emotions, but a certain emotional darkness seems dominant in his relationship with Gertrude as well. The Freudian Oedipus complex has been so repeatedly discussed and we have become so used to productions in which Hamlet and Gertrude fondle one another that we are apt to forget that in Elizabethan upper-class families, at least, parent and child relations were more restrained, more formal than is the norm today. Of course, the fact that a number of early modern families lived in accord with such a familial pattern does not mean that they all did (Ingram 142–43). One must be cautious about superimposing a theory about Renaissance family behavior onto the play.[31] But *Hamlet* does suggest that its protagonist's relationship with his mother little partakes of the "chum" familiarity between parent and child that many persons value today. A weighty degree of formality in Hamlet's relationship with Gertrude is evident in the first scene in which they appear together. When Gertrude asks him not to return to Wittenberg, his response is not, as a modern counterpart might have couched it, "Hey, Mom, give me time to think for myself," but "I shall in all my best obey you, madam"(I. ii. 120). Although he is an adult, Hamlet's deference reveals him to be abiding by the early modern code of familial hierarchy in which the father came first in ranking, the mother second and the children third. This same sense of hierarchy is also pronounced during the bedroom scene in which Hamlet upbraids his mother for her reprehensible marriage. Almost immediately Gertrude attempts to gain dominance in her verbal battle with her son by asserting, "Hamlet, thou hast thy father much offended" (III. iv. 10). She draws upon her hierarchical role as his mother. His reposte inverts the situation. He says, "Mother, you have my father much offended" (11), making her the target of blame. After several verbal thrusts, Gertrude, her control of the situation melting, utters, "Have you forgot me?" (14). Much of the shock the scene offered the original audience resulted from Hamlet's trampling on the customs of respect and deference mandated by the Elizabethan idea of the hierarchical family. In confronting her, he momentarily casts aside a barrier of status and formality that has always separated them.

Possibly too much emphasis could be placed upon this distancing formality. Without doubt affection exists between Hamlet and Gertrude; without doubt this affection has been mutually expressed. It would be folly to posit for Hamlet a childhood of parental neglect, yet the Elizabethan hierarchical system colors Hamlet and his mother's relationship with a tincture that is possibly difficult to reproduce in the modern, "more democratic" family, in which children are encouraged to express themselves and become individuals. Nevertheless, the play does reveal that mother and son have never revealed deeply held secrets and troubling feelings to each other. As his first soliloquy makes clear, Hamlet is stunned to realize that his mother is in love with his uncle. Likewise, Gertrude misjudges the unplumbed depths in her son. At the beginning of the play she is unaware of the effect her marriage has had and is having upon him. She fails to comprehend the causes of his bizarre conduct, falling into line behind Polonius with his theory that Hamlet's gloom is caused by love melancholy. At base mother and son have never been able to communicate deeply with each other; in modern parlance they have found it difficult "to dialogue."

A certain distance between parent and child manifests itself in Hamlet's encounters with his father's ghost. Never is there any display of affection or remembrances of past joys. Zeffirelli's restructuring of the ghost's revelation scene so that Hamlet (Mel Gibson) and the elder Hamlet's spirit (Paul Scofield) sit down for a father and son chat, although intriguing with its novelty, is off-center. The same could be said for the depiction of the ghost in Steven Pimlott's generally fine 2001 production of the tragedy for the Royal Shakespeare company. Alone with Hamlet on the battlements, the specter breaks into sobs. In the text the elder Hamlet appears in armor, betokening unrest and forthcoming conflict, and the traditional way of presenting the ghost as an iron-willed commander is more in line with Shakespeare's intention. As was the case with his mother, arguing that Hamlet and his father never felt affection for each other or expressed it would be amiss, but again, in their bizarre conversation upon the battlements of Elsinore, duty and vengeance override any need either may feel for father and son bonding.

Certainly emotional, as all of us to some degree are, Hamlet suffers because the circumstances of his upbringing and the intricacies of his very personality itself have made it difficult for him to understand and express his emotions. Likewise, the sensation-seeking currents of his personality are underdeveloped. Clearly he enjoys fencing, and having practiced it, is ready for his encounter with Laertes, but perhaps he has done so only to be ready to use a sword as a brand of vengeance. At base, however, he does not seem especially interested in physical activity, sports, or exploring new situations and locales. Interestingly enough, Ophelia's lament for Hamlet's apparent madness — spoken at the conclusion of the nunnery scene — calls attention to the intellectual aspects of the prince's personality.

> O what a noble mind is here o'erthrown!
> The courtier's, soldiers, scholar's eye, tongue
>   sword,
> Th' expectancy and rose of the fair state,
> The glass of fashion and the mold of form,
> Th' observed of all observers, quite, quite down!
> And I, of ladies most deject and wretched,
> That sucked the honey of his music vows,
> Now see that noble and most sovereign reason
> Like sweet bells jangled out of tune and harsh,
> That unmatched form and feature of a blown youth
> Blasted with ecstasy [III. i. 153–63].

Significantly, Ophelia does not praise him for skills in archery, deer hunting, horsemanship or other activities which would be marks of a sensation seeking nature.[32] Her words emphasize his insistence on personal order and his intellectual pursuits. Perhaps the trait he is most deficient in is sensation. In fact, nowhere in the play do interests in activity, novelty, or advertising self-confidence — all traits frequently at the forefront of sensation type personalities — seem of major value to Hamlet. If this reading of his psyche is just, then we possibly have another cause of his delay. His psychetypology makes executing Claudius difficult because of the relative underdevelopment of his sensation, action-taking side. As

Coleridge has surmised, his psyche retreats from action and hides from it by fortifying itself within walls of speculation.

Ophelia's lamentation at the loss of the Hamlet she knew, nevertheless, suggests that prior to the play's beginning Hamlet possessed something like a unity of being. The circumstances of the play upset whatever degree of psychic equilibrium Hamlet might have had. In the throes of his predicament, the feeling and sensation sides of his soul begin asserting themselves, destroying his attempts to refashion a unity of being by recreating himself as a stoical man.

Dark deeds at Elsinore have trapped Hamlet in a torture chamber of psychological turmoil. He needs to escape, but can find no doorway to the reunification of his being. Psychic energy from his libido seeks an outlet, but finds none. Hamlet's psychological turmoil spills out into his exterior actions, blighting his relationship with his Ophelia, intensifying his "war" with his mother, and obstructing his desire to enact vengeance, as the neglected function of feeling and the inferior function of sensation create an inner melee in their attempt to overmaster his dominant functions of thought and intuition.

Hamlet's complex relationship with Ophelia starkly reveals the chaotic workings of his psyche. Whatever the stage of their romance prior to her breaking it off, Hamlet soon comes to doubt its worth. In his first soliloquy he utters "...frailty thy name is woman!" (I. ii. 146), giving vent to a cynicism that will darken his feelings for the daughter of Polonius. Gertrude's surprising conduct — hastily remarrying in an era in which the majority believed a widow should remain unmarried to honor her husband — has tortured Hamlet's view of his mother. He is also disturbed by canon law's classification of a marriage between sister-in-law and brother-in-law as incest. His mother's double violation of social norms unsettle his feelings, causing him to project his bitterness toward his mother upon all women. Here we see full-blown the prince's psychological propensity which Coleridge described as "running away from the *particular* in[to] the *general*." Unable to channel his feelings toward his mother in a fashion based upon a conviction of her inner nobility, he begins to distrust, and, at times, perhaps, even to hate her. His animosity toward Gertrude spreads to womankind in general, then is sporadically directed toward Ophelia, rising violently into consciousness in the famed nunnery scene, when, suspecting her of collusion with her father and the King, he berates her. He rails against women for being sly, alluring, seductive and treacherous, inveighs against the sex act itself as an engenderer of sinners, and well-nigh accuses Ophelia of being a prostitute. Later, during the play within a play scene, his violently bitter feelings toward her have abated.

He wishes to sit beside her, but still feels compelled to jibe at her about sexuality: "Lady, shall I lie in your lap?" Seizing upon the words' sexual implication, the befuddled Ophelia utters, "No, my lord." Hamlet adroitly masks his double-entendre, saying "I mean, my head upon your lap?" and then underscores his words' intended sting at sexuality when he says, "That's a fair thought to lie between maids' legs" (III. ii. 110–18). Cynical remarks about romantic love, as we have seen, are generally mitigated by wit and whimsy and the overriding comic structure of the plays in the comedies. In *Hamlet,* as well as in *Troilus and Cressida*, such remarks manifest the protagonist's acid bitterness, hint at a possibly murky reality, and reveal the spirit-numbing poison of disenchantment.

After Claudius rises from his chair and disrupts the play, events rush forward pell-mell. Hamlet accosts his mother in her bedchamber and slays Polonius. The King, then, dispatches him with Rosencrantz and Guildenstern for England. Shakespeare provides us with no evidence of an encounter between or a parting involving Hamlet and Ophelia before the voyage for England. Very likely Hamlet does not see her after his staging of "Mousetrap." Caught up in the vexing currents of his mind, withdrawing from the outer world into the inner, absorbed in brooding upon his predicament, Hamlet neglects his feelings for Ophelia, and relegates them to a dusty chamber in his mind. When he next happens upon her, he encounters her body; she is dead. Suddenly learning of her death in the graveyard scene, he bolts forward — stung obviously by jealousy — after Laertes springs into the grave to embrace his sister. The two men grapple, maiming even further Ophelia's "maimed rites." After they are parted, Hamlet cries, "I loved Ophelia. Forty thousand brothers / Could not with all their quantity of love / Make up my sum" (V. i. 272–74). These words are among the play's most poignant. They express the shock of his discovery of her death, the piercing regret for opportunity lost, and desperate knowledge that the forgone opportunity will never be rediscovered. Hamlet's imprisoned feelings break forth and bolt to the forefront of consciousness, galvanizing his inferior function — his capability for sensation. For the moment the inner gates of restraint are down. Psychological frustration becomes incarnate in physical action. Having apparently leaped into the grave with Laertes, he shouts

> Swounds, show me what thou'lt do.
> Woo't weep? Woo't fight? Woo't fast? Woo't tear
>   thyself?
> Woo't drink up eisel? Eat a crocodile?
> I'll do't. Dost come here to whine?

To outface me with leaping in her grave?
Be buried quick with her, and so will I.
And if thou prate of mountains, let them throw
Millions of acres on us, till our ground.
Singeing his pate against the burning zone,
Make Ossa like a wart? Nay, a thou'lt mouth, /
I'll rant as well as thou [V. i. 277–87].

The queen's verdict — "This is mere [utter] madness"(287) — leaves little doubt as to wildness of Hamlet's behavior. Even here, however, Hamlet's rational faculties are not slumbering. Although he finds himself impelled by his own exploding emotions, the satirical jester in his psyche remains active. Laertes' grandstanding behavior more than borders on absurdity. Hamlet's very diction jibes at Laertes' extravagant wish to be buried with his sister: "And if thou prate of mountains, let them throw/ Millions of acres on us!" (83–84). As if summing up his judgment of Laertes, he cries, "I'll rant as well as thou" (287). But his description of himself as ranting directs criticism at himself as well. He experiences a kind of dissociation in which he acts outrageously, yet waxes critical of his behavior. He acts and observes himself at the same time. The barriers between taking action and playing a role collapse until unraveling the two twisted skeins of his behavior becomes impossible.

This episode is but one occurrence of a pattern in Hamlet's behavior: brooding and ratiocination followed by wild outbursts in which the sensation, action-taking side of his personality erupts into momentary dominance. These outbursts are not insane (in the generally accepted clinical sense of the patient's losing contact with reality) for during his outbreaks he maintains a detached awareness of his behavior. The outburst subsides, leaving him again entangled in tendrils of speculation.

The unforeseen death of his father and his mother's sudden marriage to Claudius, whom Hamlet despises, no doubt contribute to this pattern, but Hamlet's erratic struggles to understand his behavior and consequent outbursts are exacerbated by the sub-created world's multiplying chaos. Like Enobarbus, Hamlet needs a rational justification for his behavior; in Hamlet's instance, as Lee Jacobus observes, a proof of the King's guilt.[33] As with Enobarbus, the whirligigs of chaos wreak havoc upon a supposed rationally delineated course of action. Once Enobarbus decides that his rationalization for deserting Antony is justified and withdraws to the opposition, Antony unexpectedly sends his treasure after him, awakening Enobarbus's feeling side, evoking self-recrimination, guilt, and leading to his death. Hamlet gains proof of Claudius's guilt, but chaos will not let him act immediately. Presumably, of course, Claudius has guards who would prevent an immediate onslaught. But Hamlet's one unexpected opportunity to fulfill his duty — his chance to kill Claudius in the chapel as the latter prays — is undercut by the Prince's own chaotic psyche — the sudden, realization that by killing Claudius at prayer, he will insure his enemy's salvation. Possibly — if currents in his psyche had not eddied in this direction — he would have killed Claudius. This opportunity missed, Hamlet again confronts chaos when his killing of Polonius causes his own dispatch to England and the madness of Ophelia. Her resultant death and her father's murder then provoke Laertes to seek vengeance upon Hamlet. The uprising of the mob in support of Laertes forces Claudius to act quickly, to enact the planned murder, which of course backfires, causing the deaths of Laertes, Gertrude, and himself.

Chaos limits Hamlet's action, creating inner turmoil in the prince which finds its catharsis at times in wild, barely premeditated action, which in turn produces further chaos, resulting in further ratiocination. A closer look needs to be given to exactly how Hamlet's erratic action-taking embroils him in disaster. In the nunnery scene, during the heat of his interchange with Ophelia, he blurts out, "it hath made me mad. I say we will have no more marriage. Those that are married already — all but one — shall live. The rest shall keep as they are" (III. i. 148–51). A dangerous remark indeed, for he gives in to a compulsion to refer, albeit obliquely, to his planned murder of Claudius. (Again reason mixes with his emotional outbursts.) But by the same token, if Claudius is savvy enough to understand the hint, Hamlet is jeopardizing his own life.

A similar emotionally-wrought debacle is his insertion of lines referring to the elder Hamlet's assassination into *The Murder of Gonzago*. Although this plan occurs to him when his mind is at a white-hot pitch of inspiration at the conclusion of the Hecuba speech, its implementation is not the result of an outburst. For obviously he has time, as he later writes the lines and waits for the beginning of the play, to reconsider his plan and, if need be, reject it. Here occurs an intriguing variation on the pattern outlined above. Hamlet's psychogenic need to take action rises into his consciousness and momentarily dominates it, perhaps bedazzling his reason. Indeed, it is unclear whether he ever considers the potential dangerous upshot of his stratagem. By proving Claudius' guilt by having a murder portrayed similar to the one Claudius committed, Hamlet reveals his knowledge of his enemy's guilt to that very enemy. Again he confronts an unintended result. Convinced of Hamlet's knowledge of the crime, Claudius plots his adversary's death.

Even more disastrous is Hamlet's impulsive killing of Polonius. The murder occurs in seconds. Fearing that the Prince intends to harm

Gertrude, Polonius cries out. Without hesitation, Hamlet stabs through the concealing arras, giving the counselor a mortal wound. "Is it the King?" he asks, underscoring his uncertainty. The implication is that for a moment, for a dynamic and ultimately inexplicable moment, his sensation side rose into psychic dominance, impelling his action, causing him to forget that he had just left the praying Claudius, obscuring the fact that the concealed person could not be the king. Hamlet's reaction to the shout, as we have seen, embroils him further in chaos.

Again microcosm and macrocosm team to thwart ambition and produce anguish. By stressing this pattern in Hamlet, I do not by any means negate such classic interpretations of the cause of Hamlet's delay as the unconscious workings of the Oedipus complex, Hamlet's need to justify the action to himself, his need to prove the King's guilt to Denmark, or his wish to discover a means of escape after he kills the King. These and other reasons for the prince's delay have been debated for decades. Many of these need not be mutually exclusive. Hamlet's suffering from Oedipal manifestations need not obviate his concern with killing the king and escaping from the monarch's guards. Whatever complex of reasons stays the prince's hand, the psychetypological struggle recurs, creating in Hamlet a hell from which he cannot escape. Unlike Sartre's *No Exit,* in which hell seemingly is other people, Shakespeare's *Hamlet* portrays a bitter world in which hell is the self. Presumably Sartre's unhappy trio—Garcin, Estelle, and Inez—could leave their infernal room furnished in French Second Empire Style—by simply choosing to do so. Hell is not other people as Garcin believes, because in Sartre's view one is capable of mustering the fortitude to make the existential decision to recreate his own being. One can always walk away from the persons and situations producing vexation. The world of *Hamlet* negates this easy and optimistic panacea. It is a world in which the hell is both other people and the self. Hamlet cannot make an existential decision either to commit the murder or walk away from his grim charge. He remains trapped in a hell of psychological chaos.

Hamlet's plunge into the depths of chaos whirls him into another depth as well: that of relativism. When, as with Enobarbus, reality for the prince refuses to be codifiable, Hamlet begins to doubt the certainly of knowledge. As he tells Rosencrantz when the latter protests that he does not think Denmark a prison, "Why then 'tis none to you, for there is nothing either good or bad but thinking makes it so. To me it is a prison" (II. ii. 249–59). Clearly he is not insane; that is, he does not believe that Denmark is an actual prison of brick and mortar. Yet his quip points to the differences between the ways human beings perceive reality.[34] Like Troilus and Antony, Hamlet struggles with reason's inability to grapple successfully with values. His skepticism as to the worth of his mother, as to the goodness of women, and as to the nobility of the human species in general has spread until it even challenges the conviction that vengeance against Claudius is virtuous or worthwhile. Hence, we have another possible reason for Hamlet's delay.

Does Shakespeare offer Hamlet a way out of this chaos? Perhaps the best answer contains a yes and a no. Despite the play's apparent sense of cosmic anarchy, the workings of Providence are manifested. "God be at your table!" (IV. v. 44), Ophelia pleads in her madness, and as far as Denmark is concerned, her prayer is answered. As in *King John*, divine power acts, but only obscurely. In *Hamlet* it seeks to cleanse the throne of Denmark from its stains of usurpation and fratricide.[35] Hamlet senses a manifestation of the divine when he feels impelled to open the letter being delivered to the King of England by Rosencrantz and Guildenstern and, thereby, learns it is the warrant for his death. Hence, he is enabled to take the crucial countermeasure of changing the document to condemn its two unfortunate barriers. As he sums up the situation to Horatio, "Our indiscretion sometimes serves us well / When our deep plots do pall, and that should learn us / There's a divinity that shapes our ends/ Rough-hew them how we will" (V. ii. 8–11). The next day the ship is approached by the pirate vessel — another seemingly supernatural occurrence, enabling the prince to return to Denmark to complete his mission. Upon his arrival at Elsinore, he may be seen to have undergone a "sea change"; he is more calm, more reserved, more ready to confront the future and its possible trickery, and more prepared to face, if need be, his own death. Not that he is a model of stoical reserve: His outburst in the graveyard occurs after his return. But Hamlet is bolstered by a faith that, as he tells Horatio in a paraphrase of St. Matthew's words on Providence, the time for him to enact vengeance will be provided. Before his departure for England, Hamlet had relied too heavily on himself, rough-hewing things however he willed. Now he will await a divinely-granted opportunity.

And it is granted, through ambiguously, and in a manner which makes the divine manipulations appear indistinguishable from chaos. Unable to wound Hamlet in accord with the rules of fencing, Laertes pricks him when he is not looking. In the ensuing outburst of rage, Laertes and Hamlet's swords fall upon the floor, enabling Hamlet to pick up the poisoned sword to use against the plotter.[36] Similarly Claudius's intricate plot to rid himself of the Prince backfires when Gertrude unexpectedly drinks from the poisoned stoup of wine and Laertes' before-death accusation of Claudius exposes the monarch's machinations and justifies Hamlet's role of executioner. In the final confrontation with his enemy, Hamlet's sensation seeking side rises to the fore without any hampering from his intuitive and thinking functions. At length he has found a kind of unification of the self, albeit not a permanent one. What finally enables him to kill Claudius is an involuntary repetition of the now embedded pattern of the thinking-intuitive nexus of his personality reaching an stalemate in its search to justify bloody action: an impasse that leads to an eruption of the action-taking inferior function into consciousness and activity.

Very likely, if questioned about the circumstances concluding *Hamlet,* many Elizabethans would have confidently judged that divine intervention helped Hamlet to serve as God's executioner and to cleanse the throne of Denmark. No argument can gainsay this interpretation. As Laura Simms has argued, attempts to prove or disprove preternatural influences inevitably founder into intellectual cul de sacs.

> The ceaseless conundrum of whether one is predestined or somehow the author of a particular fortune or fate seems impossible to solve through human logic. Any explanation is limited to how I tell or hear the story. What religion did I grow up with, or what philosophy have I come to adopt? How far back can I trace the cause, effect, or ultimate sources of a particular incident? How vast is my perception? [7].

These factors indeed subvert any effort to muster logical proof.

But the question lingers: If the Prince is God's chosen warrior, then why does Hamlet die? Why doesn't the divine power place him firmly on the throne instead of allowing the realm to succeed to Fortenbras, a hotheaded warmonger?

Here again the text propels our attempts to understand it back into ambiguities. No simple pattern of distributive or political justice emerges. The divine power demands the death of Claudius but seems not to be as concerned with his replacement by an able prince. Is Gertrude likewise punished for her sins? Or is her taking the fatal swallow circumstantial? If she dies for her sins, what of the relatively blameless Ophelia? Was her death accidental?

Likewise, Hamlet's death is shrouded in mystery. Critics who adhere to the view of Providential intervention informing the action of *Hamlet* often see the Prince's death as an instance of retributive justice enacted because of his killing Polonius.[37] The crucial passage cited to support this idea follows:

> For this same lord,
> I do repent; but heaven hath pleased it so
> To punish me with this, and this with me,

That I must be their scourge and minister.
I will bestow him, and will answer well
The death I gave him [III. iv. 179–84].

Without doubt Hamlet considers that he will be punished for the old man's death, yet proving that the Prince's death results from heavenly judgment is difficult. For one thing Hamlet repents of his crime, an action summoning forth debate concerning whether God punishes penitent sinners.[38] Furthermore, Hamlet sees himself enacting the role of a Providential scourge, thus killing Polonius in accord with divine decree, punishing the sins of Polonius and being punished for his own sins by being forced to enact the crime. The text then raises another perplexing theological enigma: Does a just God punish sinners for sins that He himself has decreed?

Of course, theologians and philosophers can present theories to account for or seemingly justify these contradictions, but none of these tenets can definitively resolve the conundrum; that is, no one can prove that Shakespeare had in mind, for example, a particular ramification of Calvinistic predestination while penning these lines. In other words, Shakespeare was writing poetry, not illustrating theology. Various interpreters may see shadowings of dogma in the passage but cannot prove that the passage illustrates or confirms these beliefs. Hamlet's death may or may not be punishment for the death of Polonius. Readers are free to abide by their own theories, but since God does not step upon the stage and explain His workings as in a medieval morality play, the extent and purposes of heavenly intercession in *Hamlet* can be only conjectured, not proven by citing a passage from Luther, the Psalms, St. Augustine, or Calvin.

Thus, although divine intervention influences the action of the play, its scope and some manifestations are obscure. But one aspect of it is disturbingly clear: it does not grant Hamlet peace this side of the grave. Nor does he like Dante at the conclusion of the *Paradiso* behold a beatific vision of the concentric circles of the divinity, symbolizing the triune God. In the grip of that "fell sergeant, Death" (338–39), Hamlet yearns only that Horatio tell his tale; that is, clear is name by portraying a version of himself that will be acceptable to himself. He is unable to complete his instructions to Horatio: "The rest is silence" (360). Neither the unfolding of events nor the intercession of a heavenly power bestow upon him anything like a sense of fixed or discovered selfhood.

Yet the play does not obviate the possibility of Hamlet's salvation and "consequent" individuation beyond the grave. In fact, the text makes this prospect almost certain when Horatio says, "Good night, sweet prince, /And flights of angels sing thee to thy rest!" (V. ii. 361–62). It is mostly unlikely that Shakespeare would have expected an irony-minded audience to judge Horatio as misguided, foolish, or blinded by friendship.

On this point Shakespeare's *Hamlet* shares much with Sir Thomas Malory's *Le Morte d'Arthur*. Throughout the many pages of Malory's superb romance, Lancelot seeks to perfect a sense of self through loyalty to King Arthur, through his many deeds of valor, and through his adulterous love for the Queen. He is never successful; in fact, the tumultuous events of Malory's final book destroy whatever momentary balance between these conflicting demands that Lancelot is able to muster. With the fall of the Round Table, Lancelot is bereft of his lord, his vocation, and his mistress. He retreats from the world of action to the cloisters of a monastery, but still he has not achieved total individuation. Only with his death does Lancelot complete his quest for self-hood through his salvation. Malory impresses upon his readers the fulfillment of Lancelot's quest by two means: The Bishop's beatific dream-vision of Lancelot being born upward into heaven by angels, and the condition of the body — a smile upon the face as well as a sweet smell emanating from the corpse.[39]

Hence, in providing his protagonist with no sense upon this earth of a final discovery of the self, Shakespeare's tragedy is much more in line with Malory's late medieval view than with the plentiful modern paperbacks of pop psychology. Here we come to the center of much of the play's darkness. When asking my students, why Hamlet dies if he is to be understood as a heaven-sent avenger, I have not infrequently encountered the view that death is kind to him. No longer having his father, his mother, or Ophelia, having suffered so much, and fulfilled his mission only at so great a cost, Hamlet has little left to live for.

Whether or not the God of the world of the play is being kind to the Prince by engineering his death, this view points to a crucial, disturbing aspect of the drama's conclusion. Shakespeare here touches upon a dark, unfriendly coast in his exploration of the human psyche — the suggestion that the hope for inner unity may be impossible to be fulfilled; that, to a crucial extent, the Jungian archetypal quest for selfhood may be doomed from the outset.

At times Jung himself could write glowingly of the hopes to be gained from individuation. His very concept of the self — a central guiding force distinct from the ego or consciousness — argues that each individual psyche has its own built-in Merlin figure or "wise old man" to guide one on the path to fulfillment. At times Jung advocated a mastery of one's personality based upon "complete obedience to the fundamental laws of human nature; and there can positively be no higher moral principle than harmony with natural laws that guide the libido in the direction of life's optimum" (*Types* 213). Yet Jung himself would admit that pursuing this course is not simple: "During those years, between 1918 and 1920, I began to understand that the goal of psychic development is the self. There is no linear evolution; there is only a circumambulation of the self. Uniform development exists, at most only at the beginning; later everything points toward the center. The insight gave me stability, and gradually my inner peace returned" (*Memories* 196–197).

At this time the central emblem of the self to Jung was the mandala — usually a circle containing a square. The mandala is a symbol of the heavens, an aid to reflection among Buddhists, and for Jung it came to suggest the psyche's center which one approaches but never reaches. In other words, the process of becoming an individual is on-going. Total realization of the self is an impossible goal.

This concept of "finding oneself" is difficult for many moderns, for most of us consider this process to be linear. Ordinarily we think of our searches for selfhood as a journey down life's road with the development our best selves — and happiness — at the end. To be sure, at times Jung, his followers, and psychotherapists in general speak of the search for individuation in linear terms. Indeed, the concept of a road implies the journey's end, completion, finality, fulfillment. The concept of the mandala that one circumambulates but never enters, on the contrary, offers a more uncertain, tentative nonlinear paradigm.

While hoping to avoid oversimplifying so complex and challenging a thinker as Jung,[40] I point out that Jung's discussions of individuation often couch the concept in more inspiring, hopeful terms. For Jung this process is often enthralling, challenging, ever beckoning, at base stimulating — a great adventure. His emphasis is generally upon the vital discoveries one makes by undertaking the quest.

Indeed, although Jung was knowledgeable of darkness in the human psyche and well aware that humankind might obliterate itself from the planet, a certain recurrent optimism keeps bobbing cork-like to the surface of the often troubled waters of his thought. Despite manifesting an awareness of dangerous challenges facing mankind in the twentieth century, *The Undiscovered Self* (written in 1957), one of Jung's final writings, directs attention to his recurring optimism. For instance, in opposition to principles of Marxist collectivism, Jung asserts that the hope of humanity resides in the development of the human psyche. "Happiness and contentment, equability of mind and meaningfulness of life — these can be experienced only by the individual and not by a State, which ... continually threatens to paralyze and suppress the individual" (403).

In the same essay, Jung speculates on a momentous transformation of the human psyche — an alignment of the instincts with mankind's spirit:

> We are living in what the Greeks called the καιρόσ the right moment — for a "metamorphosis of the gods," of the fundamental principles and symbols. This peculiarity of our time, which is certainly not of our conscious choosing, is the expression of the unconscious man within us who is changing. Coming generations will have to take account of this momentous transformation if humanity is not to destroy itself through the might of its own technology and science [402].

Although concerned about the prospect of destruction on a hitherto unimaginable scale, Jung, nevertheless, presages a rebirth for humanity — a kind of apotheosis of the psyche. As his optimism rises to the fore of his discussion, Jung embraces what he understands as a potential of growth for humanity's well being. Even here, however, a certain uncomfortable vagueness manifests itself as to the nature of this miraculous change. A similar reticence, a similar lack of definition, appears elsewhere in Jung, as we have seen, as he speculates on humanity's goal of "finding itself." Although at times acknowledging that the quest may never be completed, Jung tends to emphasize that a significant portion of the trip can be made and a number of new territories conquered. In essence, his message is one that most of humanity craves to hear.

Similarly, Jung's exponent, Joseph Campbell, evinces a striking optimism as far as individuation is concerned. While not denying that life unavoidably commits us to suffering,[41] Campbell extols humanity's capacity to discover inner direction and, therefore, a meaningful destination. In his now classic discussions with Bill Moyers, published as *The Power of Myth*, Campbell iterates Jung's fundamental doctrine of the unconscious self struggling to guide the personality, then affirms, "The thing to do is to learn to live in your period of history as a human being ... and it can be done." "By doing what?" Moyers asks. Campbell responds, "By holding to your own ideals for yourself and, like Luke Skywalker, rejecting the system's impersonal claims upon you" (144). To achieve this success, Campbell argues, persons must reenact in their individual searches for meaning the basic myth of the hero and conquer the inner dragon that holds them back from self-fulfillment. In responding to Moyer's question about how to "slay that dragon in me," Campbell replies, "My general formula for my students is 'Follow your bliss.' Find where it is, and don't be afraid to follow it" (148). A few pages later he adds further illustration: "What is it that makes you happy? Stay with it, no matter what people tell you. This is what I call following your bliss." (155). A life of fulfillment granted by dedication to music, art, and poetry, by dedication to leadership, by dedication even to religious asceticism — these and other triumphs may be achieved by differing individuals following their own forms of bliss. Again we encounter a point of view that most people wish to hear.

The same may be said for the essential message found in the plethora of self-help books that has filled the bookstalls in recent decades. As our society becomes more fragmented, as we become more confused about values, as the simple life we believe our great-grandparents enjoyed seems more and more impossible for us to achieve, we want the assurance that indeed all and all manner of thing may be well. As the essence of the deluding pop therapeutic message, Bruce Thornton has singled out Dr. Joyce Brothers' assertion that "Love, power, riches, success, a good marriage, exciting sex, fulfillment are not impossible dreams. They can be yours if you want them" (53). Dr. Brothers enjoys the agreement of many of her paperback colleagues. For several decades Dr. Wayne Dyer has been promising to lead his readers to a "Promised Land of No-Limit Persons," individuals always think for themselves, do not hide their lights under bushels, and relish life as unabashed and forceful achievers. While at times drawing upon overgeneralizations about the sexes, Dr. John Gray offers to lead his readers to a secular Mecca of happiness and harmony.

In *Hamlet* Shakespeare presents the disarming possibility that the conflicting currents of the self cannot be fully channeled into one smooth course.[42] The fortunes of Hamlet, moreover, indicate that the quest down the road to selfhood may be a frustrating search for a never-reached wonderland, that our circumamublations about the self may never smoothly circle the center.

Curiously enough, Shakespeare's perception of humankind's quest for happiness— at least as far as it is embodied in *Hamlet*— is much more in line with that of Sigmund Freud, Jung's erstwhile mentor and later rival, than it does with Jung's. In one of Freud's most provocative works, *Civilization and its Discontents*, published ten years before his death, the famed psychiatrist devotes extended focus to humankind's need for happiness. From birth human beings are dominated by their need to gain gratification — the so-called pleasure principle — yet complete satisfaction of this psychogenic demand is doomed. Or, as Freud himself couches the dim reality, "and yet its [the pleasure principle's] programme is in conflict with the whole world, with the macrocosm as much as with the microcosm. It simply cannot be put into execution, the whole constitution of things runs counter to it; one might say the intention that man should be *happy* is not included in the scheme of *Creation*" (772). The causes of humanity's unhappiness are threefold: (1) fragile and decaying bodies, subject to diseases; (2) hurricanes, tornadoes, and other destructive forces of nature; (3) complex, varied, and often sad or hostile relationships with others. The resulting frustrations of will and desire create inner havoc. Freud goes on to argue, "The goal toward which the pleasure-principle impels us— of becoming happy — is not obtainable; yet we may not — nay, cannot — give up the effort to come nearer to realization of it by some means or other" (774). Humanity then adopts numerous strategies for coming "nearer to realization of it," ranging from the ascetic withdrawal from the world to the sensualist's immersion in its pleasures. But none of these offer guarantees of happiness. No panaceas exists. In fact, some strategies may bring misfortune in their wakes. While not categorically dismissing some momentous shift in the human psyche, possibility produced by new means of child rearing and education, Freud does not share Jung's optimism; in fact, the father of psychoanalysis generally manifests a dim view toward such utopianism. In concluding the essay, Freud sums up his skepticism as follows: "I have no consolation to offer them [his fellow human beings]; for at bottom this is what they all demand — the frenzied revolutionary as passionately as the most pious believer" (802).

Both *The Undiscovered Self* and *Civilization and its Discontents* offer their authors' views within a decade of their deaths, when, we might assume, their individual concepts, theories, and values had been more or less solidified. Yet although he was aware that humanity may indeed destroy itself, Jung ultimately maintains an optimism: The individual can reach higher and higher self-awareness and individuation. Freud, however, considers humankind's confrontation with what this study calls chaos and sees scant chance of victory.

The view that Hamlet's death is indeed merciful to him gives us reason to return to and reexamine his psyche at the drama's conclusion. Certainly his sense of belonging to a world capable of providing him with a joyful sense of existence has been devastated. Likewise, without his father, mother, and Ophelia, he is bereft — except for Horatio— of vital relationships with other human beings.

One, nevertheless, cannot underestimate humanity's resiliency in rebounding from depression, anxiety, and other debilitating psychological difficulties. Arguing, however, that Hamlet, had he lived, would never have regained a sense of personal direction would be fatuous. But at the moment after he has accomplished his mission, all doors are closed to him. Almost isolated, cut off from his past, unable to integrate the opposing currents of his psyche, he is lost upon his own inner psychological moor. Death, in a sense, would be merciful to him. He himself considers his death a balm when he stops Horatio's attempted suicide by telling him, "Absent thee from felicity awhile, / And in this harsh world draw thy breath in pain / To tell my story" (V. ii. 349–51).

Hamlet is, in one sense, Shakespeare's most disarming tragedy. It suggests that individuation, self-hood, control of one's psyche — however one may wish to define the goal — may well be impossible, at least for a number of luckless persons. Perhaps more than any other of Shakespeare's tragic heroes, the prince dies adrift, without a psychological rudder. Although he is buoyed to some extent by a somber resignation to providential workings, for him both his inner world and the outer world of Denmark are both bleak, hollow, devoid of spiritually-warming meaning. More than any other Shakespearean tragic hero, Hamlet dies remote from any personal sense of identity. Of course, Lear's identity has been demolished, but painfully and gradually it is remade as he comes to express his feeling side in loving Cordelia. Her death savagely frustrates his newfound capability for loving; it does not disintegrate his new-found selfhood. Death comes too quickly to him for his psychological dismemberment. He dies, in fact, believing that Cordelia still lives. Romeo and Juliet both die having in a sense fashioned an identity: that of passionate, sincere lovers.[43] Likewise, Antony and Cleopatra die having achieved identities as lovers. Antony meets death still feeling ennobled by his love for Cleopatra, and she applies the snake to her breast, aspiring to a beyond-the-grave reunion with her lover and to a psychic harmony in the hereafter. Coriolanus, still the victim of his rampaging emotions, encounters death with his psyche unintegrated, yet he seems shockingly unaware of his lack of developed selfhood. Although, Timon undergoes a sundering of his psyche, he is spared a sense of psychological "lostness": He is anchored in his newly found hatred. Perhaps only Othello, Brutus, and Macbeth experience something like Hamlet's stunning dissolution of the psyche. As we have seen, the eruption of Othello's thinking side causes him to murder the person he loves most. Brutus loses his sense of inner direction when his intellect fails him in his attempt to defeat the armies of Antony and Octavius; his attempt to fashion for himself an inner unity based on stoicism disintegrates, and he attempts to recall this self by dying stoically. Macbeth seems to fashion an identity, but discovers that he has not done so. At the play's conclusion, he is as bereft of inner moorings as Hamlet is. But Macbeth's psychological degeneration occurs suddenly. Until the end of the play Macbeth has been able to ballast his psyche because of his faith in the witches' prophecies and his dependency upon his wife. Only when these props are kicked from under him does he realize how formless his psyche has become.[44] Presumably, after the play's end, his soul has been claimed by darkness, but psychologically Macbeth has already joined Hamlet in the ranks of those suffering in an inner hell.

I exclude Troilus from the list of tragic heroes simply because to many readers his play is a dark comedy rather than a tragedy and his loss of Cressida does not produce a tragic fall such as Lear's or Othello's. Yet, interestingly enough, the play written about the same time as *Hamlet*, as we have seen, concludes with its male protagonist bereft of direction and lacerated by bitter emotions.

On the other hand, a backward glance at *Richard II* is in line. In many ways different, Richard and Hamlet share some disarming similarities. In having lost psychological direction, in musing upon the nature of selfhood and misfortune, Shakespeare's unfortunate king, like the Prince of Denmark, has reached a grim cul-de-sac in his search for individuation. As we have observed, as his misfortunes mount, Richard's inferior function of thinking begins dominating his consciousness until shortly before his death, in prison, fluid speculations prepossess him. He begins his final soliloquy by attempting futilely to find a means of comparing his prison to the world. Although he struggles for the rhetorical strategy to hammer it out, the metaphoric connection in his mind indicates that he feels that he has unwittingly been imprisoned all his life; his choices, wishes, and desires paradoxically confined even though he was monarch. He moves then to confusion about Biblical texts.

> The better sort,
> As thoughts of things divine, are intermixed
> With scruples that do set the word itself
> Against the word, as thus, "Come, little ones,"
> And then again,
> "It is as hard to come as for a camel
> To thread the postern of a small needle's eye [V. v. 11–17].

Disturbed by conflicting passages, Richard cannot easily find peace in scripture. He then turns to philosophical musings.

> Thus play I in one person many people,
> And none contented. Sometimes am I king,
> Then treason makes me wish myself a beggar,
> And so I am. Then crushing penury
> Persuades me I was better when a king;
> Then am I kinged again, and by and by
> Think that I am unkinged by Bolingbroke,
> And straight am nothing. But whate'er I be,

Nor I, nor any man that but man is
With nothing shall be pleased till he be eased
With being nothing [31–41].

Like a rowboat amid a storm at sea, Richard is tossed and pitched about. Unable to drop a mental anchor, he can take comfort in no moral or philosophical stance. He cannot gain sustenance from a stoical acceptance of poverty and imprisonment, nor can he convince himself that indeed he was better off in regal trappings. He is daunted by the recurrent sense that I "straight am nothing." Like our prisoner in the room with five doors, Richard cannot help but keep attempting to escape through the ceiling hatch only to find himself in a similar prison fashioned of quandaries. He comes to believe that all ready-made philosophic pills for dealing with misfortune are ineffective. Human beings cannot help but keep hoping, like Samuel Beckett's Vladimir and Estragon, for betterment. For Richard the longing can end only with death.

Like Hamlet, Richard feels alienated from himself and the world about him, uncertain where to turn, what stance to assume. The personalities of both have, in a sense, become fluid. However, Richard's melancholy realization that he is lost does not seem to be as acute as Hamlet's, simply because Richard is assassinated as he is coming to a full realization of his unhappy impasse, whereas Hamlet has lingered long in the prison of his inner hell. Managing to survive a while longer with his death wound, Hamlet presents his summary of events to Horatio. It is unremittingly dark.

Hamlet, then, is not alone in presenting us with a protagonist whose quest for individuation fails. Other tragic heroes share his failing. But his failure is the most intricate, most minutely detailed, the most disheartening, and therefore, the most unnerving. In Hamlet we see writ large the possibility of, perhaps inevitably, of our own ultimate failures.

Shakespeare's horrific sense in *Richard II* and *Hamlet* of the human psyche's amorphism may be likened to that of Eugene Ionesco's in his pseudo-detective drama *Victims of Duty*. The play begins with its protagonist Choubert spending an uneventful evening at home with his wife when a detective arrives. The operative seeks information about the apartment's previous owner, particularly whether the man's name was "Mallod" with a "d" or "Mallot" with a "t." Choubert denies any acquaintance with or knowledge of the man. Convinced that the answer must be in Choubert's unconscious, the detective becomes a psychoanalyst and begins delving into his "witness-victim's" psyche. The quest to find the answer to the question of the previous tenant's identity metaphorically attempts to answer the riddles of existence and to comprehend the essence of the human personality. The quasi-mesmerized Choubert begins a symbolic quest into his own past and into the depths of his unconscious. As the detective-psychoanalyst delves further and further into the protagonist's self, Choubert journeys deeper and deeper into a profound inner pit, but then scales slopes to soar into the brightness of the sky, while at times disappearing from view of the detective and his wife (that is, reaching depths and heights they can neither share or understand). Frustrated, the detective cries, "We keep going from top to bottom, from bottom to top, from top to bottom, up and down, round and round, it's a vicious circle!" (303). Yet detective's faith abides that he will find the solution(s). "I don't believe in the absurd, everything can be comprehended in time ... thanks to the achievements of human thought and science" (309). But the detective is unable to lead his victim to any resolution. As Nicholas, another character, describes the situation, "We are not ourselves.... Personality doesn't exist. Within us there are only forces that are either contradictory or not contradictory" (308). Focusing attention on the drama's emphatic comparison of the human psyche to a dark hole, Martin Esslin has described the situation thus: "But Choubert, however deeply he descends into his subconscious, can find no solution there, only a gaping hole of nothingness. Far from containing the hidden solution to the riddle of existence, the subconscious mind opens into a bottomless pit, the absolute void" (156).[45]

The metaphor might well apply to the psyche of Hamlet, with this modification: The gaping hole is awhirl inside with conflicting magnetic fields—the four functions. Hamlet is never able in this world to achieve psychological equipoise. By implication, the best he can hope for is inner harmony beyond the grave.

In *Hamlet*, Shakespeare, as we have seen, suggests a dark possibility that Jung and Campbell often avoid: The view that individuation may not be possible — at least for a large number of persons. To be fair to Jung and Campbell, it must be asserted that to them total realization of the self is impossible; the development of the psyche is unending. But both, as we have seen, tend to portray the quest for selfhood optimistically, stressing the exuberance, joy, and satisfaction of the forward march. Shakespeare's Hamlet cannot fall into step with their ranks. He cannot extricate himself from the warring forces in the pit of his psyche. For the playwright his protagonist's psyche can achieve nothing approaching inner unity. Shakespeare's play does not necessarily disagree totally with Jung and Campbell; rather, it shifts the emphasis to psychogenic forces that cannot be harmonized. Deciding which view is more nearly correct is impossible. Terms such as "individuation," "inner forces, " and "inner self" are too imprecise and murky to undergo scientific measurement and codification. When a patient breaks off analysis, arguing that he is still depressed and confused, a therapist can tell himself that the patient did not persist long enough, try deeply enough, *will* success powerfully enough. Such an argument is unanswerable. One can always posit that if a different run had been made on the gridiron, the game would have ended victoriously.

However, with the forces of chaos thwarting apparently logical courses of action in Denmark and the ultimately unmanageable forces of the human psyche defeating self-realization, the world of *Hamlet* is a world where nothing can ever be taken for granted; it is indeed a world of tragedy. Bruce Thornton has succinctly expressed the essence of tragedy's view of humanity's condition.

> The tragic vision, then, does what the English poet and critic Matthew Arnold said the Greek tragedian Sophocles did — see life steadily and see it whole. The tragic hero looks into the grim limits of human life, and rather than turn away or cower before them, strives to achieve something worthwhile — despite those limits, despite the certainty of failure, despite the unforeseen consequences of success. After all, humans are tragic, not because they fail, but because they *succeed* in transcending, if only for one brief dazzling moment, those limits. Their aspirations create brilliance at the same time as they create the conditions for degradation and suffering. Yet in that very struggle we find our dignity and worth as human beings [56].

In *Hamlet*, Shakespeare cedes to the possibility that what we have come to think of as "individuation" may not be possible for all persons. It is a likelihood that disturbed him. As we have seen, he again dealt with this grim prospect in *Troilus and Cressida* at almost the same time as he wrote *Hamlet*. He would return to this restless possibility, in different ways, in *Othello, Coriolanus,* and *Antony and Cleopatra*.

SEVEN

Shakespeare's Romances: The Return to Eden and the Return of the Goblins

Shakespeare's dramatic romances have entertained and inspired generation after generation of theatergoers and readers. As with the comedies, this appeal may seem surprising for the stuff of the romances seems diametrically opposed to what moderns would recognize as the stuff of serious literature. These intriguing plays contain storms at sea, miraculous realms, improbable separations and equally improbable reunions, oracles, divine maneuverings, and extraordinary reconciliations which jar notions of probability. In short, these plays offer the fanciful. They seem dramatized folk tales or fairy tales—hardly subject matter for term papers in graduate level seminars concerned with English literature.

Yet many term papers, articles and books has been written on them. We recognize at least two of these works as masterpieces. Gone are the days of the Victorians who regarded these plays as "Shakespearean dotages," products of a tiring Will Shakespeare's flagging imagination. Still we have trouble classifying them and indeed trying to understand them. Attempts to reduce them to a common denominator invariably founder. Terry Eagleton's view that "The 'resolutions' of the late comedies thus rest not only upon a reactionary mystification of Nature but on a logical mistake" (93);[46] that is, they in essence present a naive spiritual essence—certainly provokes scholars and students to study the plays more closely. Still we have the feeling that Eagleton's analysis does not answer all of our questions. It is as though while peering through his critical telescope, Eagleton focuses attention on a particularly intriguing crater but misses the image of the entire moon. As Charles Frey and Frank Kermode (947) have suggested, the romances are difficult to analyze, unamenable to strict formulation.

The complex design of their weaving cannot be reduced to a common thread.

Given this observation, a further discussion may seem futile. Nevertheless, each strand identified should help in the comprehension of the whole, even if the goal to understand the design of the whole may prove unavailing. Much of the essence of Shakespeare's romances can be thrown into sharp relief by understanding that during the period of their writing the feeling side of Shakespeare's personality was struggling to reassert itself, to break from inner trammels and soar Ariel-like to freedom. It wanted to escape a Machiavellian hell and reestablish a personal Eden.

As has been shown, in the tragedies the emergence of the inferior function of thinking in plays such as *Othello* and *Timon of Athens* threatens the world of emotions, of love, of concord, indeed, in the later play almost calling its existence into question. In the romances there is a need to jump past the objections of the rational warder of cynicism's hold on the psyche and to assert feeling values despite all. Much of the uniqueness of Shakespeare's dramatic romances results from this psychological thrust.

Before pursing this line of inquiry, I wish to present two observations which may shed some light upon the nature and value of the romances. One is that in turning his attention to the romance form, Shakespeare — consciously or unconsciously — was adopting the Sidneyean mode of literary creation. That is, he focused attention upon idealized characters rather than upon realistic portrayals of human nature.

The twentieth century so concentrated its attention upon maladjusted or abnormal characters—James T. Farrell's Studs Longian, Tennessee Williams' Blanche DuBois and Chance Wayne, Arthur Miller's Willie Loman, William Faulkner's Joe Christmas and Flem Snopes, just to offer a thimbleful of examples—that we often forget that in earlier ages writers aimed for literary merit by providing idealized characters as models of behavior. To be sure, the Elizabethans and Jacobeans had their share of robust realists—writers who sought to portray life as they conceived it — with all of its petty and flagrant corruptions, its emotional confusions, its debilitating sorrows, mordant humiliations, and repetitious pains. But authors of the era also sought to portray life as it should be, to supply examples of righteous conduct to be imitated.

In *The Defense of Poesy*, Sidney eloquently presented the idea that Dame Nature herself never

> brought forth so true a lover as Theagenes, so constant a friend
> as Pylades, so valiant a man as Orlando, so right a prince as
> Xenaphon's Cyrus, so excellent a man every way as Virgil's

Aeneas.... Which delivering forth also is not wholly imaginative, as we are wont to say by them that build castles in the air:
but so far substantially it worketh, not only to make a Cyrus,
which had been but a particular excellency, as Nature might
have done, but to bestow a Cyrus upon the world, to make
many Cyruses, if they will learn aright why and how that maker
made him [607–08].

Many moderns are prone to sneer at the idea of literature providing
examples of ideal behavior. They easily equate ideals with the syrupy goodness often associated with fifties television sitcoms such as *Leave It to
Beaver* and *The Adventures of Ozzie and Harriet.* Yet this tradition has old
and honorable beginnings. The classical world would not have sneered at
it. It formed the intellectual foundation of Plutarch's *Parallel Lives.*

Although one may feel justification in rating more highly the rugged
realists, one may well wonder about the condition of a world without
ideals. One may shudder upon contemplating an existence without examples of loyalty to friends, romantic love, familial concord, and battlefield
courage.

This valuing of ideals does not mean, of course, that writers like Sidney and Spenser shunned portrayals of evil. Certainly *The Faerie Queene*
abounds with villainous characters and personified vices, such as Duessa,
Archimago, Pyrocles, and Acrasia, and Sidney's *Arcadia* provides us with
the unforgettable Queen Cecropia. (Indeed, Sidney's literary standpoint
also valued portraying examples of vices to be shunned!) Nor does this
literary stance mean that Spenser and Sidney uniformly created lackluster
allegorical embodiments of goodness. The moral weaknesses and failures
of Spenser's Red Cross, Guyon, Britomart, Artegall, and Calidore are obvious. Likewise, Sidney's heroic princes, Pyrocles and Musidorus, undergo
hardship and pain because of their folly and wrong-headedness. The central characters of these two poets imperfectly adhere to exemplary patterns; at certain points, nevertheless, these fictional heroes seem to become
momentary embodiments of these abstract concepts. Great variety and
complexity distinguish the fictional characters of these two poets, yet Sidney and Spenser — and those who utilized their mode of literary creation —
sought to furnish ideals by which humanity, hopefully, may steer its course.

In Shakespeare's romances, the characters are often portrayed as
embodiments of evil or are idealized. *Cymbeline*'s wicked queen, her brutal oafish son Cloten, *The Tempest*'s Antonio and Sebastian, *Pericles*'
depraved Antiochus and his incestuous daughter are all fundamentally
evil without much individualization; they are representations of the shadows and dark animas and animuses. On the other hand the prominent

young female characters—Marina, Perdita, and Miranda—are reproduced from the pattern of the blessed damozel. They tend to be modest, reticent, chaste, loving—promising renewal of society through their capacity to bear children. Only Imogin strikes us as spirited, determined, individualistic. Of the major male characters only Leontes and Posthumous draw readers into the inner vortexes of complex troubled personalities. As intriguing as he is with thought-provoking suggestions of an inner depth, Prospero lacks these characters' volatile power. Autumnal, sage, often ruminating, he seldom allows a glimpse into inner fires. Like the heroes of Sidney and Spenser, the male protagonists of the last plays, for the most part, totter upon the brink of evil and even fall into its abyss, yet emerge from their ordeals with renewed integrity and gained wisdom. Like Spenser's Redcross Knight, Shakespeare's Posthumous succumbs to evil impulses yet regains control of himself and is reunited with his lady. After sixteen years of penitence, Leontes is again worthy of Hermione. After facing many perils and undergoing heartaches, Pericles is reunited with his wife and daughter. Although his wife is deceased, Prospero reclaims his dukedom and sees his daughter advantageously married. In other words, they achieve ideal states or states in which the ideal may be closely approximated: the Jungian process of individuation has been or is about to be completed. In a sense this pattern evokes what Northrop Frye has called the "Myth of Deliverance" (49), an archetypal pattern based upon the inherent conflict between the mundane world of confusion, disappointment, and imperfection and the ideal world of stable joy. The "Myth of Deliverance" gains its power by vicariously allowing the reader to escape from the real world of mutability into the imaginary world of near perfection, but such release is only momentary. The joy evoked by the archetype recedes as the reader closes the book and the world of diurnal flux and flow encroaches. As Laurence Coupe has expressed the concept, a tension almost always exists in the literary work between these two concepts of time, a status wherein the ideal is attained and the daily grind (57–63). The ideal can be envisioned, but not lived in. This intractable disparity need not cause despair. As Keats suggests when he addresses the immobile lover on the grecian urn, a certain worthwhile pleasure abides in vicariousness: "Though winning near the goal, do not grieve; / She cannot fade, though thou hast not thy bliss, / Forever wilt thou love, and she be fair!" (ll. 18–20). One can bask in the radiance of the ideal. But the reward need not be exclusively passive. As Coupe reminds us, the mythic hero can be "a force for endlessly productive imperfection, rather than for arid and static perfection" (46). The heroes and heroines of Shakespeare's romances will never achieve Utopia, but their steps are on the pathway to Eden.

The second observation is that the romances are contained within a basically religious framework. Perhaps this statement seems too obvious to be stressed. However, critics have long sought to deny a theological dimension to these later plays.[47]

The romance pattern that Shakespeare drew upon in writing these intriguing dramas was tailor-made to include a religious dimension. As has long been recognized, Elizabethan romances, prose and dramatic, share a lineage going back to Greek ancestors. Popular during the Hellenistic era, prose romances featured the unravelings of mysteries; the adventures of suffering heroines and valiant heroes; despair at and denunciation of the seemingly malevolent quirks of Fate; and at the end a vindication of Providence as a benignant power. For a variety of reasons, these extravagant tales captured the imagination of the Renaissance, and a host of imitations flowed. Among other bequests, the Greek romance provided its Renaissance imitators a ready-made structural pattern for expressing the concept of benign power, however obscurely, controlling the cosmos.[48] And use this pattern the Renaissance practitioners did. For despite the tribulations of the hero and his apparent subjection to chance, the Renaissance imitations of the Greek romance stressed the beneficent control of the cosmos. In fact the unstated motto of many of these works might well have been "Trust the gods, and all comes right in the end." Writing of the trials the romance hero undergoes, Robert Gram Hunter observes that "Those trials are never meaningless, however, for there are powers above man who judge and finally reward (or punish) his conduct" (137).

To many modern critics the acts of providential intervention in Shakespeare's final plays appear to be too outlandish to be taken seriously. The divine intercessions in these plays, however, were not so extravagant to Elizabethans. As best as we are able to determine, the romance appeared first in Elizabethan literature as prose fiction and then passed to the stage. Since the religious elements of the form were apparently well established before playwrights began writing romances for the stage, it would be just to look at the function of the role of Providence in the prose romances as an aid to understanding the use of divine invention which dramatists found in the form.

A look at Robert Greene's prose romances would be illustrative. I have selected Greene for three reasons: he made wide use of the form's theological potentialities; he was apparently one of the first dramatists, in his play *James IV*, to adapt the type to the stage; and undoubtedly he influenced Shakespeare in following and developing this genre: Greene's *Pandosto* is, of course, the source for *The Winter's Tale*.

In the letter of dedication to his romance *Menaphon*, Green indicated he considered his tale more than an extravagant fantasy. He wrote that his story was concerned with the deeds of Fate in human life. After calling attention to the sorrows that his patroness, Lady Margaret Hales, had recently been enduring because of her husband's death, Greene wrote the following in a letter to her:

> I thought It my dutie to write this pastorall historie, conteyning the manifolde iniuries of fortune, that both your Ladiship might see her [fortunes] inconstant follies, and beare hir frownes with more patience, and when your dumpes were most deepe, then to looke on this little treatise for recreation; wherein there be as well humors to delight as discourses to aduise [Rollins and Baker 752].

Greene makes explicit two purposes In writing the tale: first, to tell an entertaining story (a highly sensational one at that) and second, to write a "treatise"" on a more serious level concerning the "iniuries of fortune" and to include a "discourse to aduise" in order to comfort the lady. In the letter Greene does not make clear the means by which he hopes to offer her comfort. I suggest that he attempts to do so by illustrating the belief that a benign Providence overrides and controls the misfortunes of life and makes use of such misfortunes to create goodness.[49] This view gains support from the fact that in other romances, such as *Pandosto* and *The Card of Fancie*, Greene evinces the same preoccupation with providence's creation of final goodness after the characters have suffered numerous mishaps. To illustrate how those beliefs were accommodated by the romance form, I shall examine *Menephon*. A summary of the intricate plot will be necessary.

As the story begins, pestilence is ravaging Arcadia. Damocles, the king, sends a messenger to Delphi to learn how to end the blight. The oracle replies with a long, obscure prophecy, too lengthy to be quoted in its entirety. He says that when Neptune yields forth Arcadia's wonder, when swelling seas shall neither ebb nor tide, and when other marvels have occurred, Arcadia will receive great happiness. Failing to understand these riddles, Damocles loses hope.

Meanwhile, his daughter — Sephestia, exiled because she has married Maximus, a man of lower degree than she — arrives upon the shores of Arcadia from a shipwreck, with only her uncle Lamodon and her infant son. Apparently Maximus has perished in the shipwreck. Distraught because of Fate's senseless vagary, Sephestia questions the justice of the universe and almost succumbs to despair — actions typical of the heroine of

Greene's romances. Lamodon attempts to bolster her sinking fortitude by telling her that she must accept the decrees of Fate and live for her infant son. The shepherd, Menaphon, who has only a minor role in the tale bearing his name, discovers and takes them to his cabin. There Sephestia assumes the name of Samela and decides to spend the rest of her life as a shepherdess. Soon she meets Melicertus, a shepherd who resembles her late husband, and because of this similarity, begins to fall in love with him. Likewise, because she resembles his late wife, he finds himself attracted to her. Nevertheless, because both prefer to remain faithful to their deceased spouses, they do not marry.

As the tale progresses, the infant, Pleusiddippus, becomes a precociously courageous child. While wandering on the seashore, he is captured by pirates and taken to Thessaly, where he is given to the king. Recognizing the courage, pride, and manliness of the child, the king of Thessaly decides to rear Pleusiddippus in the court and eventually to marry him to his own daughter.

Complications develop years later, when the aging Damocles, hearing of a beautiful shepherdess in his land, disguises himself as a shepherd, observes Samela, and, unaware that she is his daughter, lusts for her. Meanwhile, Pleusiddippus, now a young warrior, quarrels with his fiancée the Princess, and, having likewise heard of Samela's fabled beauty, journeys to Arcadia to win her love. The events which follow occur rapidly, with many reversals and complications. In brief, Damocles and Pleusiddippus, both spurned by Samela, become partners in crime and capture her. Melicertus and Pleusidippus fight in single combat for Samela, but the battle is a stalemate, whereupon the treacherous Damocles orders his troops to capture Melicertus and Samela. Realizing that he cannot seduce Samela by entreaties or gifts, Damocles accuses Melicertus and Samela of fornication and sentences them to death. Then, as Damocles and the court assemble to witness the execution and the unfortunate lovers ascend to the hangman's block, the gods intervene. A mysterious prophetess appears and declares the prophecy fulfilled. Pleusiddippus, having come from the shipwreck when he was an infant, is the wonder of Arcadia given by Neptune; the stalemate between him and Melicertus was the waters that had neither ebb nor tide.[50] She unravels further riddles, then identifies Sephestia as the king's daughter, Pleusiddippus as her son, Melicertus as Maximus, who, having thought Sephestia dead, assumed a new identity as a shepherd. Then the prophetess vanishes.

Afterwards comes what might be called a bestowal of Grace. Damocles and Pleusiddippus are converted from vice and treachery to penitence. Damocles accepts Sephestia and Maximus' marriage; Pleusiddippus marries the Princess of Thessaly. The two kingdoms are united. The age of Arcadia's happiness and prosperity begins.

Clearly *Menaphon* cannot be taken as a forerunner of the school of Zola. From the standpoint of realism, its plot, characters, and their actions are absurd, but to Greene the tale was a vehicle for the fulfillment of a serious purpose, a means of consoling Lady Margaret Hales and relieving her "dumpes" caused by the death of her husband. One must, therefore, be wary of assuming that Greene's story is merely a *potpourri* of sensationalism. Rather I suggest that Greene is attempting to offer consolation to the lady by illustrating the belief that the "misfortunes of life" are but apparently horrendous and that no matter how grievous and painful they may be, they are part of a beneficent divine plan.

As I have indicated earlier, this concept of a benign Providence controlling the action was fundamental to some of Greene's other prose romances. *The Carde of Fancie* relates a similar intricate tale, in which interest is centered upon the sorrows of separated lovers and references to the fates abound. Likewise, Providence acts at the end to set all right and to unite kingdoms in harmony and concord. *Pandosto* reveals a similar attitude toward Providence. Although, however, peace and harmony reign at the conclusion, Pandosto, unlike Shakespeare's Leontes, cannot overcome the guilt resulting from his past misdeeds and kills himself. Thus, to an extent, it departs from the standard view of Providence represented in Elizabethan romances.

The key, of course, to the resolution of *Menaphon*'s plot and to the comprehension of the romance's philosophical suggestions is the prophecy, couched in riddles, appearing at the beginning and at the end of the tale. Not every misfortune which occurs in *Menaphon* is hinted at by the riddle, but most are, and the tale presents an almost schematic correlation between the dark prophecies, the bizarre events, and the misfortunes which occur. Although the catastrophes which involve the principal characters are grotesque, these troubles are links In a providential chain of events which ultimately rescues Arcadia from the plague, brings about the country's rebirth, and ushers in an era of prosperity.

The providential chain of happenings, however, is pervaded by mystery. The tale supplies no inkling as to why the gods have caused the plague to descend upon Arcadia or why they have selected the particular tribulations of Sephestia, Melicertus, and the rest to end the pestilence and to bring about the era of prosperity. Nevertheless, all the characters and their misfortunes are parts of a supernatural plan. Although they act as though they have free will, they in essence resemble pieces on a chessboard, moved about by the gods to achieve a predetermined end. No reason is given why these persons have been chosen as the chess pieces. Divine motivation is beyond human understanding. Yet, like Job, after having undergone their trials, the characters receive blessings manifold more then they had.

Pericles, Cymbeline, and *The Winter's Tale* are all structured on the basis of the riddled prophecy. Likewise *The Tempest* is based on a providential design. Prospero believes that the Fates have given him the opportunity to settle the scores with his enemies, an opportunity that he must seize by the forelock, or possibly lose forever. No reason lingers as to why we should not take Shakespeare's repeated use of the providential design seriously as an expression — on some level — of belief, not as a mechanical use of a convenient plotting device. (If he were indeed the arch antireligionist proposed by some writers on the romances, why wouldn't he have expunged references to the gods from his final plays and left all the miraculous events clearly up to happenstance?)

But why does this overt religious dimension appear in these final plays? This question is, in fact, part of a larger query. Why did Shakespeare turn from writing tragedies such as *Hamlet, King Lear,* and *Macbeth* and sail toward uncharted literary waters of the romances? Solutions have been presented for decades. Some scholars have argued that being a shrewd man of the theater, Shakespeare sensed the shifting of the sands of public taste and saw the power of Fletcherian tragicomedy, although the literary jury is still out as to whether Shakespeare or Beaumont and Fletcher inaugurated this popular dramatic trend. That doughty old-time Shakespearean E. K. Chambers, on the other hand, averred that Shakespeare, mired in dwelling upon the darker sides of life, suffered a nervous breakdown and, thereafter, forswore the writing of tragedies, works expressing the very anxieties that sundered whatever equanimity he might have had (*William Shakespeare* I, 86). The theory that Shakespeare's semi-retirement to Stratford, indirectly created the shift in his dramatic interests is also provocative; that his return to rural Warwickshire, the reestablishment of his relationship with his wife Anne, his reacquainting himself with his daughters, now burgeoning into womanhood, reawakened an appreciation of humanity, a faith in basic virtues, a hope for a younger generation's promise. Another recurring hypothesis holds that after enduring some spiritual crisis, Shakespeare rediscovered religious faith.

Another, and brutally frank, theory has the backing of the often brutally frank A. L. Rowse. "What does one do when sick with disillusion? One turns from a world gone sour to the world of romance, to poetry, and the inner life of the imagination, in a sense one comes home again" (118).

None of these possibilities need be disqualified. Indeed, each may express a portion of the truth. What seems central to whatever shift of outlook and sensibility Shakespeare experienced is an intensified stirring of the feeling aspects of his psyche. As we have seen, in the tragedies of *Othello* and *Timon of Athens* and in *Hamlet*, Shakespeare expresses an implied disillusionment with what has come to be called in Jungian terms "individuation" or more commonly called "finding oneself." Although progress can be made toward integrating the conflicting functions of one's personality, total inner harmony — the angelic state sought by the Renaissance philosopher Pico della Mirandola in his *Oration on the Dignity of Man* — is impossible. Superior function and inferior function can never be fully reconciled, and in terms of the tragedies thinking and feeling can never become one. Unable to harmonize these aspects of his psyche and thus committing his tragic error, Othello kills himself. Realizing that his superior function has mislead him into undervaluing his inferior one, the embittered Timon withdraws from humanity into antipathy, despair, loneliness and fatal isolation. Like *Hamlet*, these plays suggest that instead of reaching a solid core as one ventures further in the exploration of the psyche, what is discovered is a labyrinth of conflicting thoughts and feelings, an inner chaos as baffling and daunting as the outer one of insurmountable exterior world. (We might recall Ionesco's Choubert.) In Shakespeare's tragedies the Delphic oracle's admonition "to know thyself" becomes an unsettling invitation to confusion and despair. The romances, then, represent an dynamic turn in Shakespeare's psychological venturing — the emergence of a need to affirm the feeling aspects of the psyche *in spite of* this disillusionment.

And indeed, in the romances, as we have seen, the protagonists, do find themselves or, to a rewarding extent, approach this goal. Prospero perhaps offers us the most provocative example. A thinking-intuitive personality type, Prospero earlier isolated himself amid his studies, leaving the governance of Milan to his unscrupulous brother Antonio — a grave error in judgment, for Antonio seizes power for himself and exiles Prospero and Miranda. During his twelve years of exile on the island, Prospero has learned of his folly in trusting Antonio and neglecting his responsibilities in favor of his intellectual pursuits. And when the ship containing his enemies draws near the island, he is ready to act to reclaim his dukedom. In Jungian terms, he has approached individuation by developing his hitherto neglected sensation or action-taking potentialities. He has taken a vital step towards integrating opposing aspects of his personality. (Yet as we shall see, questions arise as to Prospero's having finally achieved happiness.) Central characters of the other romances also in a sense "find themselves" or at least enable themselves to partake of Dryden's "common quiet" through bonding with others.

What comes to matter supremely in the romances are human relationships—friends with friends, fathers with children, husbands with
wives. Gonzalo and Prospero, Posthumous and Pisano, Polixenes and
Leontes, Prospero and Miranda, Alonzo and Ferdinand, Pericles and Emilia
and Marina, Hermione and Polixenes, Posthumous and Imogen, Ferdinand and Miranda, Perdita and Florizel—the pairs are emphatic, Sidneyean ideals made flesh.

The emphasis is also upon loyalty, friendship, and love restored after
rupture, even after apparent destruction. Despite Leontes' paranoid accusations and his frantic attempt to poison his long-time friend, he and Polixenes in *The Winter's Tale* are able to place the bitter past behind them and
renew their devotion and concord. Moreover, Leontes, despite the asper-
sions of his wife's character and the death of their son Mamillius, is able
to embrace Hermione again. In *The Tempest* Prospero is able to forget
sharp differences and overcome his dislike of Alonzo. In *Cymbeline*
Posthumous is able to rejoin Imogen in marriage even though, having
believed her adulterous, he has ordered her murder. Cymbeline, freed from
his bewitching fascination with the evil queen, is able again to enfold his
daughter Imogen in his arms. These plays present a bolstering faith that
the knots can be untied, old wrongs can be righted, and tarnished relationships can regain their luster. Humans need not linger in prisons of self-
recrimination, loneliness, and guilt. The passage of time and the capacity
to forgive can free them.

These plays not only celebrate the renewal of old love relationships,
but the birth of new ones, particularly heterosexual unions whose end is
marriage. Ferdinand finds Miranda; Florizel's love for Perdita wins royal
approval; Posthumous again wins his Imogen. With these unions comes
the hope of posterity, and maybe—just maybe—the future generation will
not make the mistakes of its forebears. Perhaps they will not become disillusioned with concord, with friendship, with love. Like Shakespeare, they
have learned the value of these relationships.

In these senses Shakespeare has indeed come home. Again he is drawn
to and finds meaning in the Edenic world of the comedies. But does this
emphasis upon revitalized love and friendship, upon the obscure but
beneficent manipulations of the gods, mean that Shakespeare at last has
arrived at a philosophy or a religious view providing him with tranquil-
ity and an optimism that never wavers? Not necessarily, I think.

What we have is not a systematic philosophy constructed during the
final years of his dramaturgic career. Rather, his psyche's need to emphasize the feeling side of relationships is leading him to value love in varied
manifestations. Or, to couch the matter in other terms, Shakespeare evokes

the archetype of deliverance both to express his own psychological needs and to inform these plays. Why his libido projected psychic energy in this way at this juncture in his life is beyond the scope of this study, indeed, if not beyond our ascertaining. Clearly some manifest need existed in his psyche to reassert the function of feeling and to partake — if only imaginatively in its blessings—friendship, sexual love, and familial concord. To experience again the Edenic sense of basking in the glow of one's functions, to feel at harmony with one's self and the universe. Sage as he was in understanding "the world's false subtleties" (sonnet 138, l. 4). Shakespeare doubtlessly did not embrace a Pollyanna view of the human condition. But he could — and most likely did — welcome the Sidneyean aspiration of upholding ideals— ideals in Shakespeare's case of faithful love, bitter differences reconciled, and familial and inner harmony. Perhaps, he thought, if human beings cannot obtain such goals of living, at least they can have models to aspire to. While evoking the "Myth of Deliverance," Shakespeare could well have shared the view emphasized by Coupe, that myth can be "a force for endlessly productive imperfection, rather than for arid and static perfection" (46).

But the cynical demon of Shakespeare's psyche is still on the sidelines, filing its nails like Joyce's god in *A Portrait of the Artist as a Young Man*, smirking as the lovers embrace. When naive Miranda exclaims, "O brave new world / That has such people in 't!" (V. i. 185–86), Prospero replies, "'tis new to thee" (86). Experience has taught him not to be overly optimistic, and a certain melancholy darkens his triumph. Prospero has regained his dukedom, but only after a stretch of years, when old age is advancing upon him and when, as he says, "Every third thought shall be my grave" (V. i. 315). The optimism of *The Tempest* is not unqualified.

Indeed, what of the chess game between Ferdinand and Miranda? "Sweet lord, you play me false"(V. i. 173) says Miranda. She is accusing Ferdinand of cheating! He replies, "No, my dearest love, / I would not for the world" (74–75) to which Miranda replies, "Yes, for a score of kingdoms you should wrangle, / And I would call it fair play" (176–77). Discomfiting questions wrinkle our brows. Was Ferdinand indeed cheating? Does this betoken future "cheating" in the modern sense? The scene takes on sinister implications when we recall the almost archetypal grim connotations of a chess game. In our own age, from modern classics like Eliot's "The Waste Land" to cinematic thrillers like *From Russia with Love* to cult TV series like *The Prisoner*, the chess game is seen as indicative of unprincipled maneuverings and ruthlessness. This association was known among Jacobeans. In Chapman's *Bussy D'Ambois* the Guise and Henry III sit at the rear of the stage absorbed in a chess game, these two enemies suggesting the maneuverings of the court. Middleton in *A Game at Chess* figures forth the entire English-Spanish confrontation over the question of Prince Charles' marrying the Infanta as a game of chess between the white and black sides. Later, Middleton in *Women Beware Women* would use a chess game between the uppercrust bawd Livia and Leonteo's mother to counterpoint the onstage seduction of Leonteo's wife, Bianca, by the Duke. Are we not at least to question the future happiness of Miranda and Ferdinand? And what of Miranda's assertion that she would be for him, even if he were wrangling for kingdoms like a disciple of Machiavelli? Is this not naive romanticism? Is it the kind of faith needed for mature marriage?

Of course, one of the most important questions about *The Tempest* is whether the conversions occur. Few would doubt the sincerity of Alonzo's repentance. But what of those of Sebastian and Antonio? The text provides few clues. The pair of schemers have little to say after Prospero resumes his power and greets them. I have seen some productions in which Antonio and Sebastian join in concluding jocularity, apparently cleansed of ambition and avarice. In the 1940s, however, W. H. Auden wrote *The Sea and the Mirror*, a poetic sequel to *The Tempest*, in which most of the characters have their meditative says. Auden's Antonio, clearly unrepentant, counterpoints the reveries of other characters with his cynical "Me: I am I, Antonio, / By choice myself alone" (318) and with variations of this line, all emphasizing the character's ruthless individualism. Most modern productions line up behind Auden and other skeptics. While commenting upon the role of Prospero, which he had recently played, Derek Jacobi speculated that the exiled magician, facing Antonio after the gap of years, has an unsettling realization. Assuming that his magic has converted his wayward brother, Prospero looks at the man, and "He knows his brother hasn't changed" (135). Sam Mendes' Royal Shakespeare Company 1993 production of the play underscored Antonio's lack of repentance. James Hayes, the actor assuming the role, approached the stage's apron and scowling, averted his gaze from the reconciliation's and merriment. Clearly many modern productions of what may well be Shakespeare's last play suggest that all indeed will not be well.

But can one make too much of these dark suggestions at the end of *The Tempest?* Few audiences members leave the theater on an emotionally low plateau of suspicions. Played as the text seems to guide readers, the production's hopeful elements overcome the darker ones. Viewers feel joyful at the proposed union of Ferdinand and Miranda, even though doubts may batter moth-like against the boundaries of their thoughts.

In *The Tempest*, Shakespeare, ever the fox, never the hedgehog, does not offer us a clear-cut philosophy, a catechism, a statement of beliefs.

Rather, waves of feeling dominate his closing creations. In the romances he shows the polished sides of his intellectual coins, but he reminds us that the bright fronts conceal tarnished, begrimed backs and vice versa. We may accept the bright side of the coin as the only side and we may do the same with the dark; but these are only part of the truth. Shakespeare clearly was aware that often there are no clear answers. As Lee Jacobus wisely points out, "Indeed, as the Shakespeare canon tells us, lack of certainty is the hallmark of being human" (159). Perhaps if pressed to answer whether life is worth living, Shakespeare, upon reflection, would have endorsed Flaubert's well-known comment to de Maupassant, used in the latter's novel *Une Vie*: "You see, life isn't ever as good as you think, and it isn't ever as bad either"(238).

Here we enter the uncharted and potentially perilous waters of the problem of belief. Did Shakespeare experience a reawakened faith in romantic love and friendship? Did he develop a renewed faith in forgiveness? Did he undergo a religious reawakening or conversion? Did he readjust his perception of what was real, what was obtainable by human beings? What would he have said about his philosophy of life after having set aside his pen upon the completion of *The Tempest*? Of course, individual students of the plays are entitled to their opinions and theories. But the only answer is that scholars and students cannot know and, barring the discovery of the diary of William Shakespeare, they shall never know.

As stimulating as these questions are, at base we have to realize that, in a vital sense, they are unimportant. We have the final plays of Shakespeare.

Long before Foucault and Barthes proclaimed the death of the author, T. S. Eliot offered some provocative judgments in his classic essay "Shakespeare and the Stoicism of Seneca" upon the problem of the relationship of poetry and belief.

> I doubt whether belief proper enters into the activity of a great poet, *qua* poet. That is, Dante, *qua* poet, did not believe or disbelieve the Thomist cosmology or theory of the soul: he merely made use of it, or a fusion took place between his initial emotional impulses and a theory, for the purpose of making poetry. The poet makes poetry, the metaphysician makes metaphysics, the bee makes honey, the spider secretes a filament; you can hardly say that any of these agents believes: he merely does [138].

Of course, Eliot, like Foucault and Barthes, overstates a case. When *Hamlet's* Player King muses that "Our thoughts are ours, their ends none of our own" (III. ii. 211), he may well be voicing a generalization which

Shakespeare felt to be universally valid or at least valid in a significant number of cases. Or the Player King could be expressing a dictum that occurred to Shakespeare in a flash of inspiration and which the poet seldom reflected upon afterward. We cannot know. Of course, one can justifiably look through the pages of the complete works to find recurring sentiments, maxims, and values and conclude that Shakespeare believed that something was true. One can, for instance, highlight the disastrous results of rebellion portrayed again and again throughout the plays and conclude that by and large Shakespeare opposed insurrections against the crown. But one cannot know whether upon occasion, when the Elizabethan economy was seemingly going haywire or when King James seemed to disappoint the hopes of the English, Shakespeare ever privately sanctioned the taking up of arms against the establishment. At times one can be fairly sure that a sentiment expressed by a literary character is one the author shared; at other times one cannot be certain.

Perhaps, on the other hand, in the most absolute sense one can never be sure. Let us return to the view that Shakespeare was very likely against rebellion and also look at *King Lear,* in which rebellion breaks out to support a French invasion dispatched to restore Lear to the throne. Since the evil Goneril and Regen hold sway over Britain, our sentiments—along with Shakespeare's—are drawn to Cordelia and her French allies. Can we conclude that if Shakespeare had ever believed that an absolutely evil ruler sat upon England's throne, he would have welcomed a French invasion? Or would members of his audience have done so—given their traditional mistrust of the French? Here speculations border upon the meaningless and unanswerable. Presumably circumstances never presented Shakespeare with such a dilemma, and so soul-shaking a choice to him was beyond the pale of probability. Most likely he made use of the rebellion and French invasion because they were dramatically useful and gave scant regard to their ideological implications outside the theater.

Thus we return to Eliot's view that the job of the poet is to create poetry; that of the creative writer — whatever the genre — is to produce creative writing. All ideas in a work of literary creation, even those the author might have firmly held, are in some definite but perhaps ultimately indefinable sense — transmogrified by the constructive powers of imagination. In this sense, therefore, it is profitless to argue whether Shakespeare "believed" the ideas "contained" in the dramatic romances.

More accurately, we might say that at a crucial time in Shakespeare's life and artistic career, the feeling function of his personality intensified an inner need to express itself. To borrow Eliot's term, a "fusion" happily took place between Shakespeare's psychological pressure and the aesthetic machinery of the Greek romance and the theories of Sidney, which were readily at hand, and other factors. Hence we find idealized portraits of what should and ought to be. Whether or not Shakespeare believed that loves as innocent and pure as Perdita's and Florizel's were realistic and likely to survive the test of time is beside the point. Likewise may be said of the efficacy, permanence, and the wisdom of forgiveness as in the stories of Posthumous and Imogin, Polixenes and Leontes, and Prospero and his enemies who deposed him. Shakespeare has imagined subcreations in which these phenomena present themselves as realities. Nor can we say that values of these ideals in the plays are fanciful, for romantic love, enduring married love, and forgiveness do exist in the large world outside the theater. Shakespeare's final plays, then, provide the shimmering, mist-like quasi-Edenic worlds that do and do not reflect actual experience. Drawing the line of demarcation between these two is not possible at all times to the approval of all persons. As Yeats stated in a January 4, 1939, letter to Lady Elizabeth Pelham, "Man can embody truth but he cannot know it" (922).

Would these patterns of fusions have held? In *The Tempest*, the reemergence of cynicism is beginning. Recently Park Honan has suggested that *Henry VIII* and *Two Noble Kinsmen* adumbrate a reawakened pessimism at the end of the poet's career (376–78), but we know too little of how much Shakespeare shared the authorship with Fletcher and when the plays were written to support this thesis. We cannot know whether Shakespeare, had he returned to full-time playwrighting, would have focused attention on tragedies. His part time retirement to Stratford became permanent. The rest of his career is silent.

Like many other tools for understanding literary characters as well as the intricacies of the human personality, the study of psychetypes can take us only so far. It cannot quantify or qualify currents within the playwright's psyche. Therefore, this study has attempted to be suggestive and exploratory rather than definitive. Yet it is predicated upon the firm belief that at times suggestions and approximations are the best that — in fact if not all — we can do in understanding certain literary and psychological phenomena. By directing attention to the recurrent conflict thinking and feeling modes of apprehension, we gain a better understanding not only of the writings themselves, but, to some extent, of the psyche of the playwright.

For instance, this present study has a profound pessimistic current in the Shakespearean corpus, one that sees little efficacy in political action, dim hope for human beings to achieve happiness, and a disturbing commingling of good and evil in human experience. Although this complex of dark beliefs and feelings is strong in Shakespeare, we cannot say that the playwright is simply a pessimist. Foxy in his approach, Shakespeare ever views the multifacetedness of reality. Skeptical about political action as he is in *Julius Caesar* and *Troilus and Cressida*, in *Antony and Cleopatra*, order prevails. Although a pessimistic current of thought and feeling is strong in Shakespeare and, of course, needs investigation, we should not deny that other — and at times more hopeful — currents exist. Again how these conflicting currents shaped Shakespeare's dramatic art is impossible to determine. I suspect, however, that at times Shakespeare choose certain concepts for dramatization; at other times the ideas chose him.

Psychetypology can, of course, reveal to readers significant aspects of Shakespearean characters other than those studied here. Certainly the conflict of thought and feeling in characters not included here may be studied. This investigation has, of course, said little of purely sensation and intuitive types. Certainly delving into these functions in appropriate characters can elucidate plays and the emotional and philosophic currents within these dramas.

But the awareness and study of psychetypes may well help us to better understand issues confronting us in our baffling and unnerving age. In an era in which, as Elwell points out, dizzying social change instead of utopia generates further social problems demanding solutions which will inevitably create further social problems, individuals feel adrift and lost. As Moyers observed to Campbell in one of their conversations, modern western society lacks any traditional pattern by which a boy, under the tutelage of the master, passes from youth to manhood. As Moyers couches the idea, "In ancient societies, the boy, for example, went through a ritual which told him the time had come. He knew that he was no longer a child and that he had to put off the influences of others and stand on his own. We don't have such a clear moment or an obvious ritual in our society that says to my son, 'You are a man' Where is the passage today?"

Campbell's response is, "I don't have the answer." Then he adds, "I figure you must leave it up to the boy to know when he has got the power"[51] (154). But evidence suggests that nowadays many young men are having difficulties in accepting adulthood roles. In a traditional society, where the mentor led youths through a carefully planned program toward the assumption of manhood, less leeway was given to the novice to exercise his individual psychetypology in finding his way. In our era of unbridled individualism, psychetypological differences are coerced to run rampant, leading us to adopt different and often conflicting strategies to cope with far-reaching and painful change.[52]

Essentially we are all on our own in very private attempts to construct a means of relating ourselves to the external world that makes sense to us. We all live in our own subcreated worlds. And we fashion these in large part in accord with our psychetypologies. We cannot travel to and enter each other's worlds, but attempting to bridge the gap imaginatively can provide us with understanding of others' viewpoints, feelings, and modes of apprehension and thus help us further along the road to our impossible goal of at last understanding reality. Impossible, of course, because all we can hope for this partial knowledge, but partial knowledge is better than none.

As we have seen, the potentiality for misunderstanding between persons of different psychetypes can lead to suspicion, distrust, and even hostility. Being aware of psychetypological differences will not, of course, subdue our conflicts and institute a promised land, but with such knowledge we may be better able to understand ourselves and others and to foster a significant degree of tolerance—certainly not an unworthy goal.

But to return to Shakespeare's final plays. If they provide no program for moral betterment, no catechism, no philosophy, we still might ask what partial understanding might they present of the world. What pattern of thought and feeling might have recurred in Shakespeare's psyche during the final stage of his career.

No answer is definitive. But perhaps some light may be shed on the problem by taking down E. M. Forster's *Howard's End* from the shelf and reading a passage occurring during a concert at Queen's Hall. When hearing the third movement of Beethoven's Fifth Symphony, Helen Schlegel habitually imagines a titanic battle occurring in the cosmos between gods and goblins. We follow her thoughts as she hears a performance.

> ...the music started with a goblin walking quietly over the universe, from end to end. Others followed him. They were not aggressive creatures; it was that that made them so terrible to Helen. They merely observed in passing that there was no such thing as splendor or heroism in the world.... Helen could not contradict them, for, once at all events, she had felt the same, and had seen the reliable walls of youth collapse. Panic and emptiness! Panic and emptiness! The goblins were right....

But the music creates a change in her fantasies.

> For, as if things were going too far, Beethoven took hold of the goblins and made them do what he wanted. He appeared in person. He gave them a little push, and they began to walk in a major key instead of a minor, and then — he blew with his

mouth and they were scattered! Gusts of splendor, gods and
demi-gods contending with vast swords, colour and fragrance
broadcast on the field of battle, magnificent victory magnificent
death! Oh, it all burst before the girl, and she even stretched her
gloved hands as if it were tangible....

Again the music creates a mutation in her thoughts.

And the goblins—they had not really been there at all? They
were only the phantoms of cowardice and unbelief? One healthy
human impulse would dispel them? Men like the Wilcoxes, or
President [Theodore] Roosevelt, would say yes. Beethoven knew
better. The goblins really had been there. They might return—
and they did ... a goblin, with increased malignity, walked qui-
etly over the universe from end to end. Panic and emptiness!
Panic and emptiness! Even the flaming ramparts of the world
might fall.
    Beethoven chose to make all right in the end. He built the
ramparts up. He blew with his mouth for the second time, and
again the goblins were scattered. He brought back the gusts of
splendor, the heroism, the youth, the magnificence of life and
death, and, amid vast roarings of a superhuman joy, he led his
Fifth Symphony to its conclusion.

But Helen's emotionally charged mind does not cease its meaningful
imaginings: "But the goblins were there. They could return. He had said
so bravely, and that is why one can trust Beethoven when he says other
things" (34–36).
    Helen's orchestrally-inspired fantasy reverberates on many levels. It
recreates the prehistoric fear that the primordial forces of chaos, exiled by
the gods of light and rationality, again will enter the realms of apparent
order and harmony, reducing all to anarchy. It manifests our fear of war
and our hope to reestablish peace. It dramatizes psychetypological havoc,
expressing dread of the inner chaos matching the outer, revealing our
struggles with potential disillusionment, depicting hope of ultimate individuation, underscoring bewilderment as to the reality of ultimate mean-
ings.
    The meditation tells more about Helen Schlegal than about Beethoven.
However, it portrays a flux of psychological states that all persons, on some
level, have experienced. Resurgent and insistent is the human need to
escape such turmoil, to evoke the archetype of Deliverance, to find an
emotional dawn and a spiritual haven. At times we may think we have

found our goal, but Forster and Helen Schlagel doubt its permanence. The cycle of chaos and the need to escape from chaos continue, but in different degrees and with different intensities in differing persons. It is impossible, of course, to decide what the results were of Shakespeare's need to reassert the primacy of the feeling aspects of his psyche — whether he regarded his own need with a measure of cynical detachment or whether he ever found what he sought as a reawakened inner harmony. Very likely, however, he would agree that the goblins could return.

Notes

1. Wilson, of course, offers other possible evidence to bolster this contention, such as identifying the John Robinson who witnessed Shakespeare's will with the John Robinson who lived at the Gatehouse and who might have been an activist Catholic. These identifications and other possibilities offered are suppositional.

2. For a detailed critique of Wilson's biography, see Thomas A. Pendleton's "Getting a Life" in *Shakespeare Newsletter* 45 (1995): 10, 16.

3. Of course, this is a generalization. In classical stoicism, a strong pantheistic strain is evident; however, for stoical writers the inner world-outer world distinction, through couched in varying terms, was an apt means of focusing attention upon the need to make one impervious to outside events.

4. Indeed a tradition of thought skeptical to stoicism extends back to classical times. Often Renaissance writers regarded the extravagant claims of this popular philosophy with a sly smile. Throughout *The Praise of Folly*, Erasmus takes playful snipes at those who would become rational supermen by quelling all emotional reactions. Folly, according to this often didactic sage, is an inescapable lot of the human condition. Certainly absolute stoicism would have seemed an absurdity to Rabelais, whose quasi-serious solution to life's problems—if indeed the fifth book of *Gargantua and Pantagruel* be his—was simply "to drink"; i.e, to enjoy life's pleasures (intellectual as well as physical). In later ages stoicism continued to come in for intellectual drubbings, as evidenced by Dr. Johnson's memorable satire in *Rasselas* when his eponymous hero, buoyed up by a stoic's lecture, returns several days later to gain further enlightenment only to discover the savant in the throes of desperation because his only daughter has died.

5. All quotations from the plays are taken from *The Complete Works of William Shakespeare*, ed. David Berington. 4th ed., rev., New York: Longman, 1997.

6. For a concise, yet authoritative account of King John's historical background, see Peter Saccio's *Shakespeare's English Kings*.

7. For other strictures on complexity theory, particularly the possibility of meaningful patterns to appear in biological phenomena, see Behe, 29–30, 155–56, 178, 189–92.

8. For an interesting classification of types of curses, see M. C. Bradbrook's "Two Notes on Webster," 281–83.

9. Dryden is, of course, in the poem referring to unrest occasioned by religious controversies and hostilities, but the "common quiet" he values may, of course, be threatened by other social conflicts.

10. Plato suggests that the truly

wise will be able to apprehend the essence of the divine and use this ultimate pattern as a template for managing society. Or, as he states his view, in discussing how society might be reorganized, " I conceive they [the philosopher rulers] will often turn their eyes upwards and downwards: I mean that they will first look at absolute justice and beauty and temperance, and again at the human copy; and will mingle and temper the various elements of life into the image of a man; and this they will conceive according to that other image, which, when existing among men, Homer calls the form and very likeness of God" [*Republic* Book V, Jowett translation].

11. A popular introduction to psychetypology and the Myers-Briggs test is Renee Baron's *What Type Am I?*

12. Indeed the similarity between Shakespeare's comedies and twentieth century musicals has not been ignored by directors, as witnessed by David Thacker's 1991 production of *Two Gentlemen of Verona* for the Royal Shakespeare company (replete with thirties' costumes, a dance band at the rear stage, pre-performance renditions of songs written by such applauded craftsmen as Rodgers and Hart, Jerome Kern, and Irving Berlin). A more recent harking back to the thirties is Kenneth Branagh's screen musical version of *Love's Labor's Lost*, which interspersed songs of the thirties amid the truncated Shakespearean text.

13. In delineating these characteristics of Shakespearean comedy, I draw primarily upon John Dover Wilson's *Shakespeare's Happy Comedies* and Roland Mushat Frye's *Shakespeare: The Art of the Dramatist*. These works may be consulted for more detailed consideration of these traits.

14. Of course, all is not smooth in friendship as in love. These relationships in the plays are at times impeded by distrust and suspicion before being emphatically reconfirmed in the conclusions.

15. Interestingly enough, while listing Shakespeare's Antony as a feeling type (165), Malone classifies the historical Antony as a sensation type (181, 186, 198).

16. The play presents no clearly intuitive individual in the Jungian sense, yet Cassandra comes close to illustrating some of the salient aspects of this type: the dependence upon personal vision, strong imaginative faculties, eccentric behavior. These qualities, however, appear not in the guise of a demonstrable personality type, but in that of a supernatural seer, a prophetess who foretells Troy's destruction. Yet even in this guise the faculty of intuition proves ineffective. In accord with classical myth, no one heeds Cassandra's warnings.

17. It is worth noting that in his redaction, *Troilus and Cressida, or Truth Found Too Late*, Dryden foreshortens the debate considerably. True, at its conclusion Dryden's Hector likewise does a *volte face*, siding with Troilus and vowing to keep Helen for the sake of the honor of Troy. But the brevity of the debate would allow one to conclude that Hector is indulging himself in some intellectual gymnastics in order to test his mental mettle against his younger brother's. Very likely Dryden felt disturbed by the length of the interchange in the original as well as the implausibility of Hector's reversal. At any rate the shortness of the discussion de-emphasizes it. In performance it would not command much attention and Hector's consistency would not be impaired.

18. Self-fashioning is, of course, an important concept in Renaissance literature. The now classic study of this

theme is Stephen J. Greenblatt's *Renaissance Self-Fashioning: From More to Shakespeare.*

19. For a rewarding basic discussion of how the concept of value applies both to Cressida and Achilles and how these characters are interlinked, see Norman Rabkin's "Troilus and Cressida: The Uses of the Double Plot" in *Shakespeare Studies*, I (1965): 265–82.

20. See especially "The Transcendental Humanism of Antony and Cleopatra" in *The Imperial Theme*, 3rd ed. (London: Methuen, 1951).

21. M. C. Bradbrook's *Themes and Conventions of Elizabethan Tragedy* is the classic study of the non-realistic conventions of English Renaissance drama. Her study underscores Elizabethan drama's cardinal differences from the realistic drama of Ibsen and Shaw.

22. Of course, in orthodox Jungian thought, the anima represents the female aspects of the male personality or perhaps rather the traits traditionally thought of as feminine — compassion, fellow-feeling, tenderness, empathy.

23. Malone identifies Othello as a continuous type and, therefore, relates his perception of time to his distress (34–35). Malone, however, does not pursue this topic in detail.

24. In fact, his apparent devaluing of sex has lead some commentators to suspect that Iago is impotent or homosexual. See Stanley Edgar Hyman's *Iago: Some Approaches to the Illusion of His Motivation.*

25. The English in Shakespeare's day were notorious throughout Europe for friendly kissing between males and females. Criticized for their actions, the English did not assume such a greeting betokened lust. The original audience would most likely not have read a sinister undercurrent into Cassio's kissing Desdemona and fondling her hand.

26. It is worth noting that a sim-

ilar psychological change occurs in Troilus. After witnessing "Diomede's Cressida," Troilus, a feeling type as we have seen, adopts a cynicism similar to that of Thersites.

27. Robert S. Miola has provocatively argued that, perhaps both consciously and unconsciously, Shakespeare drew upon Seneca's *Hercules Furens* in depicting Othello's homicidal fury. If so, the Senecan archetype provided a ready "mold" for the portrayal of a rampant inferior function. The coming of madness by its very nature, of course, illustrates the surging of the irrational into the psyche. Whether or not Othello can be considered clinically insane, the play's use of this "convention of madness" makes for the dramatization of inner discord and the conquest of psychological equilibrium by unwonted psychic currents. Hence, Othello's "conventional madness" offers an appropriate vehicle for depicting the welling forth of the inferior function.

28. Graham Bradshaw has argued that Claudio's crime is not premarital intercourse per se, but his having got Juliette with child (213–16).

29. Malone suggests that Coleridge himself was an intuitive.

30. In a flashback in his movie version of *Hamlet*, Branagh shows a nude Hamlet and Ophelia embracing in bed. West attempts to lacerate views of Ophelia's modesty and maidenhood by viewing her as "disreputable" (17–32).

31. For conflicting views on formality and "coldness" of the Elizabethan family, see Stone, 4–7, 135–41 and 151–218, and Ingram, 125–28 and 142–45.

32. One might object that her classifying Hamlet as a soldier indicates a strong sensation quotient in his personality. But clearly, unlike young Fortenbras, Hamlet does not hunger after battlefield exploits and paths of

glory. Ophelia's reference, rather than indicting a psychological bent, bares evidence that he has undergone the soldierly training a Renaissance prince would have been expected to undergo. Being studious and dedicated, he has done well in military training.

33. While not directly discussing Hamlet's behavior in terms of Jung's thinking function, Jacobus observes "Hamlet's capacity for action is dependent on his knowledge of the situation — whether apparent or real knowledge. As his uncertainty increases, his capacity for action diminishes: he needs to be possessed of the truth in order to know what to do" (81). However, tending to see it as the sole reason for Hamlet's delays and downplaying other, perhaps more troubling, psychogenic factors, obscures crucial dimensions of the drama. A case in point is Jacobus' assertion that Hamlet acts to kill Polonius because "he was confident that it was the king" (85). Rather, Hamlet's brutal behavior in this episode results from an irrational outburst, an interpretation suggested by the fact that he has just left the king supposedly at prayer. A moment's reflection should have centered his awareness upon the unlikelihood of the king's somehow beating him to Gertrude's chamber and hiding behind the arras. His very asking, "Is it the King?"(III. i. 27) underscores that he was not certain when he thrust the sword through the hanging. Rather what we have in the slaying of Polonius is a spontaneous reaction, brought about by Hamlet's inner turmoil.

34. Given Shakespeare's recurrent interest in prisons, Hamlet's comparison is especially telling of how he views his personality. In the history plays in particular, but also in other works as diverse as *Measure for Measure*, *Pericles, Prince of Tyre*, and *Two Noble Kinsmen*, Shakespeare was drawn to prison scenes. In essence, for Shakespeare imprisonment not only forces the prisoner's withdrawal from the world but also a self-search as the prisoner attempts to understand the causes leading to the imprisonment. From here the incarcerated may move on to speculations upon time, death, and God. Hence, being imprisoned in Shakespearean drama often leads to melancholy rumination.

35. For a provocative discussion of divine intervention in *Hamlet*, see that in G. D. F. Kitto's *Form and Meaning in Drama*, 321–28.

36. The text is unclear as to whether Hamlet, realizing the sword is poisoned, seizes it and intentionally wounds his foe or whether in the excitement, mistakenly picks up Laertes's dropped weapon. I have seen convincing productions making use of each interpretation. But either view would fit the exchange into the overall pattern of events. Laertes' abrupt decision to wound Hamlet could be viewed as a random event provoking Hamlet to exchange the foils.

37. A classic essay dealing with such issues as Hamlet's serving as a divinely-chosen agent and the prince's possible guilt and retribution is Fredson Bowers' "Hamlet as Minister and Scourge " in *Transactions and Proceedings of the Modern Language Association of America* [PMLA] 70 (1955): 740–49. For an essay taking issue with some of Bower's findings, see Harold Skulsky's "Revenge, Honor, and Conscience in *Hamlet*" in PMLA 85 (1970): 78–87.

38. In light of Hamlet's subsequent jibes about Polonius (IV. ii and iii), we may well wonder how deeply his feelings of penitence flow within his psyche.

39. For a discussion of individuation in *Le Morte d'Arthur*, see my "The Sword and the Shadow: A Jungian Reading of Malory's 'Tale of

Balin'" in *Journal of Evolutionary Psychology* 12 (March 1991), 2–16.

40. In fact Jung at times suggests that humankind's scope of action is severely limited by an inner psychological determinism. In "Psychology and Religion," he observes, "each of us is equipped with a psychic disposition that limits our freedom in high degree and makes it practically illusory." Later in the same essay he stresses, "Always, therefore, there is something in the psyche that takes possession and limits or suppresses our moral freedom" (*Essential* 246). As we have seen, however, generally the optimistic, sensation-seeking currents in his psychic predominate and direct the essential flow of his philosophy.

41. In fact, Campbell emphasizes the need to harmonize oneself with misfortune and sorrow, a task to be accomplished by contacting one's inner self (*Power* 160, ff.) Here we see a tendency not to deny evil as Hegel and Emerson did, but to stress the individual's capacity to overcome it. But Campbell, nevertheless, reveals a propensity to mitigate the power of evil. Clearly the famed mythographer's personality owned a strong sensation seeking component. He repeatedly recounts joyful immediate experiences such as hearing church bells ring and reacting cheerfully to students comments, etc. Possibly those given to orienting themselves to the world by involvement in new and exciting experiences are in general better able than thinking and feeling types to fend off the melancholy Weltanschauung which often dogs persons of these latter typological categories; hence, a possible reason appears for Campbell's tilting the balance toward optimism. If these observations are true and Campbell had sensation as a primary or secondary orientation, we may again see further evidence of Jung's dictum that psychetypology determines a person's interpretation of reality.

42. Curiously enough, in a conversation with Moyers, Campbell touches upon this very possibility: "Hamlet was given a destiny too big for him to handle, and it blew him to pieces. That can happen, too" (151). Neither Moyers nor Campbell pauses to consider the implications of this dilemma but pass on to a discussion of mythology and death.

43. Whether, of course, had they lived, their passionate involvement would have lasted beyond a year is another matter.

44. Of course, it might be argued that Macbeth does regain something of his earlier identity as a heroic soldier by fighting valiantly as Malcolm's forces enclose him, but he fights valorously in defense of his own now evil character. Whatever the sense of direction his courageous last stand gives him, his regaining anything like an integrated psyche is doubtful.

45. Of course, Ionesco's play couches the concept of the personality's non-existence in extreme, therefore, emphatic terms. Obviously the personality does exist. People are not interchangeable. We do not all share the same attitudes, feelings, and memories. A sense of self-awareness exists in the normal personality. Many factors obviously contribute to this sense of the self's existence — moral values, beliefs, opinions, conditioned patterns of behavior. Perhaps memory is a prime ingredient of what we think of as the personality. In cases of acute amnesia, we may recall, persons completely lose a sense of their identities. An intriguing treatment of this concept of memory equaling identity occurs in A. E. Van Vogt's classic science-fiction novel *The World of Null-A*. Gilbert Gosseyn, the protagonist, is killed but awakens to find himself in another place but in an

identical body. Gosseyn's sense of who he is survives because his memory survives the transferences.

The concept of the fluidity of the personality as I use it here, then, is a relative term. Certainly degrees of fluidity exist. On one level are those who experience irregular thoughts, afternoons of depression, moments of uneasiness while generally moving through life with a basic sense of inner concord and control of their lots in life. At the other extreme are the psychotics who lose their senses of identity because they believe they are Lincoln, God, or Hitler. Some of these persons do commit acts of violence. In between is a vast band of people who, because of depression, neurosis, acts of God, human cruelty, and so forth, feel confused, out of step with their surroundings, and alienated from their sense of self. It is with this large middle band that this study is largely concerned.

46. To Eagleton, Shakespeare's faith in Nature as manifested in his final plays is misplaced because the poet fails to observe that Nature creates evil and subversive forces as well as those of growth and harmony.

47. For instance, Robert Adams sees the religious elements of these plays as incidental (see especially 19, 75–76, 120–21). Throughout *Shakespeare: The Invention of the Human*, Bloom disputes that Shakespeare had any clear religion (see especially his comments on *The Tempest* on pages 667–68 and 681). For another jaundiced view of Shakespeare's having a religion (perhaps an informing religious scheme), see Macrone, 41–42 and 52.

48. The concern with Providence's control and manipulation of bizarre happenings seems to have been a basic and original element of this kind of romance. In his comprehensive and still useful *The Greek Romances in Elizabethan Prose Fiction*, S. L. Wolff

points to its presence in the Greek romances (4–5) and notes its centrality in the *Aetheopica*, in which a beneficent providence guides the action. He observes that providential control also appears in the *Clitophon and Leucippe* of Achilles Tatius. However, in this later work a tendency for Providence and Fortune to be used as separate forces exists (see 111–18). Hence, one may conclude that the providential elements in the romances were readily available for the Elizabethan use.

49. Wolff noted the prominence of strokes of Fortune in Greene's romances and finds that the frequency of Greene's references to Fate "amounts to an obsession" (84). Although Wolff sees some intellectual depth to Greene's use of Providence and Fortune, he feels that, for the most part, they are used simply to motivate bizarre events and actions. While the poet does, of course, use Fortune in this manner, I do not believe that this practice of necessity negates sincere concern with illustrating the workings of Providence (see 380–332).

50. Curiously enough, Ionesco's *The Bald Soprano* includes an episode suggestive of that in *Menaphon* in which husband and wife, bound together at the stake, discourse about their lives without recognizing each other. At a gathering at the Smith's, Mr. and Mrs. Martin sit down beside each other and, upon discovering that they have several similarities, including residence at the same address, conclude that they are in fact husband and wife. Of course, Ionesco uses the episode as a vehicle for humor, whimsy, and satire upon bourgeois conformity which renders people indistinguishable. That Greene could treat a similar episode with seriousness while to moderns it could be portrayed only as burlesque suggests something of the disparity

between Elizabethan and modern narrative and dramatic conventions.

51. In the section of their conversation under consideration, neither Moyers nor Campbell discusses problems young women may encounter upon maturing and taking positions in the postmodern world. But in his conversations with Fraser Boa, Campbell offers some provocative points on this topic. In the traditional society women assumed adult roles not through elaborate tribal rituals but through beginning menstruation. The rite of passage for a woman "was normally just to sit in her hut and realize what was happening to her, that she was now a vehicle of a transpersonal power" (*Way* 93). A few pages later Campbell argues that today's women are confused because of their pursuing roles previously restricted to males. He insists "that women are not contemplating what's happened to them. Rather they are thinking, 'Gee, I want to be a success-ful store manager or artist or professional.' So they're sold the active role of the male instead of taking active delight in the being role of the female" (98). Whether or not one accepts, either in part or in their entirety, Campbell's theories of the maturation of human females, in our atraditonal era, both pubescent males and females certainly face a rougher task in "finding themselves" than their primitive counterparts. In a society in which, as Elwell reminds us, social change begets social problems leading to further social change then further problems, providing universally valid guidelines for both sexes is well nigh impossible.

52. I am, of course, not advocating a return to primitivism or the establishment of a rigidly structured society. Our individualism is a good few of us could have reasonable peace of mind without, yet we have to pay an unhappy price for our boon.

Bibliography

Adams, Robert. *Shakespeare, the Four Romances*. New York: Norton, 1989.

Allen, Diogenes. *Christian Belief in a Postmodern World*. Louisville: Westminister/John Knox Press, 1989.

Allen, Joan. *Candles and Carnival Lights*. New York: New York University Press, 1978.

Andrews, John F. "Derek Jacobi on Shakespearean Acting." *Shakespeare Quarterly* (Summer 1985) Vol. 36, No. 2, 134–40.

Arnold, Matthew. *The Poems of Matthew Arnold*. Ed. C. B. Tinker and H. F. Lowery. London: Oxford University Press, 1950.

Auden, W. H. *Collected Poems*. Ed. Edward Mendelson. New York: Random House, 1976.

_____. "For the Time Being." *Collected Poems*. Ed. Edward Mendelson. New York: Random House, 1978.

_____. "The Joker in the Pack." *The Dyer's Hand and Other Essays*. New York: Vintage Books, 1968.

_____. "The Sea and the Mirror." *Collected Poems*. Ed. Edward Mendelson. New York: Random House, 1976.

Baron, Renee. *What Type Am I? Discover Who You Really Are*. New York: Penguin, 1998.

Bate, Jonathan. *The Genius of Shakespeare*. London: Picador, 1997.

Battenhouse, Roy. *Shakespearean Tragedy, Its Art and Its Christian Premises*. Bloomington: Indiana University Press, 1969.

Behe, Michael J. *Darwin's Black Box*. New York: Free Press, 1996.

Berlin, Isaiah. *The Hedgehog and the Fox: An Essay on Tolstoy's View of History*. New York: New American Library, 1957.

Bethell, S.L. *Shakespeare and the Popular Dramatic Tradition*. 1944. New York: Octagon, 1970.

Bevington, David, ed. *The Complete Works of Shakespeare*, 4th ed., rev. New York: Longman, 1997.

Bloom, Harold. *Shakespeare: The Invention of the Human*. New York: Riverhead Books, 1998.

Bodkin, Maud. *Archetypal Patterns in Poetry*. 1935. New York: Vintage, 1958.

Bowers, Fredson. "Hamlet as Minister and Scourge." *Transactions and Proceedings of the Modern Language Association of America* [PMLA] 70 (1955): 740–49.

Bradbrook, M. C. *Themes and Conventions of Elizabethan Tragedy.* 1935. Cambridge: University Press, 1952.

_____. "Two Notes Upon Webster." *Modern Language Review* XLII (1947) 281–91.

Bradshaw, Graham. *Shakespeare's Skepticism.* 1987. Ithaca: Cornell University Press, 1990.

Brown, John Russell. "All's Well That Ends Well." *The Shakespeare Hour.* Ed. Edward Quinn. New York: New American Library, 1985.

Bruce-Mitford, Miranda. *The Illustrated Book of Signs and Symbols.* New York: DK Publishing, 1996.

Campbell, Joseph, with Bill Moyers. *The Power of Myth.* New York: Doubleday, 1988.

_____, with Fraser Boa. *The Way of Myth: Talking with Joseph Campbell.* Boston: Shambhala, 1994.

Campbell, Oscar James. *Comicall Satyre and Shakespeare's Troilus and Cressida.* 1938. San Marino, CA: Huntington Library, 1959.

Casty, John. *Searching for Certainty: What Scientists Can Know About the Future.* New York: William Morrow, 1990.

Chambers, E. K. *Shakespeare: A Survey.* 1925. New York: Hill and Wang, 1958.

_____. *William Shakespeare: A Study of the Facts and Problems.* Oxford: Oxford University Press, 1930.

Charney, Maurice. *All of Shakespeare.* New York: Columbia, 1993.

Coleridge, Samuel Taylor. *Shakespearean Criticism.* Ed. Thomas Middleton Raysor. Vol. 1. London: Dent, 1960.

Conrad, Joseph. *Lord Jim.* London: Dent, 1946.

Coupe, Laurence. *Myth: The New Critical Idiom.* London: Routledge, 1997.

Crichton, Michael. *Jurassic Park.* New York: Knopf, 1990.

Cruttwell, Patrick. *The Shakespearean Moment and Its Place in the Poetry of the Seventeenth Century.* 1954. London: Chatto and Windus, 1970.

de Bary, Oscar James, *et al. The New Testament,* 4th ed., rev. Sewanee: University of the South, 2000.

Duncan-Jones, Katherine. Introduction. *Shakespeare's Sonnets and a Lover's Complaint.* London: Folio, 1989.

_____. *Ungentle Shakespeare: Scenes from His Life.* London: Arden Shakespeare, 2001.

Eagleton, Terry. *William Shakespeare.* Oxford: Blackwell, 1986.

Eliot, T. S. "Shakespeare and the Stoicism of Seneca." *Selected Essays,* 3rd ed., rev. London: Faber and Faber, 1951, 126–40.

Elwell, Frank W. *Industralizing America, Understanding Contemporary Society through Classical Sociological Analysis.* Westport, CT: Praeger, 1999.

Esslin, Martin. *The Theatre of the Absurd,* 3rd ed. London: Penguin, 1980.

Fitzgerald, F. Scott. *The Great Gatsby* in *The Viking Portable F. Scott Fitzgerald.* Ed. Dorothy Parker. New York: Viking, 1945, 1–168.

Flannery, Christopher. "*Troilus and Cressida:* Poetry or Philosophy?" *Shakespeare as Political Thinker.* Ed. John Alvis and Thomas G. West. Durham: Carolina Academic Press, 1981, 145–56.

Forster, E. M. *Howard's End.* 1910. London: Edward Arnold, 1947.

Fraser, Russell. *Young Shakespeare.* New York: Columbia, 1988.

Freud, Sigmund. *Civilization and Its Discontents.* Trans. Joan Riviere in *Great Books of the Western World,* Vol. 54. Chicago: Encyclopædia Britannica, 767–802.

Frey, Charles. "Interpreting *The Winter's Tale.*" *Studies in English Literature* XIII (1978): 307–30.

Frye, Northrop. *The Great Code: the Bible and Literature.* London: Routledge & Kegan Paul, 1982.

Frye, Roland Mushat. *Shakespeare: The Art of the Dramatist.* Boston: Houghton Mifflin, 1970.

Gilovich, Thomas. *How We Know What Isn't So: The Fallibility of Human Reason in Everyday Life.* New York: The Free Press, 1991.

Greenblatt, Stephen. *Renaissance Self-Fashioning: From More to Shakespeare.* Chicago: University of Chicago Press, 1980.

_____. *Shakespearean Negotiations.* Oxford: Clarendon Press, 1988.

Greene, Robert. *The Life and Complete Works in Prose and Verse.* Ed. Alexander Grossart. New York: Russell and Russell, 1964.

Harrison, G. B. *Shakespeare at Work, 1592–1603.* As *Shakespeare Under Elizabeth,* 1933. Ann Arbor: University of Michigan, 1956.

Hazlitt, William. *The Round Table and Characters of Shakespeare's Plays.* London: Dent, 1969.

Honan, Park. *Shakespeare: A Life.* New York: Oxford, 1998.

Hughes, Ted. *Shakespeare and the Goddess of Complete Being,* rev. ed. London: Faber and Faber, 1993.

Hunter, Robert Gram. *Shakespeare and the Comedy of Forgiveness.* New York: Columbia, 1965.

Hutcheon, Linda. *Poetics of Postmodernism: History, Theory, Fiction.* New York: Routledge, 1988.

Hyman, Stanley Edgar. *Iago: Some Approaches to the Illusion of His Motivation.* New York: Atheneum, 1970.

Ingram, Martin. *Church Courts, Sex and Marriage in England, 1570–1640.* Cambridge: Cambridge University Press, 1988.

Ionesco, Eugene. "Victims of Duty." *Plays,* Vol. 2. Trans. Donald Watts. London: Caller, 1958.

Jacobus, Lee. *Shakespeare and the Dialectic of Certainty.* New York: St. Martin's, 1992.

Jays, David. "The Green-Eyed Monster: Ray Fearon, Zoë Waites and Richard McCabe Talk About Love and Jealousy in *Othello.*" *Royal Shakespeare Company Magazine* (Summer 1999): 4–5.

Jung, Carl G. "Approaching the Unconscious." *Man and His Symbols.* Ed. Carl G. Jung and M. L. von Franz. New York: Doubleday, 1964, 18–10.

_____. *The Undiscovered Self* in *The Essential Jung, Selected Writings.* Ed. Anthony Storer. 1983. London: Fontana Press, 1998.

_____, et al. *Man and His Symbols.* New York: Doubleday, 1964.

_____. *Memories, Dreams, Reflections.* Ed. Aniela Jaffé. Trans. Richard and Clara Winston. New York: Vintage, 1965.

_____. *Psychological Types.* Bollingen Series XX, *The Collected Works of C. G Jung.* 1921. Princeton, N.J.: Princeton University Press, 1971.

Kalmey, Robert. "Shakespeare's Octavius and Elizabethan Roman History." *Studies in English Literataure* XVIII (1978): 275–88.

Keats, John. *The Complete Poetry and Selected Prose of John Keats.* Ed. Harold Edgar Briggs. New York: Modern Library, 1951.

Kermode, Frank. Introduction to *The Tempest* in *Oxford Anthology of English Literature,* Vol. I. New York: Oxford, 1973, 944–47.

Kitto, G. D. F. *Form and Meaning in Drama: A Study of Six Greek Plays and Hamlet.* New York: Barnes and Noble, 1964.

Knight, G. Wilson. "The Othello Music." *The Wheel of Fire*, 4th. ed. London: Methuen, 1972.

_____. "The Transcendental Humanism of *Antony and Cleopatra*." *The Imperial Theme*, 3rd ed. London: Methuen, 1951.

Labriola, Albert C. "'With Himself at War': Internal Conflict in Shakespeare's Brutus, Claudius, and Macbeth." *Journal of Evolutionary Psychology* (1990): 124–34.

Macrone, Michael. *Naughty Shakespeare.* 1997. London: Ebury Press, 1998.

Malone, Michael. *Psychetypes: A New Way of Exploring Personality.* 1977. New York: Pocket Books, 1978.

Maupassant, Guy de. *Une Vie.* Trans. by Katharine Vivian. London: Folio, 1981.

Miola, Robert S. "Othello *Furens*." *Shakespeare Quarterly* 41 (1990) : 49–64.

Montaigne, Michel de. *The Complete Essays,* trans. M. A. Screech. London: Penguin, 1987.

Nuttall, A. D. *Two Concepts of Allegory: A Study of Shakespeare's* The Tempest *and the Logic of Allegorical Expression.* New York: Barnes and Noble, 1967.

O'Connor, Flannery. "A Good Man Is Hard to Find." *Flannery O'Connor, Collected Works.* Library of America. New York: Literary Classics of the United States, 1988, 137–53.

O'Connor, Gary. *William Shakespeare: A Popular Life.* New York: Applause, 2000.

O'Rourke, James. "'Rule in Unity' and Otherwise: Love and Sex in *Troilus and Cressida*." *Shakespeare Quarterly* 43 (1992): 139–58.

Peck, M. Scott. *In Search of Stones.* New York: Hyperion, 1995.

Pendleton, Thomas A. "Getting a Life: Ian Wilson's *Shakespeare: The Evidence.*" *Shakespeare Newsletter* 45, 1 (1995): 10, 16.

Polkinghorne, John. *Quarks, Chaos, and Christianity.* New York: Crossroad, 1996.

Rabkin, Norman. "*Troilus and Cressida:* The Uses of the Double Plot." *Shakespeare Studies,* I (1965): 265–82.

Richards, I. A. "Poetry and Beliefs." *Critiques and Essays in Criticism.* Ed. Robert Wooster Stallman. New York: Ronald Press, 1949, 329–33.

Rollins, Hyder E., and Herschel Baker. *The Renaissance in England, Non-Dramatic Prose and Verse of the Sixteenth Century.* Boston: Heath, 1954.

Rowse, A. L. *Discovering Shakespeare: A Chapter in Literary History.* London: Weiden and Nicolson, 1989.

Saccio, Peter. *Shakespeare's English Kings: History, Chronicle, and Drama.* New York: Oxford, 1977.

Schoenbaum, S. *Shakespeare's Lives.* Oxford: Clarendon Press, 1970.

_____. *William Shakespeare: A Compact Documentary Life,* 2nd ed. New York: Oxford University Press, 1987.

Sidney, Sir Philip. "The Defense of Poesy." *The Renaissance in England, Non-Dramatic Prose and Verse of the Sixteenth Century.* Ed. Hyder E. Rollins and Herschel Baker. Boston: Heath, 1954.

Simms, Laura. "Misfortune's Fortune." *Parabola* 25, 4 (2000): 6–10.

Skulsky, Harold. "Revenge, Honor, and Conscience in *Hamlet.*" *Transactions and Proceedings of the Modern Language Association of America* [PMLA] 85 (1970), 78–87.

Spenser, Theodore. *Shakespeare and the Nature of Man.* 2d. ed. New York: Macmillan, 1949.

Spoto, Angelo. *Jung's Typology in Perspective,* rev. ed. Wilmette, Ill.: Chiron Publications, 1995.

Spurgeon, Caroline. *Shakespeare's Imagery and What It Tells Us*. 1935. Cambridge: Cambridge University Press, 1968.

Stockholder, Katherine. "The Other Coriolanus." *PMLA* 85 (1970): 228-36.

Stone, Lawrence. *The Family, Sex, and Marriage in England, 1500–1800*. New York: Harper & Row, 1977

Thornton, Bruce S. *Plagues of the Mind: The New Epidemic of False Knowledge*. Wilmington, Del.: ISI Books, 1999.

Tillyard, E. M. W. *The Elizabethan World Picture*. 1945. London: Chatto & Windus, 1960.

_____. *Shakespeare's History Plays*. 1944. New York: Collier Books, 1962.

Tolkien, J. R. R. "On Fairy Stories." *The Tolkien Reader*. New York: Ballentine, 1966.

Tucker, Kenneth. "The Sword and the Shadow: A Jungian Reading of Malory's 'Tale of Balin.'" *Journal of Evolutionary Psychology* 12 (March 1991): 2–17.

von Franz, M. L., and J. Hillman, *Lectures on Jung's Typology*. Dallas: Spring Publications, 1984.

Weidhorn, Manfred. "The Relation of Title and Name to Identity in Shakespearean Tragedy." *Studies in English Literature* ix (1969): 303–19.

West, Rebecca. *The Court and the Castle*. New Haven: Yale University Press, 1958, 17–32.

Wilson, Ian. *Shakespeare: The Evidence*. London: Headline, 1993.

Wilson, John Dover. *Shakespeare's Happy Comedies*. London: Faber and Faber, 1962.

Wolf, S. L. *The Greek Romances in Elizabethan Prose Fiction*. New York: Burt Franklin, 1961.

Yeats, W. B. *The Letters of W. B. Yeats*. Ed. Allan Wade. New York: Macmillan, 1955.

Index